A COMPL

MA

AND

CASSANDRA
EASON

A COMPLETE GUIDE TO MAGIC AND RITUAL

HOW TO USE NATURAL ENERGIES
TO HEAL YOUR LIFE

PIATKUS

First published in 1999 by
Judy Piatkus (Publishers) Ltd
5 Windmill Street, London W1P 1HF
www.piatkus.co.uk

Reprinted 1999

A catalogue record for this book is available from the British Library

ISBN 0-7499-1962-0

Edited by Esther Jagger
Designed by Sue Ryall

Set by Phoenix Photosetting, Chatham, Kent
Printed and bound in Great Britain by
Butler & Tanner Ltd, Frome and London

Contents

Introduction: Where to Begin	vi
SECTION ONE **Essential Rituals**	1
1. Traditional Magic	3
2. The Gift	14
3. Formal Magic	20
4. Colour Magic	39
5. Thoroughly Modern Magic	57
SECTION TWO **Rituals for Special Purposes**	69
6. The Magical Home and Garden	71
7. Love Magic	83
8. Money Magic	94
9. Defensive Magic	107
SECTION THREE **Magical Beings**	117
10. Witches and Earth Guardians	119
SECTION FOUR **Magic of the Natural World**	133
11. Natural Magic	135
12. Weather Magic	169
13. Seasonal Magic	186
14. Earth, Air, Fire and Water Magic	210
15. Magical Times	223
Further Reading	248
Useful Addresses	250
Index	255

Introduction: Where to Begin

Have you ever touched wood for luck? If so, you are practising an old form of tree magic, for the Celtic Druids would touch the sacred oak to appease the tree spirits if someone had made a rash promise, or to ensure success in an important venture. In Ancient Greece the oak was the sacred tree of Zeus, while in Christian times the power of touching wood was transferred to the sacred relics of the wood of the cross kept in many medieval churches. During the Second World War, Winston Churchill would knock on wood in the House of Commons when announcing good news.

If you spill salt, ten to one you will cast some over your left shoulder. Why? In all cultures salt, necessary for life, was considered sacred. If you spilled this precious substance, it was very unlucky and summoned up dark spirits who lurked behind your left shoulder. So you threw salt into their eyes. It is no accident that Judas Iscariot, in Leonardo da Vinci's painting of *The Last Supper*, had knocked over the salt cellar.

Few people will kill a spider, yet they will happily spray out of existence a stray woodlouse or a whole nest of ants in the yard. Spiders have a long tradition of being protected. They were talismans to the Ancient Etruscans in business and money matters. Spiders were also sacred to Mercury, the Roman god of commerce, thieves and moneylenders. If a small spider lands on you, it is said to ensure that money will come into your life very shortly. According to legend, when Mary and Joseph were hiding with Jesus in a cave during their flight to Egypt a spider rapidly spun a web across the cave mouth so that it appeared undisturbed. Herod's soldiers passed by, thinking the cave must be empty. For this the spider was given holy protection as well as being remembered in the tinsel on our Christmas trees. No wonder we cannot zap them with an easy conscience.

If you break a mirror, even a tiny make-up mirror, it's seven years' bad luck unless you put the pieces in a bag and bury them in the back garden. Yet every day we drop drinking glasses with impunity. Illogical? Early man saw a reflection in lakes and streams and believed he was seeing his soul. Smash your mirror and you smash your soul. The Romans were convinced it would take seven years for the soul to regrow. So seven years' bad luck would follow while the missing spirit grew back. Bad witches and vampires have no reflection in a mirror, it is said, because they have no soul.

Even many logical people today still hark back to these and countless other superstitions rooted in the magical beliefs of our ancestors. They may carry lucky charms or amulets, or possess a lucky dress or suit that will be worn at a special interview or on an important date. For magic is a part of our psychic fabric and the old rituals, far from being no more than mumbo-jumbo, do offer ways of focusing our energies and building the confidence that enables us to succeed or find love or happiness, as they did for our ancestors.

As a child you believed that if the Sun came out on a cloudy day as you made a wish, that wish would come true. You blew thistle-down to help the fairies on their way – if one flies upwards to the Sun you may have helped the queen of the fairies, and she will shower happiness upon you in return.

This childhood magic gets lost as we learn more about how the world is supposed to work. But when bad luck strikes out of the blue – an unpredictable financial reversal, a sudden job loss or an illness – we may be suddenly thrown off an apparently ordered life path and logic and reason fail to provide the answers.

Suddenly you must have money to fix the car or roof and you are way beyond your credit limit. Then you return to your childhood, clutching your four-leaf clover or your lucky pig and wishing with all your heart that gold coins would shower down from the sky or that you could see the object of your dreams standing at the door with a bouquet of red roses and a pizza for two.

That is where magic can help. We must return to the same inspiration and the enthusiasm that we possessed as children to make the world what we will. The difference is that as adults we know that the thousand pounds or the lovely princess or movie star will not materialise out of thin air, and that we do still have to work and plan and wait. But magic can give the impetus for good things to happen. It can calm a whirling mind that keeps us awake all night and leaves us exhausted the next day. It can provide the energy and will to carry on and to succeed whatever the obstacles. The powers lie within us and in the natural energies inherent in Water, Fire, Earth and Air, in the Moon, Sun and stars, in storms and rainbows, flowers, trees and herbs – all those tools that our forebears regularly used to bring happiness into their lives.

This book offers a variety of methods from many traditions, and updates rituals to accommodate the modern world of computers and digital cameras. For magic is a living, growing tradition, and above all one that can and should be adapted to our own unique qualities and world view. There is no right and wrong in magical methods. Even in Chapter 3, on Formal Magic, you will find a variety of suggestions to discover what works for you, for there are countless traditions that differ in emphasis and practice.

What Can You Achieve with Magic?

There is nothing weird or dangerous in this book, no writing in blood nor gathering fingernail and hair clippings to bind others to our power; no summoning of spirits or demons; no curses nor hexes which rebound only on the sender. The essence of good magic is free will. You can use ritual to attract someone who might make you happy, if you are realistic and do not demand too much of the cosmos – a 6-foot-3 Adonis with biceps of steel and a villa in the south of France, or a stunningly attractive heiress. But you cannot and should not attempt to bind someone to you against their will, hard though it is to let go of someone you love and need.

If a partner does not want to return to you and the children, or is a serial adulterer, even if you could bind him or her with a knot or candle spell, the end result would be unhappiness. If you are passed over for promotion in favour of an under-qualified newcomer who happens to be the boss's nephew, raining curses on his head will only give you a headache. Life can be totally unfair and, while magic can help you to cope, to dust yourself down and to go forward after reverses in health and fortune, it should not be expected to steer you through life's minefield totally unscathed.

Practitioners who tell you that you can have anything if you take it, and that you should let no one stand in your way, do not recognise the responsibilities that go with love. We may not want to walk away from an elderly relation, children or partner for whom we have a deep affection but no passion.

Magic can and does make life better and happier, and can rekindle passion and hope and offer freedom in small ways. It is part of the real world and can improve every aspect of that world, but it should not be an escape from reality as some people try to make it. It depends on action and going out into life with enthusiasm and openness. Practitioners who promise that, if you buy one of their spells you only have to wait for fame and fortune to come knocking, are only interested in their own fortunes. Magic is the impetus of the plane taking off from the tarmac, but fuel and skill are needed to keep the aircraft flying and to enable it to reach its destination.

How to Begin Your Rituals

This book can be read in any order as all the sections are self-contained, although inter-related. But you may find it useful to read Chapters 3 and 4 on Formal Magic and Colour Magic early on. My words and chants are intended for guidance. Feel free to adapt them, for the best rituals depend on personally expressed thoughts and words. All you need for the rituals in this book are everyday items that you can buy at any supermarket or garden centre. That said, crystals, lovely candles and artefacts can mark out this area of life as special and declare that we count as individuals.

Caring people will often spend money on family and friends and give to charity, but forget to give to themselves. At fifty I am only just learning that I do exist separately from my family and that I do matter: my crystals, oils and magical statues mark out my own space, and the rituals occupy my special time when the demands of others take second place. In busy lives just five or ten minutes a day will ensure that the core person thrives.

If you are short of money, even the most profound ritual will work with a household candle and stones from the seashore or local park. The magic is in us all, and the most powerful magicians can work with nothing more than a handful of sticks or stones in an urban park or back yard.

We are all special, unique, and have a life path that, if followed with courage and determination, will offer happiness and spiritual fulfilment and achieve our unique destiny. If we respect and value ourselves and trust our instincts and inspiration, that is the most important magic of all.

Keeping a Magical Journal

Most magic practitioners have a special book in which to keep notes about rituals, herbal remedies, and a list of relevant correspondence for colour, moon phases and astrological associations. In addition, some people use their journal for divination, using tea leaves or the clouds in the sky to suggest images that can hold the key to a current issue or question, or perhaps the more formal methods of runes, tarot or the *I Ching*, an ancient form of Chinese divination.

Perhaps the most important thing is to keep a record of significant dreams and meaningful coincidences: for example, when you meet a school friend, with whom you had lost touch, in a bar halfway across the world at a time neither of you should have been there if you had followed your expected itineraries. We always think we will remember the premonitions children make without realising the significance of their words – the times they read our minds or make brief but tantalising remarks about a previous existence. These moments do get blurred as the kaleidoscope of life whirls faster, yet they are a rich part of family history. Preserve, too, the family legends that get embellished over generations but have a kernel of truth, for they are part of the heritage we can bequeath to our descendants.

The Book of Shadows is the name given to the more formal handwritten reference book that is usually held by the high priestess of a coven, containing useful information such as myths about various deities, ceremonies and significant dates for gatherings that may be based on astronomically calculated dates and so vary slightly each year. Gerald Gardner, who founded the Gardnerian witch tradition, believed that the Book of Shadows or Grimoire should be hand-copied from teacher to student. Like the various Wiccan traditions (see Chapter 10), the contents of these books vary considerably. In recent years many have been published, usually privately, and you can even get Grimoires on the Internet. However, it really is best to devise your own book of rituals, and it can be a lovely legacy to any younger relative who would appreciate such knowledge of herbs and flowers and the customs of their forebears. In the older tradition, some witches were said to have burned their Book of Shadows before death. Few of these books are really old, as the ability to write did not become common among ordinary people until the beginning of the twentieth century. But the ideas were handed down verbally, often through the female line.

Invoking Psychic Protection

If you work only with positive intent and avoid carrying out any psychic activity when you are feeling exhausted or angry, you should not need complicated rituals while you work. Equally, the most complex protective rite will not protect those who dabble with darker magic or try to control spirits.

However, it is important to mark the beginning of a more formal ritual so that you can create a personal space that is special and different from the everyday world. When you have released your wishes or banished a destructive habit or redundant relationship, you can then close off your psychic energies so that they are not buzzing round in your head all night or affecting your everyday life. In Chapter 9 I have suggested a variety of techniques, some of which can be adapted to protection before and after ritual.

Some people invoke four of the archangels to stand in each corner of the room: usually Michael, the Archangel of the Sun and the warrior to stand in the south; Gabriel, the messenger, to stand in the west, Raphael, the traveller with his pilgrim's staff, to stand in the north; and Zadkiel, the Angel of Wisdom, to stand in the east (sometimes Uriel, the Angel of Salvation, is substituted as the guardian in the east). Others ask God, the Goddess (the archetypal female principal) or a named chosen deity for protection, or invoke the blessing of Light and Benevolence, before beginning psychic work. Afterwards they thank their guardians and see them fading like pillars of light; see Chapter 2, on protective magic, in my book *The Complete Guide to Psychic Development*, (Piatkus, 1997) for a description of how to close down the chakras or psychic energy centres of the body.

Below is a general protective ritual that could form the basis for your own ceremony.

A Ritual for Opening and Closing Magical Energies

Before performing a major ritual or formal magic:

- Bath, using no more than eight drops of a gently protective and purifying oil, such as geranium, lavender, rose or sandalwood, to a bathful of water (check the label on the oil bottle for instructions regarding exact quantities). Alternatively, tie a handful of lavender flowers or rose petals in a muslin bag and place it in the bath: as the water runs in, the herbal fragrance will infuse the water. Or hang the bag just below the hot tap and let the water run through it.
- Draw nine continuous protective clockwise circles around yourself in the water, seeing the fragrance entering your pores and filling you with harmony and tranquillity.
- Prepare everything you will need for the ritual and leave it on a low table, unless you have a special magical altar or altar stone.
- You may have a special magical place (see Chapter 3), indoors or out, but wherever you work, sprinkle a pinch of salt dissolved in water in each of the four corners, beginning in the one closest to the north.
- Burn a cleansing incense that will promote psychic awareness, for example frankincense, rosemary or sandalwood, in the centre of the room.
- If it is dawn or dusk, beginning in the north and moving clockwise light a candle in lilac, purple or pink at each of the four corners of the room, seeing four protective pillars of light expanding until they fill the whole room or garden.
- If it is daylight, set a clear quartz crystal from a square dark box in each of the four corners, seeing light accumulating in them and

rising so that they arch in a rainbow over your head and beneath your feet, filling the whole room with the spectrum of light.

- Finally, hold a chunk of uncut amethyst or rose quartz between your hands and, breathing slowly inwards, inhale the colour and exhale any darkness, doubts or anxieties left from the day. See yourself enveloped in a protective ellipse of pink or lilac through which no negativity can penetrate.
- If you are carrying out a formal ritual you can create a magic circle within the protection of the room to concentrate the power and protection.

When you have finished the ritual, if it is formal you will uncast the circle first, as described in Chapter 3. If not:

- Begin by moving to the candle in the westernmost corner, seeing the light gradually returning to it. Blow out this candle.
- Moving anti-clockwise, go next to the south and repeat the ritual, then move to the east and end in the north.
- If you have used crystals visit each corner anti-clockwise, seeing the light fade in turn.
- Wash each crystal under running water and anoint it with salt before drying it gently with a cloth and returning it to the box.
- Leave the incense to burn and hold your crystal again in both hands, letting the light fade from around you.
- Circle the crystal with a pendulum nine times anti-clockwise to cleanse it, or wash it in salt and water.
- Quietly tidy away your tools, placing any discarded candle wax or non-vegetable matter in a brown paper sack or any recyclable material – the kind you get in grocery stores in the USA. Seal it and dispose of it in a lidded bin.
- Any herbs, flowers or vegetable ash can be placed on a compost heap or buried.
- Now follows what Wiccans call the 'cakes and ale', an ancient formal ritual of dedication that in ceremonial magic takes place before the circle is uncast and forms an important part of any rite; informally, this can be a light meal served to any friends who have shared the ritual or eaten by yourself.

I find the act of clearing away forms part of the vital grounding process that is essential to mark the return to the world. For me, the clearing away and preparing of refreshments allow the physical body to come to the fore while the spirit stills. You can then move straight from the meal to either quiet contemplation listening to music, perhaps the sounds of the ocean or a rainforest on CD, or chatting with friends or family until bedtime.

Section One

Essential Rituals

1

Traditional Magic

Magic began with the desire of men and women to control their environment; to have homes safe from fire, storm and thieves; for themselves and their families to be healthy and strong; to have sufficient food and material comforts; and above all to be loved. The needs and hopes of ancient man were not very different from our own.

Much modern magic is derived from the early celebrations of the passing year and family life cycle that predate written records. When we decorate our Christmas tree – that today may be made of plastic and come in a kit – we are following the tradition of families long, long ago who hung up evergreens at the time when the days were at their shortest to persuade the other trees to return to life. Our modern fairy lights are descended from tallow torches hung on the trees to lend power to the Sun to shine again after it had reached its lowest position in the sky.

These rituals followed age-old patterns that were heralded not only by the annual cycle of festivals, but linked with the annual appearance of a certain herb or flower. For example, a woman who wished to become pregnant would wander naked in her garden at midnight on St John's or Midsummer Eve and pick the yellow St John's wort in order to produce a baby before the next midsummer. But she would be competing for the herb with young maidens who would gather the herb before the dew was dry on the morning of St

John's Eve before they had eaten. For their efforts, tradition promised them marriage within the year. If they subsequently slept with the herb under their pillows, they would dream of their true love. Before going to sleep they would recite:

Good St John, please do me right,
And let my true love come tonight,
That I may see him in the face,
And in my fond arms him embrace.

A less romantic version of this ritual involves placing an onion wrapped in a handkerchief under the pillow.

Different Kinds of Magic

But whether folk customs or more formal ceremonies, the underlying principles were the same. The types of magic practised around the world can be categorised under the following headings, although the details of the rituals might vary.

Sympathetic Magic

This involves performing a ritual that imitates what you would desire in the outer world, for example putting a doll in a toy cradle next to your bed while making love as a way of increasing your chance of conceiving. Hunters around the world would act out the symbolic slaughter of the animal they sought before setting out on the chase.

Contagious Magic

This kind of magic involves acquiring the power of a symbolic object or animal. For example, some hunters might wear the pelt of a lion to bring them the beast's courage and ferocity. A couple wanting a baby might make love next to one of the old fertility Earth symbols, for example on the phallus of the Cerne Abbas Giant in Dorset. The magic can also work the other way: young couples would make love in the fields on May Eve to encourage the Earth to be fertile.

Attracting Magic

This type embraces both sympathetic and contagious magic to bring yourself something you desire. For example, if you wished to move house you might carry out a ritual involving a symbol of a new home, such as a key, placing it on a map in the area to which you wished to move and visualising yourself moving into your new house.

Banishing and Protective Magic

These involve driving away negative feelings and fears by casting away or burying a focus of the negativity. For example, you might carve on a stone a word or symbol for some bad memories you wished to shed, and then cast the stone into fast-flowing water.

Knot Magic

Tying a knot in your handkerchief to remember something is a relic of an old form of folk magic that was gradually adopted in the more formal tradition into cord rituals of power. The idea is quite simple: you tie up power in your knot and either undo it when you need energy or success or keep the knot tied as a reminder of the power invoked in the original tying. I have used both methods. It is believed that knot magic dates back to the Ancient Babylonians more than four thousand years ago. In medieval and Tudor times witches would tie knots in ropes and sell them to sailors to release for wind when their ships became becalmed.

Knot rituals have also traditionally been performed for binding spells to restrict negative influences and in love spells. The knot is a symbol of true and lasting love given to lovers as a talisman with the words: 'So long as this knot endures so shall our love.'

The lovers' knot appears in runic inscriptions throughout northern Europe and may well have been linked to the goddess of love and fertility, Freyja, with perhaps some long-forgotten religious significance. Woven from undyed fibre, it was made to attract a lover or bind an inattentive one. The actual or potential partner's garter or neckerchief would be secretly obtained and tied with a garter or ribbon from his intended into a true lover's knot. By this means it was said he would love her forever.

The girl would say:

Three times a true lover's knot I tie secure.
Firm be the knot, firm the love endure.

She would then sleep with this bound to her bedpost from the new to the full Moon.

Knots were also tied in undyed cords for wishes. Nine knots would be made, one after the other in a kind of 'ladder', sometimes with nine small cords each about a foot long. In each knot a nut or seed would be secured: almonds for love, hazels for wisdom, small shelled walnuts for fertility, sunflower seeds for happiness, cloves or sesame seeds for prosperity, apple pips for health and poppy seeds for harmony and reconciliation. Sometimes ears of corn would be woven through the ladder. The ladder would be preserved for good fortune for a year and a day or until the wish came true. Sometimes there would be a mixture of seeds and nuts for an all-purpose good luck knot talisman.

In Ancient Babylon wise women would knot black and white cords with twice times seven knots and bind them round an afflicted part of the body. This was especially effective for headaches.

An energising knot ritual for power

Like the witches of old who tied up winds in their knots, you can make an empowering knotted cord by plaiting silks or cords and tying them together with nine knots in ascending power. You can combine colours according to needs (see Chapter 4) or use the Norse scarlet tradition from which the love knot came.

Begin by focusing on what it is that you want, and as you tie each knot build up the power by chanting faster and faster. You can vary the chant according to your needs, but I would suggest this as a good all-purpose chant:

Knot one renew
My power; knot two
In courage be, and so
Knot three.
The power is more,
I make knot four,

And so I strive
Within knot five
With fate not fixed,
I tie knot six.
My strength I leaven
And tie knot seven,
I master fate,
And so knot eight.
The wish is mine,
Within knot nine.

There are many versions of this rhyme. Say it on your own faster and faster nine times, each time tying another knot until you have all nine. At the end shout 'The wish is free' and pull the cord taut. You can either hang the knots as a talisman or undo one each day (see also the knot ritual in Chapter 14). If you use nine multi-coloured scarves, the effect is quite stunning.

Another version of this ritual is useful if you urgently need instant energy or a boost of confidence. Tie the nine knots loosely one on top of the other, and at the end of the chant undo the knot and toss the cords or scarves into the air with a cry of empowerment.

Knot wishes

Another traditional method for both healing and wishes was to knot a thin strand of thread around the wrist or bind it in a garter, while making a wish: 'When this knot decays, my wish will come true/my illness will depart.'

Magical Number Squares

From early times mathematicians have been fascinated by 'magic squares'. Numbers are laid out in grids three-by-three, four-by-four and so on so that all the rows, columns and diagonals add up to the same total. Such squares were considered of mystical significance.

Folk songs such as 'Green grow the rushes, O' with its refrain of 'One is one and all alone and ever more shall be so', mingle pagan and Christian imagery with magical number meanings. 'Two, two the lily white boys covered all in green' referred to the Oak and Holly Kings, who were twins and respectively ruled the light and dark halves of the year.

In Ancient Egypt and among the Phoenicians of Asia Minor mathematics became the province of a priest-scribe caste who, as they plumbed the hidden depths of numbers, found that they were governed by rules related to everyday life. As a result numbers became intrinsic to magical ritual. They were believed to hold the key to everything – a belief that has held sway up to the twentieth century, when Albert Einstein proclaimed his belief in a logical universe which could be explained mathematically. 'I cannot believe that God would play dice,' he said, rejecting the proposition that the universe and the forces behind it were a random accident.

In a simpler way, folklore attempts to explain the connection of events and numbers. Most people have a lucky number which they can point to as having an uncanny significance in their life. We talk of troubles coming in threes and unlucky thirteen (many modern buildings do not have a thirteenth floor and go straight from twelve to fourteen – even Canary Wharf, the super-modern complex in London's Docklands, bows to this tradition).

The Ancient Chinese sages and the Pythagoreans – the followers of the Greek philosopher Pythagoras – attributed certain powers to numbers. They saw one as the source of all numbers, standing apart from the pack. After that, they believed that odd numbers were yang, male, positive and dynamic and even numbers were yin, female and negative (in the sense of positive and negative poles of electricity and receptivity).

Each number also had its personal characteristic – and to understand these characteristics it may help to see the numbers as diagrams as the ancients did and to use them as a focus for magic (see also the section on colours and numbers in Chapter 4).

○ One, all alone and the prime source of everything, stood for reason, which the Pythagoreans saw as the ultimate force.

○ ○ Two, the first even and therefore female number, stood for opinion.

● ● ● Three, the first odd number (remember that one was seen as special in itself) and therefore the first male number, stood for potency.

○ ○ ○ ○ Four, the balanced 'square' number, stood for justice.

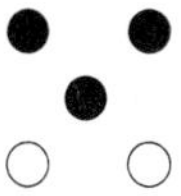

Five, which was created by the union of three, the first male number, and two, the first female number, stood for marriage.

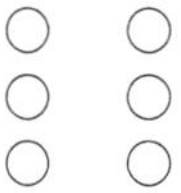

Six held the secret of cold.

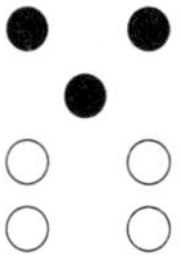

In seven could be found the secret of health: three, for, potency, together with the balanced number four.

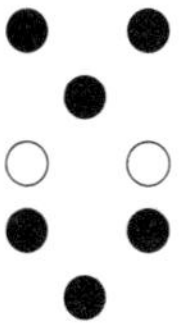

Eight held the secret of love: this time the potent three was added to five, the number of marriage.

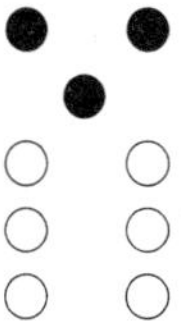

Nine held the secret of harmony: five, for marriage, together with four, for justice.

From these roots sprang the mystical art of gematria or numerology. The ancients did not have our numeral system, which was adapted from Hindu numerals by Jewish and Arab scholars and arrived in Britain around 1490. But they soon found that using diagrams for numbers was far too awkward. One solution, adopted first by the Hebrews and later by the Greeks, was to give each letters of the alphabet a numerical value. It followed that if each letter had a numerical value, words too would have a numerical value – the value of the individual number letters added together.

The following table is based on the Pythagorean system of numbering letters and is most often used in numerology. For a fuller description of the Pythagorean number system and of numerology, see my book *The Complete Guide to Divination* (Piatkus, 1998).

1	2	3	4	5	6	7	8	9
A	B	C	D	E	F	G	H	I
J	K	L	M	N	O	P	Q	R
S	T	U	V	W	X	Y	Z	

First you need to work out the number values of the individual letters of your name. You should use the name with which you feel most comfortable, perhaps the forename and surname that friends would use if sending you a birthday card or message on the Internet. Mine is generally:

CASSEASON = 311151165

The most powerful forms of magic are secret. If you prefer, you can add to this name so that it cannot be identified by others from its numerical form – substitute the log-on name you use on an office computer or the Internet to your first name instead of a surname.

Alternatively, you can use a secret power name – witches always have a special name. Many people in earlier times would not use a child's first name or indeed any of his or her real ones for the first year, for fear of enchantment. There is nothing fanciful in having a secret name; it can be very empowering. Many a closet tiger will one day have the courage to speak out or walk away from a destructive situation. Native American children would adopt a name according to the power animal that contacted them during their adolescent initiation, when they would live apart from the tribe for a few days and commune with the natural world.

Perhaps you see yourself as a Cordelia or Boudicca instead of the name you were given after some aunt who never went further than the south coast. Use your wish name and a surname with which you are most comfortable, whether a professional, married or maiden name. Again, create one that symbolises how you would wish to become and add those numbers to your power name.

Using magical number squares

We are going to use the numbers you have found with your magical name in a magical number square. Magical number squares can be used in a variety of ways as a basis for candle wishes, as talismans, or in rituals of empowerment. I have a tambourine marked with such a square which I regularly use as a source of the power inherent in the magical square.

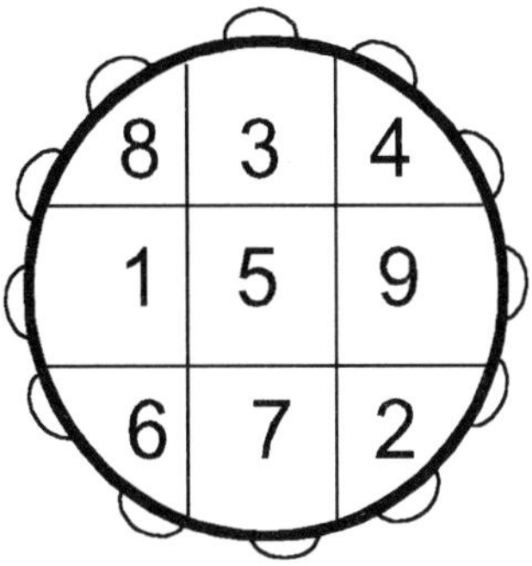

Why is this a magic square? Because the rows, columns and diagonals all add up to fifteen. This is the most usual and potent form of number square.

- You can draw a number square on paper, card or fabric, or engrave it on metal, or carve it in wood. It will serve as a protective and empowering talisman.

Making your lucky talismanic shape

Your special talismanic shape will be created by tracing the numbers of your name on the magic square. Let's take as an example my name (C A S S E A S O N = 3 1 1 1 5 1 1 6 5). Traced out on a magic square (zigging and zagging where we have the three ones) it looks like this:

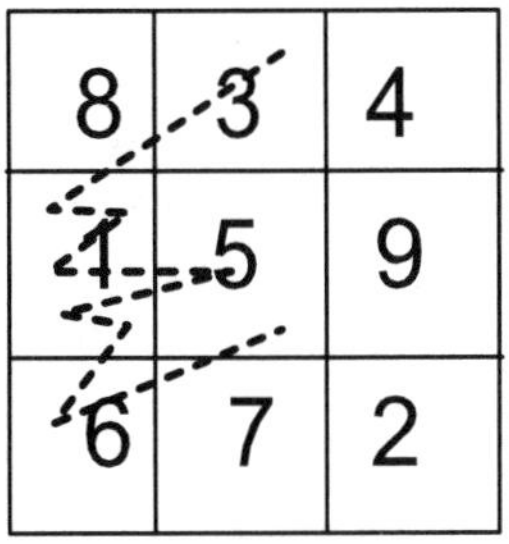

which gives the sign of 

- You can carve or draw your own symbol on a piece of wood or pottery as your very own magic sign. It can be used on talismans and for wishes, drawn or painted in colours that are associated with specific needs, for example red for courage and pink for mending quarrels. The shape can be transferred to a thin scroll of paper and worn in a small silver tube on a chain round your neck, or etched on metal or wood to make a talisman.

Talismanic wishes

If you have a specific need or wish, write out the numbers of that need. It can be something as simple as

Money = 4 6 5 5 7

or more complex, in which case you can reduce it to the key words. So 'Joe will fall in love with me' could be reduced to the more manageable:

J o e l o v e m e = 1 6 5 3 6 4 5 4 5

- Create your magical number shape by tracing over the magic square in the appropriate colour on paper.
- Then, in the age-old tradition, light a gold or silver candle on a fireproof tray and burn your wishes. Men and women over the centuries have offered petitions to the gods in this manner or on sacrificial fires, and have sent their pleas or thanks into the cosmos.
- Blow out the candle and send the light to whoever needs it, not forgetting yourself.

A tambourine or drum number ritual for power

Drumming for power and altered states of consciousness features in the shamanic practices of almost every culture, and still thrives among the shamans of Siberia and the Arctic Circle. I discovered that, as well as using the numbers for divination, it was very empowering to draw a number square formation on top of a drum or tambourine and tap out the numbers of a person's name in the order they occur, creating the talisman in sound. You can shake a crystal on top of your tambourine or drum if you prefer, bouncing it on each number of your name in turn on the number square. I found the concentration helped to build up the power. The grid of nine numbers that I draw on the drum is an ancient Northern tradition formation and would be marked out in front of a shaman's hut. It was believed that this number order in itself contained magic.

- If you have a child's drum or tambourine, make either a number square using numbers or the dot formation I described above.
- A permanent marker is ideal for drawing the dots or numbers and the grid of nine, itself an ancient sacred division from the Northern magical tradition.
- Write out the numbers of your first name on paper and memorise them. If a number is repeated, you can drum the number a second time or shake the crystal twice on the same number.
- You can also use this method for a single-word wish, for example the numbers of the name of someone you desire or the numerical value of health.

2

The Gift

In the modern world, gifts have become inextricably linked with consumerism. But the concept goes back to the earliest rituals when offerings – incense, precious gems, sometimes human sacrifices – were made to deities in return for rain, sunshine, growth and fertility. The wishing well, discussed in Chapter 11, originates in the custom of dropping coins into a well to buy healing or fertility from the spirit of the waters.

Treasure hoards have been discovered at the bottom of wells used by the Celts and Romans. For example, more than fourteen thousand coins, bronze figurines, jewellery, glass, pottery and a human skull have been excavated from the shaft of Coventina's well in Carrowbaugh, Northumberland. The skull was probably used for dispensing the water, since the Celts regarded the head as the source of wisdom. The heads of great leaders would be cut off immediately after death while it was thought the life blood was still flowing, to offer protection and guidance to the land.

On Hallowe'en on the Isle of Lewis in the Outer Hebrides, tributes of ale were offered to the sea god Shony and a fisherman would wade out into the waves to pour the ale on the water and ask for a fine catch. This was customary in sea-going communities throughout the year, as was a ritual in which sailors' wives would preserve a bottle of sea water collected when their husbands put to sea. The bottle would be kept in a safe place and, just before the earliest time that the returning boat might be sighted on the horizon, the women would pour the water back into the sea, saying: 'I have returned safely what is yours, return now safely what is mine.'

Ran, the Viking sea goddess, was said to love gold above all things, and when going to sea sailors would carry a golden coin to appease her if they drowned and in the hope that she would entertain them in her halls. Even today fishermen in East Anglia wear a gold earring. The custom is variously said to ensure keen eyesight or they would get a Christian burial if they died far from home. But it has echoes of paying Ran. The custom of placing pennies on the eyes of the newly deceased also dates back to the Classical belief of paying the ferryman to cross the sacred rivers to the Underworld.

The custom of offering the first fruits to the gods in return for future good harvests is almost universal. At Lammas Christians and pagans alike have baked bread from the first grain harvest and placed a loaf on the altar as an offering. The first eggs laid after the spring equinox were brightly painted and offered at the shrine of the Anglo-Saxon goddess Eostre, known in the Northern lands as Ostara, goddess of spring. Easter was named after her, and giving eggs is still a central feature of this festival.

In many cultures gifts to the sacred ancestors would invoke their protection for the clan or tribe. Among the living, gifts were always taken when a tribe went visiting: they were a guarantee of protection and hospitality while under the host's roof. Even today, few people would turn up for a weekend or for dinner without a bottle of wine or bunch of flowers at the very least.

Once the magical offering has been made, the host, deity or natural force undertakes to grant favours or offer protection. Thus the concept of the gift lies behind all magical offerings, whether scattering salt, casting flowers upon water or burning wish candles to the cosmos. Indeed, the religious practice of purchasing a candle and lighting it for a deceased relative follows the same principle.

Gifts Come Back Threefold

When willingly offered, gifts are said to come back threefold. Magic is like a balance sheet: you can ask for help or healing from the sea or any other natural force or the cosmos generally, and by making a symbolic offering of a coin, a crystal or a flower you are entering into a bargain.

But that symbolic offering has to be followed by a practical act of kindness or positivity without demanding an instant reward. Secret acts of generosity are doubly precious. Real life and magic are inextricably bound, so the more you can give the more you will receive – though not instantly and not necessarily from the recipient of your generosity. I was once told that if you gave a crystal away to someone who needs its healing or protective properties, you would be given another when you yourself were in need. It is far more potent to offer a crystal that has given you happiness than to buy a new one for a present.

Two years ago my personal life had hit an all-time low and a friend took me to see Mary, a gifted healer who had a caravan filled with beautiful crystals. She diagnosed that I was totally drained physically and emotionally and would become ill if I did not reverse the trend of my life – I ignored her warning, which did indeed come true. Mary gave me a piece of healing amethyst that was still within its rock for inner harmony, a browny-yellow citrine in rock for strength, a gleaming clear crystal quartz for energy, and a tiny sparkling citrine wish crystal. She would take no money for them. Her gift to a stranger was of tremendous help and comfort, and I have been careful ever since to give of my own special crystal freely, knowing that others do return in the cycle of mutual energy exchange.

Sea Rituals

We have all skimmed stones across the waves and made wishes. Because of the powerful ebbs and flows of the tide sea rituals have always been especially effective for attracting money, and the act of casting offerings upon the sea established the cosmic contract.

The turning tide is the most powerful for rituals of all kinds. It is especially so if you use the highest tide of the month (check local tide tables), and cast your offering on the seventh wave or leave it in a circle on the edge of the shore just before high tide for the sea to take. For a gradual increase in fortune or love use the incoming tide; and for banishing debt or a period of bad luck cast your offerings on the ebb tide.

A Ritual for Restoring Prosperity

This is useful after a financial setback or career reversal. Pearls and mother of pearl, natural jewels of the sea, are especially potent for attracting prosperity.

- Take two oyster or mussel shells that fit together and buy a small cheap pearl or piece of mother of pearl fashioned into a button or charm – I use mother of pearl buttons or charms. You can use a coin, but if you can give the sea something that is hers, like a pearl, the ritual is especially potent.
- Place the pearl or coin inside the shells.
- Bind the shells tightly together with seaweed secured with green twine, and either cast the shells into the seventh wave of the turning tide or place it within a clockwise-drawn circle at the sea's edge just as the tide reaches its height.
- Wish for either increased money or fertility by saying:

I return freely to you, mighty ocean, what was once yours.
I ask that you restore to me the prosperity that was once mine.

A Sea and Setting Sun Spell for Money

This spell should be carried out on a calm evening on a beach where the sea is shallow, just as the setting Sun makes a golden pathway across the sea. The setting Sun is sometimes associated with banishing magic, but for money spells it can incubate the coins. It is the time when the Sun and sea blend most naturally into a golden pathway of potential.

- You will need seven gold-coloured coins in a fabric bag, either gold-coloured or with golden thread running through it so that the Sun glints on it. Gold is the colour and metal of the Sun.
- Wade out a little way along the golden pathway and drop your first coin into the sea as an offering, saying:

Golden path across the sea,
Bring prosperity to me.

- Continue to paddle out, casting the coins along the golden pathway, repeating the rhyme or something similar till all seven are gone. If you can manage to drop each one on a wave so that the last is carried away by the seventh, the ritual will work even faster.
- Finally, walk in a golden circle of Sun water in a clockwise direction seven times and return to shore along the pathway.

I have followed this ritual many times in different variations, using moonlight and jumping from one rock pool to another. If you do carry out a Moon rite, use silver coins and a silver bag, the Moon's own colour and metal, and work on the days immediately before the full Moon or at the full Moon herself so that you can see the light reflected in the water.

A Gift of Love

Sometimes when we want a deep commitment we must risk exposing our own feelings. One of the most meaningful gifts you can offer a lover is a pomander (a fruit studded with cloves) made from an apple, the ancient Druidic symbol of enduring love. At Hallowe'en, the beginning of the Celtic year, even today we bob for apples as a relic of an ancient Druid marriage divination ceremony. This is one of the main times for love ritual and divination (see Chapter 13).

On both sides of the Atlantic the pomander has become associated with love; in more temperate climates a large red apple was used rather than the customary citrus fruits. The latter would sometimes be bought back to Britain as a present by a sailor lover or husband, who might have seen them as pomanders in houses or hostelries in Mediterranean regions. The wife or sweetheart would then create a love pomander to hang in the home in his absence to bring him home safe when he set sail again.

I first came across the concept of pomanders when I was researching a book on world healing. I discovered that love pomanders are also made by people wishing to attract love, not only from a potential partner but from an unknown lover who may not have appeared on the scene or not been recognised. So you would still make your pomander as a gift, but instead of giving or sending it, hang it up as an offering to someone who would make you happy. You must make and give the pomander quite freely, without imposing any demands, casting your love upon the cosmic sea and letting your gift multiply as it will.

- Use a large firm red apple or an orange to attract or ensure the safe return of a man. Use a lemon in the same way for a woman.
- Prepare a spice mixture with a mortar and pestle, or a wooden spoon in a large ceramic dish, even if you are using ready-ground spices.
- As you mix them, pour into them in your mind's eye golden rays of love, protection and healing and see the person you desire coming or returning to you.
- Push whole cloves into the fruit to form the shape of a heart and/or the person's initials, and surround this by a protective circle of cloves.
- As you push each clove into the skin, name a gift to the person you love: loyalty, honesty, laughter, compassion, strength, tolerance and so on.
- Complete the pomander with unbroken rings of cloves, again naming each gift that you would wish for your lover, such as health, abundance, wisdom, knowledge and focus.
- Roll the fruit in the spice mix and either leave it in the bowl, turning it every couple of days, or hang it up in a dry, warm place.
- When it is dry, give it to your lover or partner as a symbol of your love and increasing commitment.
- If he or she is absent, hang it from a green ribbon near a window or door facing the direction in which he or she has travelled, and give it to them on their safe return.
- For an as yet unidentified love hang it in the centre of a room, so that he or she can come from any direction.

3

Formal Magic

Formal or ritual magic has a place in the practices of solitary practitioners as well as those who might wish to come together with a group of friends for a special need. Such people might want to send healing to a mutual friend, or to prevent pollution in a neighbourhood or the environment generally.

Ritual magic can be especially empowering at a change point in your life. Although there are definite tools and stages, even these more ceremonial rites are not set but can be the focus for very creative and personalised magic. Some people shy away from this more defined method because they believe (mistakenly) that unless you use the specified tools, words and form the magic will not work. That is like telling a creative chef that unless he or she follows precise ingredients and stages in a cookery book any dish they produce will be inedible.

As with cookery, it is the point where the practitioner has the courage to move away from set forms that true inspiration begins. So do experiment: write your own poetry and chants and devise your own dance steps, speaking from the heart and soul. Try not to follow a book by candlelight or moonlight. And above all be prepared to laugh, not least at yourself.

Practising Ritual Magic

There are many different kinds of formal magic and they vary quite dramatically in focus and ritual, so this chapter's approach is based on several traditions. If you do join a coven or take a course in Wicca, you will find that each tradition has its emphasis, terminology and practices that have evolved over time and with which you may or may not be comfortable. You might sometimes use a full ceremony, but at other times follow parts of a ceremony, for example casting a magical circle and passing a symbol through the different quadrants of the circle.

When did formal magical practice begin? From paintings on Paleolithic cave walls, it would seem that our distant ancestors depicted hunters fighting and overcoming animals as a form of sympathetic magic. Tribes who still today live in ways unchanged by the modern world perform ritualistic dances before the chase: the hunters rehearse in dance and chant the progression of finding, struggling with and overcoming the wild animals, as a means of transferring ceremonial success to the actual situation.

Making a Magical Area

Magical areas are sometimes called temples or sanctuaries. What they are is a place where you can carry out ceremonies in privacy and quiet, marking off an area as either permanent or temporary. Whether a room, a patch of garden or part of a living or sleeping area, it should be large enough to create a circle 9 feet (3 metres) in diameter for a group and 5 feet (2.5 metres) in diameter if you are working alone. If you are working with friends, try to make your circle large enough for you all to sit or stand inside and to accommodate the altar in the centre, still leaving room to move round it, dance or chant.

You will also need an altar table to hold your magical items while you are working. A piece of unpolished wood from one of the magical trees such as hazel, ash, rowan or oak, or an uncut stone supported on bricks will do. Traditionally, altars are not constructed using metal. You can push your altar against the wall when not in use, unless you are lucky enough to have an attic, basement or spare room that you can set apart for magical working. Altars can be circular, square or rectangular – a round altar works especially well. If you are working outdoors, you can adapt a tree stump or flat rock as your work space. Some traditions place the altar in the north so that people can face it while standing in the south of the circle. By standing in the south you are placing yourself in the position of the noonday Sun, and thus absorb its power. You are also directly facing the north, the traditional source of magical energies. One ingenious solution I have seen to the working/storage problem was to use a chest of drawers so that the artefacts could be stored inside when not in use.

In Chapter 1 I described a detailed rite for opening and closing your psychic energies that includes purifying the entire room. This not only provides a potent prelude and close to any ceremony, but offers protection for the period you are working.

Dressing Your Altar

It is quite possible, even if you are using a communal room in an apartment or house, to leave your altar partly prepared, although items such as salt and water are best added just before a ritual. If you are subtle about placing the items it will offer a focal point for the room, as the sacred hearth does (see Chapter 6). A garden altar can be set with an outdoor candle or torch and stone figurines, perhaps shaded by bushes.

Candles

You will need one or two altar candles in white or natural beeswax. From these candles you can light all the others used in rituals. There is some debate over whether you should snuff or pinch out candles that you do not wish to burn – candle snuffers are easily obtainable, but the act of blowing out a candle is itself a magical release of power and, rather than holding the light in a snuffer, you can send it forth to all who need it. This is an excellent way of releasing power at the end of a ritual. Candle holders can be of brass, the colour and metal of the Sun, or silver, the colour and metal of the Moon. They should be sufficiently solid to carry, and if they have a wide rim there will be no problem with dripping wax.

You will also need four coloured candles – one for each of the four ancient elements – to place on the actual or visualised line or the circle. These elements, which each control one of the cardinal compass points, are said to combine to make the fifth ether or *akasha*. (See Chapter 14 for the significance of the four elements.) If you have a permanent room to use for magic you can keep your candles on brackets in the correct positions, ready to be lifted down for ceremonies. Alternatively you can keep them on furniture in the appropriate areas of the room or in your special box or cupboard.

Green is for Earth and the north. Place the candle at what would be the twelve o'clock position on a clock, aligned with north.

Yellow is for Air and the east. Place the candle at what would be the three o'clock position.

Red is for Fire and the south. Place the candle at what would be the six o'clock position.

Blue is for Water and the west. Place the candle at what would be the nine o'clock position.

An Altar Cloth

You can change your cloth according to the season or the purpose of the ceremony, or not use one at all. Highly attractive ethnic cloths decorated with sequins and glass beads or a block print design can be obtained from ethnic craft shops: try to buy from those where the profits are sent to the workers. Alternatively you can buy a plain cloth, dig out a design with a sharp knife on the cut surface of half a potato, and, using fabric paint, print your own. To do so is especially potent. If you can include the colours of the four elements, you will create a well-balanced focus of energy.

Power Statues

These are not essential, but have a place in many ceremonies as well as offering a focus and balance of the male or yang energies and female or yin. The Earth or Moon Goddess and the Horned God are ancient symbols of the union of male and female energies, but because of the demonisation of the male nature god into Satan the latter image can easily be misinterpreted.

Sometimes the mother goddess is symbolised by a large seashell and the father by a drinking horn. If you are not attracted to any particular statuettes, wait: one day you will see them when you least expect to do so. Failing that, sculpt your own from clay and create two abstract representations of male and female energies, or perhaps the two united. I have a clay wise woman painted with the ancient symbols of the moon's phases that were found on cave walls.

Keeping the Altar Alive

Decorate your sacred table with the flowers, fruits, berries and leaves of the season, or living pots of flowers or herbs that contain *prana*, the life force. Add a clear crystal quartz of energy and an amethyst.

The Tools of Formal Magic

Traditions vary as to which artefacts are necessary. It is not a question of having as many as possible to increase power, because even in formal ceremonies tools are just that – tools. If you are uncomfortable wielding a ceremonial sword or would attract undue attention if you purchased one, it would be counter-productive. Another tool can just as easily perform the same function.

So be prepared to adapt according to your means, your circumstances and preferences. Where possible, personalise your tool, either with an inscription of your own or by purchasing or making them in places that are imbued with positive associations for you.

Keep your ceremonial objects wrapped in dark material and safe in a special cupboard or on a high shelf, away from similar household items which can quite happily be adopted for less formal rituals (see Chapter 5). Apart from the safety aspect of a child finding a double-edged knife, your tools are linked to a specific and highly personal aspect of your life and so, like other personal treasures, are off limits to others.

Elemental Tools

Earth

The bell, an optional tool, is a symbol of the Earth. It can be made from either crystal or brass and can easily be obtained from an antique shop. If you do buy one that has already been used, a dedication ceremony (described on p. 28) will over-ride any negative vibrations from previous owners. You can sound the bell in each of

The pentacle

the four elemental quadrants as you pass your chosen symbol around the circle; or, if you have created a large circle, walk around it carrying the symbol while ringing the bell.

The bell can also be rung nine times at the beginning and close of each ritual, standing in the south of the circle facing north. Nine is the number of completion and perfection.

The pentacle, another symbol of the Earth, is familiar to users of many tarot packs. It can be used as a symbol of material possession, especially money and practical endeavour. You can place crystals on the pentacle, or make it the focus of the ritual, to endow it with Earth energies. It is very easy to make a pentacle. Take a suitable-sized piece of clay, wood, wax or metal; on it mark a pentagram, a five-pointed star, and enclose it in a circle as shown, in the diagram (see Chapter 5 for instructions on drawing an attracting pentagram).

- Place the Earth symbols to the north of the altar.

Air

The athame or air dagger is a ritual black-handled knife, usually with a double-edged blade, traditionally engraved with magical or astrological signs. You can obtain one from a specialist magical shop (see Useful Addresses) many of which run a mail order service. I bought a curved-blade knife with a silver-engraved scabbard from a souvenir shop in Spain.

Alternatively you can use a camping knife with a black wooden handle into which you can burn magical symbols using a pyrographic set which you can obtain from an art supplies shop. You can even paint moons, stars, spirals, suns, astrological signs or crosses on it with silver paint.

The athame is traditionally used for drawing magical circles in the Earth and directing magical Air energies into a symbol. It is sometimes additionally associated with the Fire element.

It can also be used as a conductor of energy, especially in solitary rituals. It is held above the head with both hands to draw down light and energy into the body, then brought down with a swift cutting movement, held in the right or power hand, and thrust away from the body horizontally at waist level to release this power. If others are present direct the athame not towards them but towards the altar.

A white-handled knife can also be a substitute for the sword. This can also be used for cutting herbs, cutting the Hallowe'en turnip or pumpkin and marking candles with runes or astrological signs. Some practitioners believe that you should never use metal for cutting herbs but pull them up, shred them and pound them in a mortar and pestle kept specially for the purpose. Pearl-handled knives are considered especially magical. You can obtain reproduction ceremonial swords for casting circles and, as with the athame, for drawing down energies from the cosmos. It is the equivalent male symbol to the female cauldron (see under Water, below) and can be used in love rituals and in any rite for the union of male and female, god and goddess energies.

- Place the Air artefacts to the east of the altar.

Fire

The wand or fire stick, fire symbol in the tarot, is traditionally a thin piece of wood about 21 inches (50 cm) long, narrowed at one end, rubbed smooth and preferably cut from a living tree (though some conservationists find this unacceptable unless the tree is being pruned). After a strong wind, or in a forest where trees are being constantly felled, it is often possible to find a suitable branch from which the wand can be cut.

You can make a series of wands for your ceremonies:

Ash is a magical wood, associated with healing and positive energies.

Elder wands are symbols of fairy magic and so are good for any visualisation work.
Hazel comes from the tree of wisdom and justice and is linked with the magic of the Sun. The wand should be cut from a tree that has not yet borne fruit.
Rowan is a protective wood and is therefore good for defensive and banishing magic.
Willow is the tree of intuition and is said to be endowed with the blessing of the Moon.
Crystal you can also use as a wand a long clear quartz crystal, pointed at one end and rounded at the other.

The wand is valuable for directing energies and for circling in the air; hence the image of the fairy godmother waving her wand. Do it clockwise for attracting energies and anti-clockwise for banishing them. It can also be used for drawing an invisible circle when you are working on carpet or any other surface that cannot be physically marked. It can then be used to draw attracting pentagrams in the air around the edge of the circle, beginning in the north or east depending on your entry point. In some traditions, the wand is a tool of Air.

- Place the wand or wands to the south of the altar.

Water

The chalice or ritual cup represents the Water element and can be filled with pure or scented water, or with wine or fruit juice if you are drinking from the chalice as part of the ceremony and then pouring wine on the ground. The chalice or cup used for rituals is traditionally made of silver, but you can also use crystal glass, stainless steel or pewter. The cup need not be large.

If you are using essential oils in your chalice, use a small earthenware or dark glass cup rather than metal.

The cauldron or ritual dish, another optional tool, is also a symbol of Water, although occasionally it is regarded as an Earth symbol. If a deep dish is used, it is frequently made of silver.

The cauldron can vary from a deep earthenware dish to a small iron pot with a handle that symbolises the womb of the mother goddess. The cauldron is used for brewing potions, for burning incense, as an alternative to the incense burner or as a container for flowers or herbs. You do not need to buy a special cauldron from a magic shop, as there are many suitable pots in kitchenware or gift shops.

You can also use your cauldron for scrying, especially on the old festivals such as Hallowe'en and May Eve, by using pure water and dropping dark inks or oils on the surface. With direct moonlight or a candle behind you, you may see many images that will suggest ideas or answers to matters that are concerning you.

Frequently the cauldron is translated, at least in indoor magic, to the libation dish which holds the offering to the cosmos or specific deities.

- Place the Water symbols to the west of the altar.

Dedicating your Ritual Tools

Sprinkle each tool with a few grains from a dish of salt (see under Elemental Substances, below). Hold the salt in your right or power hand with which you write, and your tool in the other. See rich golden brown energy rising from the Earth, bringing stability, strength and endurance to all enterprises undertaken.

- Circle clockwise over the new tool incense, frankincense or rosemary for the Sun, jasmine or sandalwood for the Moon, holding the incense in your power hand. Picture the pure white light of morning offering freshness of perspective, optimism and clear focus.
- Pass your tool through a golden candle flame, holding it carefully in both hands and feeling inspiration, joy and clarity pouring through the instrument.
- Finally sprinkle it with pure water, scented with roses for softer energies and a few drops of pine essential oil for purification, holding the water in your power hand and feeling the tool tempered and cooled with healing powers and altruism.

The Materials of Ritual Magic

You will need a set of small silver symbols, such as those found on a charm bracelet, for example a thimble for domestic affairs, a padlock for security at home, and a boat for travel. However, you can also use soft wax or even clay to fashion symbols, which can be any image that feels right – a flower for love, say, a coin for money, a tiny teddy bear for friendship or children. These will act as a focus for your own inner energies and the elemental energies.

Elemental Substances

Salt

This substance usually represents Earth, as it is the purest element and vital for human life and its magical significance. Use sea salt from a small unglazed pottery jar kept specially for more formal magic and healing salt baths. Immediately before the ritual tip some into a tiny pottery dish and place it to the north of the central candle on the altar or, if you use two, to the north of the altar and to the left of any other Earth symbols.

Incense

This substance represents Air, with different perfumes used for different rituals, for example: allspice for money rituals, bay for rituals concerning health, cinnamon for increasing psychic awareness, dragon's blood for sexual attraction and fertility, frankincense for success and new beginnings, myrrh for endings and banishing sorrow, lavender or rose for love, pine for courage and cleansing, rosemary or sage for memory and learning, and sandalwood for protection. Frankincense and sandalwood are good all-purpose incenses.

You will need a thurible, either an incense censer or a deep jar or secure holder in which you can safely carry your incense around the circle to the different areas. Keep your incense in the east of the altar to the left of any Air tools.

Candles

These represent Fire, as well as being used on the altar, and are a potent symbol of different needs according to the colour used (see Chapter 4 for colour meanings and Chapter 15 for more detailed use of candles in ritual). Keep candles in the south of the altar, positioned according to the ritual.

Water

This represents its own element. Use either pure spring water from a sacred spring or tap water left for twenty-four hours in a crystal or clear glass container in the sun- and moonlight. If the Water is in a special bowl keep it in the West, to the left of the chalice.

Personal Preparations

The ritual of bathing described on p. xii applies also for ritual magic. For circle work, you should not eat a heavy meal or drink alcohol for two or three hours before the ceremony.

You do not need to fast for twenty-four hours, as physical weakness not only interferes with everyday functioning but the state of otherworldliness it induces does not make true psychic awareness any greater. Abstinence from sex for twenty-four hours before performing the ritual was, and is still in some traditions, considered vital. If you are carrying out sex magic as part of your ritual (see p. 37) you may find this helpful, but two or three hours of gradually quietening your inner spirit is probably just as effective for moving into another state of consciousness. Few people can spare twenty-four hours for preparations.

After your bath, dress in something loose and comfortable. A special robe or kaftan that you keep for your magical workings is the best garment, unless you prefer to work skyclad or naked.

The Timing of Rituals

Chapter 15 contains lists of appropriate days and times for different kinds of magic. You should also try to have one personal esbat or meeting a month, ideally on the night of the full Moon, a time of maximum power. If you cannot fit in a personal esbat a month, spend at least a few minutes kneeling or sitting in front of your altar candle, holding in your hands one after the other your ritual objects and their associated substances, allowing the energies inherent in them to balance and empower you.

The Magic Circle

Intrinsic to all magic is the concept of the magic circle, to mark out a space for carrying out rituals, concentrating power and providing a protective boundary against negative influences. Earth, Air, Fire and Water, representing law, life, light and love, are central to all ritual magic and in the northern hemisphere are sited at the four compass points in any magic circle: Earth in the north, Air in the east, Fire in the south and Water in the west.

In the southern hemisphere some practitioners follow the northern tradition. However, you may wish to follow your own seasonal patterns: reverse the Earth and Fire quadrants, place the altar in the south of the circle and cast the circle anti-clockwise (known traditionally as widdershins), which is sunwise in the southern hemisphere (but not in the north). If you follow this method, you will also need to move the seasons forward six months.

Casting the Circle

You can keep a magic circle marked out with stones in a corner of your garden or painted on the floor of a room covered with a large rug. Attics are especially good.

- Find north and mark the four directions either with stones, with lines drawn on the floor or by four crystals hanging on cords on the four walls in the main marker positions.
- Once you know your directions you can mark out a circle deosil, (sunwise or clockwise) in the earth or sand with your athame, sword or wand or draw a chalk circle in your yard or on a tiled floor.
- If you need to visualise a circle, use a clear pointed quartz crystal, wand or the forefinger of your power hand and draw an outline in the air at chest level or on the ground if you prefer. Begin in the north and continue in an unbroken circle. To strengthen this circle, place attracting pentagrams (see Chapter 5) with your forefinger or wand at the four main compass points.
- Some traditions begin in the east, the direction of the rising Sun. Whichever tradition you follow, if you place your altar in the centre of the circle face the direction in which you began, on the opposite side of the altar.
- In each case, as you create the circle, visualise a golden thread circling the area and extending above your head height down to ground level so that you are completely enclosed.

- You may decide to divide the circle into four quadrants, but this is not necessary.

If you can personalise the objects you use, rather than buying expensive ceremonial artefacts that are disconnected from the real you, magic can more easily spill over into the real world where you may need action.

Creating the Triple Circle

Three is a sacred number in magic, and for special ceremonies you can create a triple circle of both power and protection.

The Salt and Water/Sacred Water Circle

Once you have created your main circle, return to the place where you began.

- Using your athame or forefinger, dip it into a bowl of water that you will not use anywhere else in the ritual, letting in radiance. Add a pinch of salt and stir it into the water three times clockwise with your forefinger, seeing the light fill the bowl.
- Standing just within the circle, walk clockwise round it, sprinkling the circle line, physical or envisaged, with your now sacred water.

The Incense Circle

Return the bowl to the altar and, lighting your incense, follow the circle line just within the salt/water line with incense. You will now have created three circles.

The Ceremony

Ring the bell nine times to mark the beginning of the ceremony, standing in the south facing north if you began your circle in the north.

- Returning to the north, ring the bell in each of the elemental corners.
- Light the altar candle/candles and the four coloured element

candles in the order that you cast the circle. In some traditions these two actions take place before drawing the triple circle. Then the circle is drawn with the athame and dedicated with the salt/water and incense.

- If an actual circle has been drawn, or you have not created pentagrams at the compass points of your invisible one, begin now in the north and, raising your athame in your power hand, create an attracting or invoking pentagram (see Chapter 5). Return the athame to your side and proceed to each of the four compass points in deosil (clockwise) order.
- Go to the altar facing north and take up the goblet or chalice. Pour a little of the wine or juice into the libation dish, or on to the earth if you are outdoors. Then raise the goblet to your own lips, in praise of the life force or cosmic energies of the god/goddess forms you may be using and asking his/her help.

You are now ready for the four stages of the ritual.

The Focus

This defines the purpose of the ritual and should be planned well beforehand so that you and any others are clear about that purpose and have appropriate symbols. The purpose can be as simple as coming together to greet the full Moon or to celebrate the harvest, in which case the ceremony would involve quite subtle build-ups and releases of power with chanting, poetry and reflection within a sacred space. Some people who attend formal Wiccan meetings are disappointed that there is not always a wild chanting, knotting of cords and ecstatic couplings: 'like an open-air Quaker meeting', was how one disgruntled would-be member once described it to me! He had watched too many B movies about black magic.

You can use a symbol placed on the pentacle on the altar or handed from member to member to charge it with their power. Sometimes a candle, a poppet or cloth doll or wax image is used to represent a person. Two candles in front of and on either side of the altar candle can be moved closer to encourage a relationship to flourish, or further apart to weaken a destructive link.

At this first vital stage the rest of the world recedes, to leave only the need or the wish or the occasion for which the esbat or meeting is held. Whether one person or a dozen are present, the essence is the same. Sometimes the symbol is placed in a fabric or paper pocket of an appropriate colour before being placed on the altar to amplify the energies.

- Concentration is the key to this first stage.

Action

This is the part where you use actions, whether physical or inner, focusing to endow the symbol with magical energies. You now move around the circle with the symbol, begin a chant or tie knots using coloured cords, seeing in your mind's eye the fruition of the wish.

You or the person acting as high priestess – witchcraft is very female-friendly – would pass the symbol or recite the intention in each of the four quarters in turn, involving both the elemental tools and substances.

- Movement is the key to this stage.

Raising the Power

The amplification of the magical energies and/or visualisation according to the focus and tools you are using, for example by chanting a word or phrase faster and faster are involved in the third stage. You could dance in a circle with increasing speed, pulling your knotted cord tighter and tighter or adding more knots. You might visualise a cone of coloured power (see Chapter 4), seeing the wish you have written or made being carried to fruition by magical energy.

Raise your athame or extend your hands vertically as high as possible above your head to absorb power from the cosmos.

- Increase is the key to this stage, until the point when the climax is reached . . .

Release of Power

This may be in a final shout, a leap, words such as 'It is free, the Power is mine', or whatever seems natural: if you have tied a knot suddenly releasing it or pulling the cord taut, seeing the whirlwind rising into the sky or the cone of light suddenly becoming a silver fountain of pure energy, spurting into the sky to form a star or a glittering rainbow. It is the moment you consign your wish to the flame, extinguish the candle and send light and energy into the cosmos. Bring down your athame or hands in a sudden slashing movement away from your body.

Cakes and Ale

Where in informal magic this part of the ceremony (see p. xiii) is primarily a grounding and return to the Earth, in formal rites it is perhaps the most profound aspect of the ritual. It dates back to the very early symbolism of eating the body of the corn god in the first loaf baked, and drinking his essence which was made by fermenting ale (the old folk song 'John Barleycorn' commemorates this custom). Ceremonial cakes generally include honey for the power of the sacred bee, symbol of the mother goddess; flour for the grains of the Mother Earth; herbs, for example a pinch of basil, cloves or cinnamon for the flowers of the Earth; orange or lemon rind or juice for the fruits of the Earth; and eggs for the power of new life.

If you are working alone take your athame in your right hand and the chalice in your left, lower the blade into the wine or water and stir it three times clockwise to represent the union of male and female, yang and yin, god and goddess forms, so that the two become one and greater than the separate parts. In a partnership or small group, if there are both a man and a woman present the woman normally holds the chalice and the man the athame. If there are a larger number of people present, the consecrated goblet is passed round the circle to sip or each person raises his or her personal chalice.

Next, if only one person is performing the rite he or she now takes the cake in their left hand and, with the athame in the power hand, scores into it the shape of a four-armed cross, at the same time saying either out loud or silently that unless such bounty is shared we are nothing, and thanking the Earth for her gifts. The spell-caster now takes a mouthful of the cake, in the time-honoured tradition of eating the magic.

If there is a group, each member will take a portion of the cake and offer gentle songs, poetry or just quiet insights that draw together those present in the spirituality created by positive magic. It is a time for words or, if alone, thoughts of appreciation and praise.

Ending the Ceremony

- After thanking all the benign powers and guardians who have assisted the ritual, ring the bell nine times to mark its closing.
- Extinguish the candles one by one in the opposite order in which you lit them, sending the love to wherever it is needed.
- Begin to uncast the circle wherever you ended the casting of it, and go round with your athame, sword, crystal or wand if it was visualised anti-clockwise. See the protective and empowering light fading gradually.
- If it is a chalk circle, rub it out ritually.

Where Are the Words?

Throughout the book I have suggested words that might seem helpful in shaping rites. But in formal magic the actions are much more prominent. Because the whole thing is more protracted, having set words would involve learning whole tracts in advance or reading from a book or paper and this can impede the naturalness of the ritual. It is better to begin with as few words as possible. Then, as you carry out the different stages, you may find yourself, even if alone, speaking quite profound and poetic phrases.

When I am giving a lecture on spiritual matters, on those occasions when I have had the courage to put aside my carefully prepared phrases, close my eyes and speak spontaneously, I am inspired, I believe, by some ancient tribal wisdom that can be accessed by any of us if we trust ourselves to float in the sea of the collective unconscious. You will know the words spoken in love, hope or sorrow by the deep unconscious memory of all people in all times and all places if you allow them to flow.

Sex Magic

This form of magic involves the release of sexual power in orgasm and ejaculation to give impetus to a need or wish. Actual sexual intercourse, as opposed to symbolic in the cup-and-athame coupling, is quite rare in formal rituals. It generally centres around the re-enactment of the Great Rite, the union of sky or corn god and Earth Mother, of the Sun and Moon, King Sol and Queen Luna in medieval alchemy, the Horned God of animals and vegetation and the Mother Goddess.

There are many myths surrounding this coupling linked with the creation of the seeds of new life and the continuing fertility of the land and mankind. The sacred marriage between Earth and Sky was practised in many cultures in spring. In Ancient Babylon, the sacred marriage took place each year between the god Tammuz and the goddess Ishtar. The festival of Akitu or Zag-Mug celebrated the rising of the waters of the River Tigris, followed by those of the Euphrates, and the coming of the spring rains, to bring fertility, at the spring equinox. Like many of the harvest gods, Tammuz died every year and was fetched from the underworld by his consort, who restored him to life.

Although one of the most potent releases of magical energy, sex magic is fraught with difficulty unless practised by an established couple in privacy or alone, again unseen by others. Some witch couples say that their bed is the most powerful temple of all, the place where they carry out their most focused rituals.

If sex is introduced to ceremonies, sometimes unwittingly by a group of friends who try magic skyclad, friendships can be strained: actions performed in the urgency of a ritual can lead to discord and deep embarrassment in the cold light of day. True Wiccan covens are quite rightly very controlled, and are aware that human weakness and passions can all too easily over-ride and debase what should be a very spiritual form of magic.

But within a relationship, sex magic can be enriching both to the relationship and spiritually. A couple, encircled by candles, would chant or silently focus their magical intention with increased intensity and speed while engaging in genital sex, climaxing together and exchanging bodily fluids as they consign their desire to the cosmos with a final cry. In some traditions, the couple engage in intercourse but at the point of ejaculation the man uses the semen to propel the intention of the ritual into the cosmos while the woman brings herself to climax. They then join again to end the rite.

Making love outdoors in a place of great magical significance, for example on the flat stone that often lies at the base of a Neolithic-standing stone, on an ancient barrow or hilltop burial mound, where earth and sky merge, can add to the potency of such a ceremony. Given discretion, late at night or early in the morning you can make magical love on seashores, in forests or sheltered by trees in your garden, joining with men and women who throughout the ages have mingled their energies with those of the fertile Earth. At high tide and with a full Moon almost anything is possible.

4

Colour Magic

Colour has played a part in many magical systems through many ages and different cultures, from the Babylonians and Ancient Egyptians onwards. In India and China colour magic goes back thousands of years, and colour energies have been a feature of healing work worldwide.

The Significance of Colour

There are many different colour associations – with planets, Sun signs, numbers and days of the week – but those that I have included accord with several of the major systems. Colours, while having intrinsic meanings, acquire additional significance according to the area in which they are applied. For example, the colour red would link you to the courage and steel of the planet Mars; the fire and determination of the Sun sign Aries; the number one; the musical note middle C; with red carnelians, garnet, red jasper, and red or blood agate; and with Tuesday, the day linked with Mars.

If you needed courage to make change or overcome opposition concerning a root or survival issue; if you had strong positive or negative feelings and needed to express them forcefully but without losing control; if you were involved in a passionate love affair or wanted to get an important project off the ground, you would need red in large quantities. So you could wear red, light a red candle, engrave the symbol of Aries and Mars on a red talisman, begin on a Tuesday, carry a garnet and eat red foods, for example beetroot, redcurrants, tomatoes and red apples. You could also weave all these into a red ritual for attaining whatever you need.

Planetary and Universal Colour Meanings

Some planets control more than one colour.

White is the colour of divinity and the life force. It contains all other colours, as Sir Isaac Newton proved in the seventeenth century when he passed a ray of white light through a prism, splitting it into a rainbow. But more than two thousand years before this scientific proof, the Greek philosopher Pythagoras declared that white contained all sound as well as colour. In magic, white represents light, vitality and boundless energy, and so is helpful where a new beginning is needed. Wear or carry white for energy, clear vision and original ideas and as you step into the unknown. It is a colour associated with the Sun.

Black is the colour not only of death, but also of regeneration. This tradition goes back to Ancient Egypt, when the annual flooding of the Nile carried with it black silt which brought new life to the land. Because of this, black cats were considered especially sacred. In magic, black is the colour of endings that carry within them seeds of new beginnings. Wear or carry black for marking the boundaries of the past and moving towards the future. It is a colour associated with Saturn, the planet of the Greek god of fate and limitations who became Old Father Time after his own time as father of the Greek gods was done and he was deposed by his son Zeus.

Red is a magical colour in many traditions, representing blood or the essence of life. The runes of the Norsemen were marked in red, while in China the pigtails of sages would be interwoven with red threads to ward off evil influences. In magic, red is the colour of power, physical energy and determination. Wear or carry red for courage when facing opposition and for change under difficult circumstances. It is a colour associated with battle because Mars, the planet named after the Roman god of war, has a dull red glow.

Orange is another colour of the Sun and the abundant fruits of the Earth. An orange tree yields a vast crop each year and its white blossoms are traditionally worn by brides as a fertility symbol. Orange is therefore the colour of fertility, health and joy. Use orange in magic for fertility, whether personal or to bring a project to fruition and to find personal happiness.

Yellow is traditionally the colour of the mind and communication and has sometimes been associated with jealousy and treachery. In medieval paintings Judas and the Devil are often depicted wearing yellow. Yellow ochre is painted on the bodies of Australian Aborigines at burial ceremonies. In magic, yellow is the colour for intellectual achievement, learning and travel. Wear or carry yellow when facing a mental challenge or when it is important to express yourself clearly or to change location. It is associated with Mercury, the planet named after the Roman winged messenger of the gods, who spanned the dimensions and was also the deity of healing, moneylenders and thieves. It is therefore also connected with business acumen and occasionally trickery.

Green is the colour of Venus, the Roman goddess of love, and thus is the colour of the heart, love and emotions. Because of its association with growth and gardens it has been connected in the Chinese and Native American tradition with money spells. Unlucky connotations of green stem from its association with fairy folk. However, if you blow gently on a dandelion clock or thistledown to help fairies on their way, you can wear or carry the colour with impunity. In magic, it is the colour for finding new love and developing affairs of the heart.

Blue is the 'healing colour' and the colour of the spirit. The Hindu god Vishnu is depicted with blue skin. In magic it is the colour of conventional wisdom and limitless possibilities, worn by Odin and other northern father/sky gods. Blue can expand the boundaries of possibility and create confidence. Wear or carry blue for idealism, when dealing with officialdom and when seeking justice. It is a colour of Jupiter, the planet called after the Roman supreme father god. Blue is also the colour of planet Earth when seen from space.

Purple is the royal colour, worn by deities, emperors and kings and also priests. It is especially sacred to the Ancient Egyptian god Osiris. In magic it provides a link with higher dimensions, with nobility of spirit and with inspiration. Wear or carry purple when you need to trust your inner voice, and for psychic development and spiritual strength.

Brown is the colour of the Earth and the Earth spirits. Rich, vibrant brown represents rooted power and instinctive wisdom. In magic, it is the colour of affinity with the natural world and acts as a protective force. Wear or carry brown when others would mislead you and you need to keep your feet firmly on the ground.
Pink Another of Venus's colours, it represents the gentler aspects of love and kindness. In magic, it is the colour of reconciliation and harmony and can induce quiet sleep. Wear or carry pink when you need to mend quarrels or to restore your own inner harmony.
Grey is the shade of compromise and adaptability. In magic it is the colour of invisibility and protection against psychic attack. Wear or carry grey when you wish to avoid confrontation and need to keep secrets. Grey is another colour ruled by Saturn.
Gold is the chief colour of the Sun and its deities, such as the Egyptians' Ra and the Greeks' Apollo. It represents the height of worldly achievement, wealth and recognition. In magic, it represents money, long life and great ambitions. Wear or carry gold for the confidence to aim high and achieve your dreams.
Silver is the colour of the Moon and the lunar goddesses Isis and Diana. It represents dreams, visions and a desire for fulfilment beyond the material world. Silver in magic represents intuition and sudden insights, especially in your dreams. Wear or carry silver to bring to the fore your hidden potential.

Astrological Colours

Wear your astrological colour or carry a talisman of the colour to affirm your core identity and unique qualities. The power is especially potent during your Sun sign period, but is also effective when you feel under threat or lack confidence.

Aries	21 March–20 April	Red, especially scarlet	Determination
Taurus	21 April–21 May	Pink	Patience
Gemini	22 May–21 June	Yellow	Versatility
Cancer	22 June–22 July	Silver	Hidden potential
Leo	23 July–23 August	Gold	Ambition
Virgo	24 August–22 September	Green	Attention to detail
Libra	23 September–23 October	Blue	Balance
Scorpio	24 October–22 November	Burgundy or indigo	Penetrating vision
Sagittarius	23 November–21 December	Orange	Clear direction
Capricorn	22 December–20 January	Black or dark grey	Perseverance
Aquarius	21 January–18 February	White	Independence
Pisces	19 February–20 March	Violet or purple	Hidden awareness

Crystal Colours

Red	Action	Garnet, red carnelian, red jasper, red or blood agate
Orange	Balance	Amber, orange beryl, orange carnelian, orange calcite
Yellow	Logic	Citrine, topaz, golden tiger's eye, yellow zircon, yellow rutilated quartz
Green	Emotions and for money-attracting rituals	Malachite, bloodstone, aventurine, amazonite, jade, moss agate, green cat's eye
Blue	Wisdom and knowledge	Falcon's eye (blue tiger's eye), lapis lazuli, turquoise, dyed blue howzite, blue lace agate
Purple	Spirituality	Sodalite, sugilite, amethyst, purple fluorite
White	Energy	Clear crystal quartz, snow quartz, white mother of pearl, white moonstone
Black	Acceptance	Obsidian (apache tear), black onyx, jet
Pink	Harmony and forgiveness	Rose quartz, pink sugilite, rhodochrosite, strawberry quartz
Brown	Firm foundations	Tiger's eye, fossilised wood, brown jasper, brown agate, brown rutilated quartz

Candle Colours for Wishes and Needs

Light an appropriate-coloured candle as part of the rituals described in Chapter 3. You can also use them as a focus for colour candle wishes when you light a candle and focus on your needs (see Chapter 3).

White	New beginnings and energy
Red	Change and courage
Orange	Happiness, health, balance and identity
Yellow	Communication, learning and travel
Green	Love, healing, the natural world and money-attracting rituals
Blue	Power, justice and career
Violet and indigo	Psychic development, spirituality and inner harmony
Pink	Reconciliation, children and the family
Brown	House and home, financial matters, possessions and older relations
Grey	Compromise and keeping secrets
Silver	Secret desires
Gold	Long-term ambitions and prosperity
Black	Endings and banishing guilt or regrets

Colours and Numerology

Each number corresponds to a colour. We all have our primary power or colour, and by looking at number values of the different letters in the name we are customarily called we can see which, if any, colours are lacking from our life. By adding the digits of any day, and the time if a particular hour is crucial, we can also see which colours can offer the maximum impact for success or happiness.

These are the usual associations, although some systems substitute rose pink at number 8.

Red	*Orange*	*Yellow*	*Green*	*Blue*	*Indigo*	*Violet*	*Silver*	*Gold*
1	2	3	4	5	6	7	8	9

The Pythagorean system, based on the nine primary numbers, is the one most commonly used for basic numerology (see also magic squares on p. 11). According to Pythagorean theory, the letters A, J and S equal one, B, K and T equal 2 and so on. The following table shows how the alphabet is broken down into numbers.

1	*2*	*3*	*4*	*5*	*6*	*7*	*8*	*9*
A	B	C	D	E	F	G	H	I
J	K	L	M	N	O	P	Q	R
S	T	U	V	W	X	Y	Z	

An Example of Number Colour Magic

Using the Pythagorean system you can find appropriate colours for magic purposes for yourself or someone else, based on the way that a name can be reduced to a single digit by continually adding together the numbers for each letter. But do remember that in different situations we may use different names. For example, I am Cassie to friends and family, Cassandra to some people and Mrs Eason to others. Just as different behaviour and different styles of dress suit different occasions, so we must mould our magic to the moment. Let's look at the example of someone called Jenny Todd.

This is the name she uses at work, and it is the one friends would write on an envelope or use when asking for her on the telephone in business situations (use this telephone or envelope test to differentiate the names by which a person is known in different surroundings).

Using the Pythagorean grid, we can break her name down to the following digits.

J	e	n	n	y	T	o	d	d
1	5	5	5	7	2	6	4	4

Next we must add these digits together: 1 + 5 + 5 + 5 + 7 + 2 + 6 + 4 + 4 = 39. We then add 3 and 9 to produce 12, then add 1 and 2 to produce 3. Therefore Jenny's overall power colour is yellow, the colour of the Sun, joy, communication, logic and learning. But in the numbers that make up her name, 3, 8 and 9 are missing. Therefore for balance Jenny should perhaps wear yellow, her power colour, quite frequently at work, plus silver and gold, perhaps in the form of jewellery. Silver represents her secret and perhaps unacknowledged dreams, and gold her long-term ambitions and the courage to make change in her life and to bring her dreams to reality.

You can also find out the power colours and missing colours for more formal occasions when you are using a different name, perhaps a maiden name you have kept at work or even another forename which family or official documents use.

For example, Jenny or Jennifer is in fact Jenny's middle name. She was christened Marianne Jennifer Todd, and this is the name that appears on her driving licence and passport. Her parents and grandparents insist on using both her Christian names when writing to her. Consequently, her colour requirements in official situations and in those involving her family may be quite different. In the former, then:

M	a	r	i	a	n	n	e	J	e	n	n	i	f	e	r	T	o	d	d
4	1	9	9	1	5	5	5	1	5	5	5	9	6	5	9	2	6	4	4

Again we must add all these digits together. 4 + 1 + 9 + 9 + 1 + 5 + 5 + 5 + 1 + 5 + 5 + 5 + 9 + 6 + 5 + 9 + 2 + 6 + 4 + 4 = 100. That gives us 1 + 0 + 0 = 1.

One equals red, so when Jenny goes home to see her parents, to visit her bank manager or any official, she has an entirely different power colour. As Marianne Jennifer she should wear red, the colour of action, fertility, passion and sudden anger that can flare up if she feels pressurised to conform.

Her missing numbers from the official name before adding are 3, 7 and 8. Therefore she should add yellow, her power colour, in her work as well as in her less official capacity (where it was also missing), indigo for stillness and her inner world, and again silver for those hidden dreams.

Without knowing anything about Jenny, we can see from her colour numbers that she needs rituals and colour power to help her to realise her inner dreams. When we learn that she is a single parent in her thirties whose parents and grandparents strongly disapprove of her bringing up her daughter alone, we can understand her need to bring joy back into her life in all its aspects, as well as quiet and rest which she is not getting.

Red indicates that her strongest feelings, both negative and positive, are directed at the older members of her family who voice unwarranted criticism when she is struggling to cope, rather than offering practical help. Jenny also has a great deal of unresolved anger with officials who have been less than constructive in helping her meet her financial and social needs. But her power colours are such that her survival and ultimate success are assured.

Colours and Music

The world was said to come into being with the first Aum or Om, and chanting a mantra or a single note is one of the best aids to meditation. What is less commonly known is that colours have their own sounds, and that by beginning a colour visualisation with a particular note, or humming notes of the missing colours in a little tune in moments of stress, you can amplify your inner colour energies.

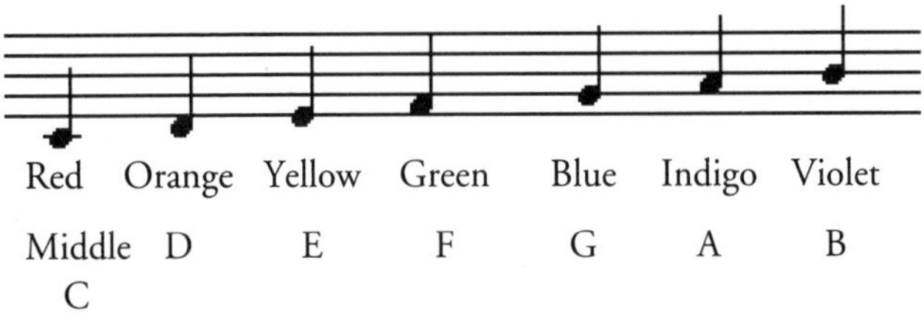

Colours and the Days of the Week

Each day of the week is also represented by a colour, so you can choose the best day to carry out a colour-based ritual. Additionally, if you have to use a great deal of energy on Saturday, which is naturally a purple or brown day, you may need to wear red or yellow to boost your system. Your power or lucky colour is also most potent on its own day.

Sunday	*Monday*	*Tuesday*	*Wednesday*	*Thursday*	*Friday*	*Saturday*
Yellow	White	Red	Orange	Blue	Green or pink	Purple or brown

Personalising Your Colour Diary

Each hour of each day has its own colour. So, although a day colour can be of help, if you have an appointment, an examination, an interview or even a date at a particular time you can also highlight a colour that will bring you fortune on, say, the third Friday in May 2000 or, more precisely, a special time on that day.

- Write down the full date of an important appointment and, if you wish to hone it even more finely, the hour, using a twenty-four-hour clock.
- By adding the digits of the time, day, month and year of the date you end up with a single digit that will give you your lucky colour for your appointment.

Simon had an interview for a new job installing computer equipment, a field in which he was well qualified, but he knew there was a lot of competition. It was on a Thursday, so he decided to wear a blue tie – blue was not only Thursday's colour but also that of the firm's logo. The actual test and interview were at 11 a.m. on Thursday, 6 August, 1998. Simon reduced the time and date to its numerical form: 11.00 06 08 1998. Ignoring the noughts, 1 + 1 + 6 + 8 + 1 + 9 + 9 + 8 = 43; and 4 + 3 = 7. Therefore the lucky colour of the interview hour was indigo, offering inner harmony and quieting nerves. Simon bought an indigo-coloured pen which he used for his selection and profile tests that began at precisely 11 a.m. He got the job.

Creating a Colour Cone

Many people talk about creating a cone of power. The cone-shaped hats traditionally associated with witches and bishops' mitres reflect this concentration of spiritual potency. The purpose of the cone, like the sacred pyramid, is to concentrate energy in a narrowing shape so that it reaches a pinnacle of power that then can be released at the end of the ritual to carry your wishes or desires into the cosmos. I found this concept hard to apply to rituals and visualisation until I started to use colours.

The easiest, most natural and, to me, most powerful way to activate a colour cone is to use a coloured focus, whether a candle, a crystal or a natural source of colour, and absorb this by visualising yourself slowly breathing in the colour and exhaling a darker or duller colour. Some people use chakra colours, associated with various energy points in your body. See my book *The Complete Guide to Psychic Development* (Piatkus, 1997) for details of chakras and colour breathing.

- Take your colour focusing object somewhere quiet – a room on your own or a secluded spot in the open air would be ideal. Sit in the position you find most comfortable and let your body relax.
- Concentrate on your focusing object, visualising its colour spreading out and enclosing you.
- Visualise the colour being gradually drawn around you like a circle of coloured light. Look upwards and visualise it forming a cone or pyramid above you. You may see the spiralling energies like a whirlwind of light, as multi-hued coloured liquids, or as miniature rainbows of which the colour you are using is brightest of all.
- You are now quite safe and enclosed, and can use this cone either to energise or protect you, according to the colour and intensity, or to send the light beams into the cosmos.
- If you need a sudden burst of energy to remove an obstacle in your life or achieve a very urgent need, you can dance around the focus of colour, whether a lighted candle, a large coloured crystal or a vivid flower whose *prana* or life force is the most powerful source of energy of all.
- After a ritual during which you have sent the coloured energy outwards from the point as light rays carrying your wishes or needs the colour in the cone will gradually fade and disappear.
- If you have been using your cone for protection while you sleep you will wake refreshed, the colour fading naturally with the

morning light, having been absorbed to refresh and cleanse the aura or etheric body around your physical frame.

You do not need to confine cones of coloured light to formal rituals, since they are entirely portable. When you have mastered the technique you can even perform it privately in a public place – all that people might notice is that you look more vibrant and radiant. You could even find opposition fading immediately as you release the coloured shaft into powerful but never-wounding words and actions that cut through inertia but maintain the esteem of everyone present. That is the real magic.

Coloured Glass Bottles

Glass bottles of the appropriate colour filled with spring water are an effective way of absorbing colour energies, and can be used in rituals of all kinds. Although water seeped in colour energies is directed primarily into healing work, drinking the water from a coloured bottle in which spring water has been kept for a Sun-and-Moon twenty-four-hour cycle, gives the strengths contained within the colour. It is therefore a quick and simple method of giving yourself an energy boost or calming stress. Although the water retains its clear colour, some people are able to detect a faint glow from coloured waters.

- If you want to transmit golden energies leave the water in a deep yellow glass bottle for a further twelve Sun hours in addition to the twenty-four-hour cycle.
- For silver, use a deep blue bottle and leave the water for an additional twelve-hour-Moon cycle.
- Water from a pink glass bottle is good for soothing children and animals and for mending quarrels.
- For pure white-light Water for instant energy, add a pure quartz crystal to a clear glass or, even better, a crystal bottle or decanter, and leave the water from dawn to noon.
- Crystals of the appropriate colour can be added to the bottle for additional potency.
- Use bottles with stoppers or corks – they can be obtained from most household shops or from antique stalls. Build up your collection so that you have the right bottle for every need.

- You can obtain smaller bottles in different colours, prepare them in advance and store them in the refrigerator for emergencies or when you need an extra boost.

There are several ways in which you can benefit from your coloured water:

- Drink or wash your face in the water, or add a few dozen drops to your bath at night. The latter is especially helpful if you are feeling exhausted but restless, and water from a pink or indigo bottle will calm you.
- Add the green water of love or the red of passion to a bath before you go out on a date to improve your charisma, while yellow will increase your confidence. People will comment on how attractive or young you are looking.
- Alternatively, sprinkle the water over a symbol that is forming the focus for a ritual, or on a special plant that you are nurturing.

Coloured Foods

These will offer a boost of colour and are a natural source of health, healing and energy. In Italy a large, fresh tomato is placed on the window ledge of the main room to encourage good health, and a second over the fireplace or on a shelf near a source of heat for prosperity.

If you need the strengths of a particular colour, eating a food of that colour in order to absorb its magical energies is a tradition that stems back hundreds or even thousands of years to the time when the horizontal cross, the old astrological sign for the Earth, decorated buns at the spring equinox. These became hot cross buns and the cross a Christian symbol, but the idea was the same: we absorb magical energies by taking them within us.

If possible, eat raw or unprocessed foods as these contain most *prana* or life force, and avoid artificial colourings because these do not contain magical energies. Here are some examples:

Red	Beetroots, radishes, red apples, red cabbage, raspberries, strawberries, tomatoes
Orange	Apricots, carrots, orange cheeses, oranges, orange melons, pumpkins
Yellow	Bananas, cheese, corn (maize), honey, honeydew melons, peaches, pineapples, yams (sweet potatoes)
Green	Broccoli, cucumber, cabbage, green apples, green grapes, green peppers, lettuce, pears
Blue	Bilberries, blueberries, blue plums, damsons
Purple	Aubergines (eggplant), blackberries, dark plums, purple grapes, purple cabbage
Brown	Brown rice, nuts, potatoes, rye bread, seeds
White	Chicken, cream, egg white, milk, onions, white cheese, white rice, onions, yoghurt

Colour Rituals

The most effective colour rituals involve a combination of candles and either poppets (dolls), sachets or packets of different-coloured materials to contain symbols of what it is you desire (see also Chapter 11 for details of poppet spells).

Ritual to Make a Garden Grow

This is appropriate whether we are talking about growing a physical garden over a place of ugliness, or a rebirth and healing of an aspect of life that has been spoiled by others.

The following ritual was carried out by Sarah, who had bought a small terraced house in a rundown area where the tiny garden had become a rubbish tip for the previous owners. To Sarah, who loved plants, the regeneration of the garden represented a source of pleasure for herself and her young daughter, as well as the regrowth of her life after being abandoned by her husband who had left her with a mountain of debts.

- Twenty-four hours before the ritual, fill a green glass bottle with spring water and leave it the full day-and-night Sun and Moon cycle.
- Begin at dawn in the open space you wish to regenerate, or in any open sheltered area if the regrowth is symbolic, on a Friday whose colour is green. If it is raining carry out the ritual indoors so that you can see the garden, and plant the seedlings as soon as the weather improves.
- Make a circle of green seedlings still in their pots, interspersed with green crystals – jade and moss agate are especially potent for gardening and healing the planet. Substitute green glass nuggets if you have no crystals.
- Sit in the rising Sun and use the pink of the sky and the green of the planet to build up your cone of healing and rebirth.
- Pick up the seedlings one by one, beginning in the east for the rising day, and sprinkle nine drops of water over each in turn, saying for each seedling: 'Receive this green light and love and bring growth where there is barrenness, hope where there is despair, healing where there is bitterness.' You can substitute your own words if you prefer.
- When you have watered your seedlings, dig a small hole for each in the earth or in a large earthenware pot or wooden trough full of earth.
- Into each hole pour a further nine drops of water, seeing the green energies filling the soil, saying: 'May the land flourish and joy return to its fullness.' Again, you can substitute your own words to personalise the rituals.
- Plant each seedling in turn, saying such words as: 'Increase in this green light towards the Sun as I will also grow from darkness to light.'
- See the light from your magical cone enclosing the plants and filling them with power, so that the light floods the sky as brilliant rays. As it does, your own cone of green will gradually fade.
- Place a tiny jade or moss agate in the flower bed or pot.
- Each morning when you rise you can sprinkle water on the plants, using rainwater you have collected in your green bottle,

again left for a full twenty-four-hour cycle, and send green light to their roots and leaves.
- If any plant dies, replace it, adapting the ritual for a single plant.

Making and Using Coloured Sachets for Rituals and Other Purposes

For centuries men and women have created tiny pillows or pockets filled with herbs for love, quiet sleep or happiness. These were usually open at one end to allow the addition of fresh herbs or flowers, or tiny crystals or symbols – for example, a silver love heart placed in a nest of pink rose petals.

These sachets would frequently be made in a natural fabric tinted with vegetable dyes and tied with ribbons of different colours sold by wandering pedlars or bought at fairs. In Chapter 6 I describe different herbs and flowers that can be added for various magical purposes.

Coloured sachets or pockets can also be used to hold symbols or tiny dolls in rituals, the chosen colour adding to the potency of the wish or needs.

- Begin a collection of coloured sachets and ribbons.
- The colour associations are listed on pp. 40–2 and you do not have to be skilled with a needle to sew together the sides of a rectangle of cloth folded double.
- Although you can buy pockets or make them from card and glue, the act of stitching the cloth fastens in your emotions and personal vibrations.
- As well as the rainbow colours, have a brown sachet for home and domestic matters; grey for compromise; pink for children, babies and animal matters; and white for pure energy.
- You may need to think about the colours used for a specific ritual, as there are no hard-and-fast rules. A new car might be yellow because you use it for travel, but it might also be brown because it involves finance and is a desired possession. However you could consider blue if owning the car would help your career – if only by making travel to work easier. So you might create a yellow sachet, sewn with brown thread and tied with a blue ribbon.

As well as using sachets for rituals, you can place a photograph of someone you love or a particular place you would like to visit in an appropriate-coloured sachet. Pop it under your pillow at night or in your bag during the day so that you can focus your desires.

Red bags, traditionally used as domestic talismans, were tied with nine red knots. They contained tiny pieces of bread and coal, a pinch of salt and a coin to ensure that the home would have food, warmth, health and enough money. In earlier times food and shelter were life-and-death matters. If you feel strongly about home issues at a particular time, red is a good colour for powerful feelings.

You can also carry a crystal in a sachet or tiny bag of the same colour to amplify its energy-bringing or protective powers. An aquamarine in a blue-green net bag traditionally offers protection at sea, while a tiny pink bag containing a piece of coral was worn by small children in many cultures to prevent them from falling. Young children especially may benefit from a pink rose quartz in a pink velvet bag beneath their pillow to bring them quiet sleep and to keep away nightmares.

A Colour Candle Ritual for a New Home

Carry out your ritual on a Saturday whose colour is brown, the colour of domestic matters and houses, and if you wish use a golden brown cloth on your special table.

- Put your astrological candle to the left on your special table. About 3 feet (1 metre) away to the right place the candle or candles of your need. Choose a golden brown one for the home and, if you wish, a yellow one for travel if you seek to change location drastically. The brown and yellow candles can stand side by side.
- In the centre place a brown sachet, sewn with yellow thread and tied with yellow or brown ribbon. It should contain a picture of the kind of home you would like, plus a tiny sketch map of your preferred location sketched in yellow on brown paper. Alternatively, you could insert into the sachet an unused key or a tiny model of a house to represent your desire.
- Light an incense stick, cone or block – allspice, cedar or frankincense, the incense of the Sun – and pass your sachet containing the photo through the smoke.

- Let all your hopes rise on the incense as you see yourself arriving at your new home. Say such words as: 'I am opening the door to my new house, carried by my wishes which I now send to the cosmos.'
- Return the sachet to the centre.
- Next light your astrological candle. Visualise yourself in the flame, framed in the coloured light of your birth colour, unpacking your furniture in your new home. Pass your sachet over the flame, saying: 'I am now making my new home my special place.'
- Return the sachet to the centre once more.
- Light the brown candle, then the yellow one. Passing the sachet over each in turn, see it bathed in the golden brown and rich yellow light and yourself, framed in the coloured light, going to sleep in your new home, saying: 'I am now totally at peace in my new home and no one can harm me.'
- Return the sachet to the centre and leave the candles to burn down naturally.
- Sleep with the sachet and picture under your pillow, and carry the sachet in your bag or car until the next Saturday when you can repeat the ritual. Use the intervening days for putting into motion plans to move.
- Repeat the ritual every Saturday until the impetus for your plans increases.

5

Thoroughly Modern Magic

When we think of real magic we picture cauldrons, swords and chalices, and indeed all of these can be used to give rituals a symbolic beauty and a link with earlier times. But it should be remembered that long ago they were not solely used by witches and wizards, but were everyday objects. Until the beginning of the twentieth century, the old cooking range with its black pot or cauldron was a feature of many urban as well as country kitchens. The witch's broom that was used to sweep out the magical circle was an everyday household implement and would be routinely placed behind a door, bristles upwards, to protect everyone within (see also Chapter 6).

In the magic of today we need not be bound to the past but can use the implements of modern living for thoroughly modern magic. The vacuum cleaner may not have the same resonance as the old twig broom, but it too can be used to banish bad vibes from the home as well as dust. When sweeping or vacuuming, move round the carpet anti-clockwise while visualising the disasters of the day or the night before – the thoughtless words, the imprints of feet stamped in tantrum – being sucked up into the waste bag for disposal along with the dirt. Then move clockwise, while visualising harmony and fresh energies being sucked into the carpet to fill the space vacated by the bad feelings.

Magic evolves with each generation, and in a hundred years our present kitchen utensils may well have been elevated to the status of magical tools. If you have the time and a ritual is special, by all means use candles, crystal and herbs. However, all too often you need magic quickly to meet some immediate crisis – we may need sudden protection, a burst of inspiration or to hold a potential lover before he or she takes the elevator out of our lives.

Magic can be practised anywhere – in the office, on the bus or train, in the car – using whatever is at hand, be they car keys, credit cards, a paper cup of coffee or even a computer. There really are no limits except for your own ingenuity, and it is possible to set up an effective defensive shield in your work area using spectacles, a paperweight or even a make-up mirror (see Chapter 9).

Modern Elemental Magic

In Chapter 14 I talk about the ancient elements of Earth, Air, Fire and Water as the basis for both formal and natural magic. They also have an important place in modern everyday magic, so I have listed some modern-day alternatives that you can use discreetly and buy anywhere.

Earth	Salt is a traditional Earth substance and you can use salt from an ordinary cruet set for the practical, grounding powers of the Earth. Alternatively try pot-pourri, an apple, any root vegetable, a plant in a pot, a coin, a cheque book or a credit card.
Air	Incense sticks are excellent for Air magic. A needle or small paper knife are substitutes for the logical, change-inducing energies of the Air, as are a set of car keys, an environmentally friendly air freshener or perfume spray, a kite or balloon, especially the silver helium type.
Fire	Candles are usually associated with Fire magic. However, you can use the flame from a lighter or a box of matches, the ring of a gas stove, a central heating radiator, a drinking glass or a make-up mirror, placed to catch the light, for instant inspiration and illumination.
Water	Oils or pure spring water, left in a crystal container for a full Sun-and-Moon cycle, are the traditional fluids used in Water magic.

Alternatively you can use a vase of flowers (which combine Earth and Water), a glass of still mineral water, a cup of tap water, fruit juices of different colours for colour magic, or even a paper cup of coffee. The local swimming pool with the water illuminated in the early morning or evening is an excellent substitute for the goddess Diana's 'mirror', a lake with the full Moon shining on it.

Earth Magic for Ending a Bad Habit

So you frequently contravene the non-smoking policy at work or can't resist the tea trolley with its calorific, cholesterol-boosting snacks. Follow the ancient magical practice of burying a bone. The bone was symbolically engraved with a sign or word indicating what someone wished to be rid of – an illness or a quarrel – and buried. As the bone decayed, so the illness or quarrel vanished.

We can adapt this ritual to modern times by burying the object of temptation, whether a cream bun or a cigarette. It goes against the grain for many of us to throw away food or cigarettes, because it seems a waste of money. In fact, we have already wasted the money on food, alcohol or cigarettes we do not need, and what we do afterwards is largely irrelevant in economic terms. If you do feel bad, put the equivalent money value of the offending item in a pot and when it is full give the cash to a relevant charity. You can use the following method for easing any compulsion or addiction.

- Fill a fairly large pot with earth and plant some fragrant flowering bulbs or herbs, such as hyacinths, lavender, eau de cologne, mint or lemon balm. The fragrance is most important.
- As you plant your bulbs or herbs say with your inner voice, or out loud if you are alone: 'I sow with this plant/flower/herb the person I wish to become, free from compulsions. Every time I smell this fragrance I am strengthening my resolve and my own self-worth, which does not need stimulants nor soothing substances to survive and thrive.'
- Pat the earth with your fingers nine times as you say these or similar words.
- When you find yourself smoking, eating or drinking at an inappropriate time or place, or overdoing it and endangering your health and well-being, take a single mouthful or inhalation.

- Then take the offending item somewhere private and shred it on a plate or, if liquid, pour it into an appropriate container.
- Bury only a very tiny quantity of the substance in the plant pot, as you do not wish to harm the herb or flower, and say once more with your inner voice or out loud: 'I bury this, that it may be taken by Mother Earth who will transform it through decay to new life.'
- Pause to smell the plant and say: 'I take with gratitude in return the fragrance of this plant as a reminder of what I wish to become.'
- Dispose of the rest of the shredded substance or pour away the liquid.
- Next time you are tempted, pause to smell the fragrance before eating, smoking or whatever, saying inwardly: 'I take with gratitude this fragrance as a reminder of what I wish to become.'
- If you still cannot resist the temptation, repeat the ritual, if possible avoiding taking even a taste of the substance. You may need plants in other places where you regularly smoke or over-eat.

Air Magic for Health and Happiness

Kites are used in Oriental rituals to carry petitions to the deities. The wishes are written either on the kites or on pieces of cloth or paper tied to the kite's tail. In a variation of this ritual, I have used balloons very successfully. I write desires on to strips of paper and tie these to the string, and in this way send them into the cosmos. Silver helium balloons are often decorated with hearts, flowers or messages and can easily be adapted to magic for different purposes. But kite magic is even better because you can let out the string and control its flight, building up the impetus of your ritual.

- Buy a very cheap children's kite in brilliant colours, or make one, and attach to the string brightly coloured ribbons according to your need. Choose, for example, yellow for travel and happiness, red for courage, orange for health and fertility, brown or gold for money (see Chapter 4 for more details).
- Write your wishes for increased or improved health and happiness on long strips of paper of the appropriate colour, being specific about your needs and your goals.

- Tie each of the wishes to the kite tails with a triple knot as you do so, saying for each,

Knot tie,
Kite fly,
Carry my wishes
To the sky.

I used to think simple ritualistic chants were trivial, and certainly you should create your own where possible. But a basic rhyme repeated faster and faster is an excellent way of building up energies, in this case within each knot, and of lulling the conscious mind that can get in the way of intuitive powers.

- Fasten the string to the kite itself quite loosely.
- Go to an open space, a common, a hilltop or an expanse of flat parkland and run with the kite until it catches the wind, gradually letting out the string so that it goes higher and higher, repeating your chant with increasing speed and volume.

Knot tie,
Kite fly,
Carry my wishes
To the sky.

- Feel the string tugging, but hold the kite back as it soars higher and further towards the light.
- Finally the kite will break free or, if it does not, cut the string, calling out:

The power is free,
The power in me
That I may be
Be [shout your wish – happy, healthy, wealthy, or wise etc.]

You have released the magical energies into the cosmos. Run and follow the path of the kite until it is out of sight. With luck the kite will be found by a child to whom it will bring even more pleasure. If you are not fit enough to run, get some children to do the running for you. They love this act, and never forget that they are the most potent magicians of all because their natural intuitive abilities have not been dulled by learning and logic.

Fire Magic for Surviving in an Unfriendly Atmosphere

At some time we all counter unwarranted hostility: as a newcomer to a firm who got the job promised to an internal candidate; from prospective in-laws who think only royalty is good enough for their offspring; in a new neighbourhood where there is a very closed community; or because you have a started a relationship with someone who was regarded as an item in an established group of friends. It is understandable if you radiate negativity in return, but quiet confidence is better, either to overcome the opposition or to protect yourself from the worst of the coldness (see also Chapter 9).

- Before going to work or meeting the hostile forces, half-fill a ceramic or cast iron pan, a naturally defensive metal, with rain-water that has been collected in a glass bowl without touching any roofs or guttering as it fell (see also Rain Magic in Chapter 12). If you have no rainwater, use spring water instead.
- Place the pan on the hob of a gas or electric stove or a camping stove, and add one pinch of dried mint or mint tea (cleansing herbs) for each person who is causing you problems (see also Herb Magic in Chapter 11).
- Do not light the ring.
- As you add the herb, name each person and say: 'Let any barriers of coldness, harshness or indifference between [name the person] and myself melt, if it is also his/her wish.' That last phrase is there because we cannot change another person's mind or will, merely make the circumstances more favourable for better relations.
- Add a pinch of dried lavender for yourself last of all, saying: 'May I be an outsider no more, excluded and alone, but wel-comed and part of this charmed circle.'
- As you say these words, mix the mint and lavender together with a wooden spoon so that the two herbs swirl round in the water.
- Light the stove and heat the water, constantly stirring it with the spoon and saying: 'Melt and mix, warm and welcome, fires of friendship, fires of compassion, fires of kindness, fan and flame.'

- When the water boils, stop stirring and allow it to simmer and evaporate until there is only a small quantity of water covering the herbs.
- Drain the herbs, saying: 'Water of fire, water of flame, bring acceptance to my name.'
- Dry the herbs naturally and add them to an open fire – a bonfire will do – or place the damp herbs in the microwave for a few seconds so that the ritual is complete.
- Repeat the ritual as necessary.

Water Magic to Get a Job

Water is excellent for getting things moving. Its power may be particularly useful for someone who has just lost their job – an all too common occurrence these days. The high-flyer is as vulnerable as the teenager just employed. The older executive suddenly faced with huge outgoings and no income can suffer a loss of self-esteem as great as someone who left school months ago but sees no prospect of a job, now or in the future. In such cases the important thing to avoid is being drained of all confidence and overwhelmed by a feeling of stagnation.

Our ancestors could recharge themselves by clear, running streams. These are not plentiful in towns, but a modern alternative is the local swimming pool which not only offers relaxation but can be a focus for potent spells, because the swimmer both directs the ritual and is the tool of the magic. Swimming pool magic is good for career matters and any area of life in a state of stagnation – love, money, promotion, confidence, health, family matters.

- Choose a time when the pool is quiet and preferably lit either by natural sunlight rippling on the water or by poolside lights.
- Stand in the water in a circle of sunlight or lamplight, and with your outstretched arms slowly make a circle in the water with both your hands so that they end up clasped at the back of you, a few inches from your body.
- This marks your present outer limits, the restrictions and stagnation around you out of which you can swim.
- Press your feet down in the water and then push yourself as high as you can, still within the invisible circle of water, saying in your mind as you do so. 'I will rise higher and higher I will succeed.'

- Repeat this nine times, each time pressing your feet lower so that you touch the bottom of the pool and are momentarily submerged. If you hate being underwater, tread water so that your shoulders are covered.
- Rise higher and higher, pushing yourself out of the water, feeling the resistance melting away before your efforts. Focus yourself on a specific goal or area in which you can and will succeed.
- Draw five creating or attracting pentagrams in the water with the index finger of your power hand (the one you use to write with). These ancient magical symbols of power can be drawn in two ways, the first with the single point uppermost to attract good fortune, and the second with it pointing downwards to banish negativity or ill health. Start yours at the bottom left-hand corner, as shown in the diagram, and continue round.

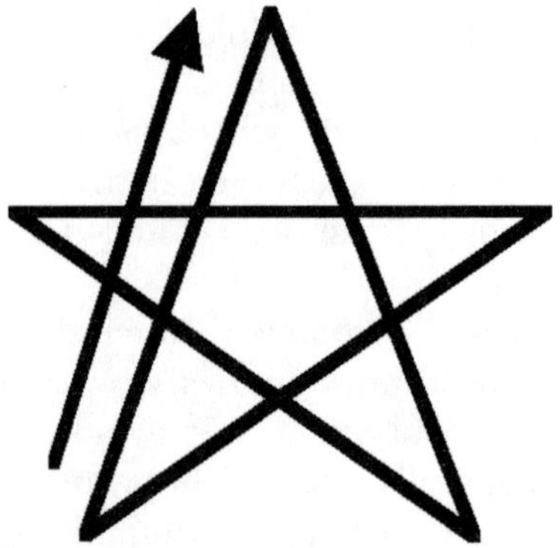

- Turn clockwise as you work, letting the light fill your watery pentagrams so that they glow with energy in your inner eye.
- Slowly visualise the individual pentagrams increasing in size and radiance.
- In your mind's eye, let them float outwards and further apart but still in a circle, as they do so releasing your potential and confidence in your own abilities.
- Wait until the pentagrams seem to float to the edges of the pool.
- Fix each visualised pentagram in an actual pool of light if possible, then swim to and touch each watery pentagram in turn, letting it fill you with inspiration, courage and determination.

- When you have touched each pentagram five times, allow them to move to form the five points of a single attracting pentagram in the centre of the pool.
- Swim the attracting pentagram formation, attracting luck, opportunities and potential prosperity.
- Gradually see the pentagrams fading and the light entering you.
- Float for a few minutes in a pool of light, opening your mind to possibilities you had not previously considered.
- Finally, return to the spot where you began and, with your hands behind you, reverse the drawing of your original circle, remaining with hands outstretched, looking at the future with renewed optimism.
- When you return home, explore five avenues of opportunity, including perhaps one you thought you were not ready to try or had rejected as beyond your scope.

Technological Magic

People often use the phrases 'the magic of new technology' or 'electronic wizardry'. In this section we will use the phrase literally, for here we will be adapting ancient rituals to modern inventions.

Computer Spells

Whatever you want – money, the guy or girl of your dreams, a new car, to move house or to travel somewhere exotic – you can use your computer as a powerful magical focus.

- Begin first with a screensaver of power. What do you feel symbolises the inner you? A tiger stalking through the jungle? A cat who walks alone? A Native American sitting in front of a tepee? Dolphins flowing through endless seas? I have seen all these images for sale quite cheaply on floppy disks or CD-Rom.
- Once you have installed your personal energiser you can use it as a focus for stilling racing thoughts at times of stress, uplifting and inspiring you as you enter the swirling world of the whales, swim with the rainbow fish or soar with mythical birds of paradise, letting their words of wisdom and healing flow through your mind.

- Choose a secret power word that you can repeat as a mantra or tap on your keyboard to lift you out of the immediate, frenetic or potentially confrontational situation into this slower, more graceful world.

Attracting and banishing rituals with computers

Use clip art to form a focus for rituals for any purpose. If you want to increase or attract something, call up, for example, an image of a bag of treasure for prosperity, a yacht for a holiday, a pile of books if you need to memorise information, a watch or clock if you need more time, a fortress for protection, a baby for fertility.

- Place the clip art image centre screen and surround it with a circle, drawn clockwise with your mouse, beginning at the twelve o'clock position if you wish to increase the power or attract the focus. Make an attracting image small initially so that, as it grows in size on the screen, so does your dream in actuality.
- If you want to attract love, call up a digicam image of the person or someone empathic that would serve as a symbol of the kind of lover/partner you would like to meet.
- Enclose the image in a square if you wish to decrease the effect or size of the symbolised factor in real life, beginning with a large picture that almost fills the square. Draw the square anti-clockwise, beginning in the north-west corner.
- You can be ingenious about symbols for both attracting and banishing computer spells – rocks for pain, balls and chains for debts, jagged lightning for stress. You can use clip art to fine-tune your needs, for example palm trees if you want to laze on a beach in Bali or craggy mountains for scaling the misty peaks of the Cairngorms.
- Concentrate on what it is you want by filling in the image with dense, vivid colour over and over so that it is embedded on your consciousness. Do you want a red car or a blue one? What about the home you want to buy? Is it a bungalow? An apartment? Use a paint program to colour in the blue door and yellow curtains, or the golden curls of the girl of your dreams.
- As you do this, picture yourself, for example, getting into your new car and starting it up, visualise the landmarks you would pass on the route home, culminating with parking your new vehicle in the drive.

- Be as detailed as you can in your visions. The richer the imagery, sounds and smells, as well as colours, the easier it is to translate the wish into the material plane. Think of the smell of a new car interior, the scent of mimosa or the cry of gulls in your holiday paradise.
- If you want to increase your salary, for example, gradually increase the size of the bag of treasure until it fills the whole circle.
- As the symbol grows larger (or smaller if it is a diminishing spell), build up the energies within you, repeating phrases in your head faster and faster. For example: 'Grow, thrive, prosperous be, desire of my dreams, come now to me.'
- As the expanding symbol touches the edges of the circle, or can shrink no smaller in a diminishing ritual, the most powerful form of any spell, the release of energy into the cosmos, takes place. In a single movement, make the circle or square disappear, leaving only the symbol on the screen and saying: 'The Power is free. The wish is mine.'

A computer ritual to improve your body shape

We all have an optimum shape and size at which we feel fit and confident. This has nothing to do with media images of very thin models, and the most important gift that magic can offer is to let us value ourselves, whatever our physical appearance, and to ignore the barbs of those who see us only as a body, whether beautiful or, in their jaundiced estimation, unattractive.

With this spell, if you are underweight you can add weight and curves to your image in the right places on your computer screen and then translate the action to the outer world. But I have concentrated here primarily on a ritual to lose fat, because many people do suffer from weight problems that can adversely affect their health. But any ritual to improve shape cannot achieve everything by magic. A sensible diet and moderate exercise are the other half of the equation, as I all too frequently choose to forget. If you do not have a computer, you can use a pencil, paper and rubber.

- Using a paint program, draw an image with your mouse to represent yourself. Save it, as you will need to come back to the image periodically and modify it as your life improves.
- Be realistic and put bulges where they exist, but do not draw in features.

- Write next to this first image one thing that would make you happy right now. Save the image and print out the whole picture.
- Choose quite modest, easily achievable goals at first: spending time alone reading a chapter of a book you enjoy, not one you need to read; having a bath or massage with oils; taking a bus trip to a place you have never been but always wanted to visit; writing the first chapter of a novel; or riding your bicycle in the early morning.
- Pin the picture behind your wardrobe door or keep it somewhere where you will see it but no one else can.
- Keep to a healthy diet and moderate exercise. If you are tempted to binge, take out your image, reread your first goal and, before eating, write another page or two of your novel, plan a trip or take a fragrant bath. If you do still want to eat, choose something you would really like and enjoy every mouthful – but maybe you will decide not to.
- When you have achieved your first goal, call up the image on the screen and erase one of the bulges or improve the shape of the outline. Set another goal for happiness, which may be related to the previous one or something quite different.
- Save the new image as well as the old one, and print out the second image and goal to keep where you can see it.
- If you are tempted to binge, take out the new improved image, compare it with the first one and work towards your new goal for a few minutes before deciding whether to eat.
- When you have achieved this goal, call up the second image on the screen, blot or smooth out another imperfection and move on to goal three, which may be more ambitious.
- You will find that after a few weeks people will compliment you on how attractive and fit you are looking, even if you have only lost a pound or two in actual weight. This is because your body is focused not on your imperfections, but on your happiness. Certainly the desire to binge should diminish.
- Continue until you are satisfied with yourself and feeling fit and have smoothed away all the imperfections on your computer image.
- Print out the first and last image, plus a list of all the steps you have taken to personal happiness, and look at them whenever you doubt your self-worth.

Section Two

Rituals for Special Purposes

6

The Magical Home and Garden

From the earliest times home has been more than a shelter from the elements; it has embodied a refuge from the outside world, an oasis of calm, a source of sustenance and renewal, and a place where we can hang up our outward persona at the door and reveal our real selves. Whether we are talking about a high-rise apartment, a rural cottage or a suburban semi, the home, whether chintzy, elegant or functional, is a reflection of ourselves. That is the theory, and perhaps the gulf between the ideal and reality explains the current fascination with Feng Shui, the Oriental art of harmonious homes and workplaces. However Feng Shui, with its insistence on everything being just so, is itself an idealised art, and the majority of people in the East live in crowded, cluttered homes and rush around trying to find enough hours in the day just as people do in the West.

The ancient traditions of the West have a less organised but perhaps richer basis, because of their diversity and an accessibility not only to experts but to everyone who seeks a happy and peaceful home. Our ancestors invoked protection upon their dwellings and abundance by using herbs, metals, fire and trees. No matter how chaotic and cluttered our homes to outward appearance, they can be sanctuaries and restorers of hope if we adapt some of the simple old ways to the modern world. If it seems that many of the spells in this book centre around herbs, trees and flowers, it is because these were the tools with which our forebears tapped the powers of the cosmos. It is the timelessness of these natural tools that can link us with the harmonies of the world of nature that lies above, below and on all sides of the most urban development (see also Chapter 11).

The Magical Hearth

In both the Eastern and Western magical systems, the hearth has long been the centre of household rituals because it was the gathering-place of present family members and believed to be the place at which departed ancestors and household guardians would also gather. Cooking, warmth, recreation and offerings to the gods were associated with the hearth. In this way the sacred became entwined with the mundane, as with so much traditional ritual, providing grounding and security and preventing the artificial divisions foisted on us today between magic and everyday living. The family gathered around the hearth for food and comfort and it was literally the focal point of the home – the Latin word for hearth is *focus*. In Hinduism too, the domestic hearth took on religious as well as family significance; Agni, god of fire, was also the god of domestic fire.

Creating a Focus or Magical Hearth

Some homes do still have fireplaces, and even if they are not used for an open fire they can form a focus for rituals for health, happiness and abundance in the home. Even if you do not have a chimney, you can still set up a symbolic hearth without a fire.

- If you have no hearth you can buy a grate or small brazier to set against a wall, surrounded by a layer of flat stones or slates on which to place offerings.
- Fill the grate, or the hearth surround if you have an open fire-place, with symbols of domestic abundance – seasonal flowers and leaves, corn tied with scarlet ribbon, coal or wood, a bowl of fruit, a skein of silk to symbolise sufficient clothing. You can also place your money bottle here (the ritual for creating one is given below) to incubate wealth (see also Chapter 8).

- If you do not have a fire that can be kindled or it is summer time, light a scarlet candle when the family are home for the night and place it in the hearth. Otherwise, light a small fire scented with pine or rosemary for cleansing any negativity the family may have brought home. Sprinkle about five or six drops of oil in total on two or three pieces of leaf, or burn the herbs or pine cones and leaves.
- Try to spend a few minutes sitting quietly in the candlelight or firelight with those you love before you engage in your various activities. Talk about your hopes and dreams, and listen to the thoughts and feelings of other family members. This short time represents the heart of the home, and whether you sit alone with your cat or dog dreaming your quiet thoughts, or let older people tell stories of their lives to the young, you can draw strength from the hearth, as people have done for centuries.
- If any family members are absent, send them love and thoughts as you blow out the candle or poke the fire nine times clockwise with a hazel stick as you say their names and send them wisdom and protection.
- Keep the family hearth well tended and replace any dying flowers or over-ripe fruit.

Money Bottles

There are so many money pot and bottle rituals from around the world that you are spoiled for choice. No home should be without a money bottle, and you should attend to it as regularly as watering your plants if you want to keep money flowing into your home.

- Choose a wide-necked bottle of clear glass or the traditional brown pottery jar with a lid.
- If possible, begin your money collection with a coin you have discovered, as there is an old magical tradition that something found is worth ten times that of something given or bought. Traditionally copper coins were used, but you can use coins of any substance or denomination. Try to add one every day.
- Whatever form of money jar you use, it should not be a source of instant change for the family, but used when it is full for

something that will make the home and family happier – perhaps the ingredients for a special meal.

Magical Housework

With increasingly busy lives and modern household appliances, we do not spend the hours our great-grandmothers and even grandmothers did working lavender polish into furniture, making soap or scrubbing floors with a herbal infusion. I can remember as a child in Birmingham, pounding the washing and rubbing polish in increasing circles into tables, chairs and dressers, worn smooth with age, until I really could see my face in them. These tasks had a mesmeric quality, and the finest scrying was done by women who gazed into the suds as they did the Monday wash or entered a semi-hypnotic trance as they scrubbed the doorstep and polished the brasses. They managed without psychic fairs and tarot packs, and as they cleaned away the household dirt and dust replaced them with positive energies. But in using the old ways occasionally we can tune into those powerful psychic energies and cleanse our homes of negativity in a way that scattering herbs or burning oils cannot do.

Endowing Household Polish with Magic

You do not need to make your own polish for household magic to be successful. Purchase unscented beeswax polish and soften it slightly by warming it in a heat-resistant bowl over a pan of warm water. Using beeswax is always restorative, for the bees are natural household protectors and act as messengers to the cosmos, transmitting family news if you tell your local hive. A friendly bee who enters your home should always be shown an exit, with thanks for calling and endowing care upon the dwelling.

- Remove the polish from the heat and, using a wooden spoon, mix in a few drops of an essential oil – lavender for harmony, pine or cedar for cleansing negativity, and rosewood for love and compassion.
- As you work, visualise the needs of your family and make wishes for a happy and safe home. Create a household mantra whose

power will be released when you use the polish. An old rhyme I heard frequently in my childhood was:

May peace reside within,
No spite, no malice pass these doors,
Health and joy shine through the windows
Food to the table, coal to the hearth
And love in times of trouble.

Such words used to seem very sentimental, but as I have grown older and learned the sorrows as well as joys of family life, and the value of a united family, they make more sense. But create your own family recipe for happiness that you can recite or that will be activated as you polish.

Before it sets, draw a symbol or letters in the wax – perhaps a heart, a flower or the name of your home. Place your polish in small screw-cap containers for use when you feel the family atmosphere is tense or you are worried about a family member.

Washing Away Negativity

There are an overwhelming array of creams, mousses and gels for rinsing away dirt and grime in seconds, although few live up to their promises with my family. But on both sides of the Atlantic a traditional way to wash floors and clean patios and yards was with an infusion of herbs in hot water, using herbs that naturally removed negative feelings along with the dirt, and attracted prosperity or luck to the dwelling. Infusions are made by leaving herbs in boiling water for ten minutes, then straining the liquid and discarding the herbs. For domestic use you can make quite a strong infusion.

- If your domestic harmony is being threatened by outside hostility or problems, make an infusion of fresh parsley.
- For quarrels between family members, make your infusion with valerian or lavender.

Essential oils are equally potent for cleansing the boundaries. An old-fashioned mop can be used in anti-clockwise circles to remove negativity or clockwise to endow protection, and should be kept for times when the home does not feel right.

- Use eight or nine drops of lemon, geranium, rosemary or tea tree oil in a medium-sized bucket of water.
- Wash the front and back doorsteps with a traditional scrubbing brush dipped in the water, marking in your mind's eye a barrier that will prevent stress or bad feelings from being carried over the threshold.
- Work next on the bathroom and kitchen or cloakroom – any area where there are water outlets that can drain out luck or happiness.
- Next sweep out any yard or patio areas in anti-clockwise circles, with a traditional besom broom if possible, to remove any lingering creeping resentments or spite that may be waiting for a door to open in order to enter your rooms.
- Wash the area with a bucket of water containing eight or nine drops of eucalyptus or tea tree oil, using your broom in clockwise circles to draw up boundaries of protection.
- Finally tip the remaining water down any outside drains to allow the negativity to flow away.
- Stand your broom, bristles up, outside the door to protect the home.

Herbs and Similar Plants for the Home

You can grow pots, window boxes or troughs of herbs near windows so that when you open them the protective fragrance enters. Tie dried bunches of lavender and eau de cologne mint to the ceiling, and sweet basil in your kitchen away from direct heat and steam. Lavender, bay or rosemary burned on an open grate in the main living area scent the room and burn away negativity.

Catnip	Grow near the front door to draw in luck and benign forces.
Cloves	Will protect children and elderly people while they sleep.
Dill	Dried seed heads hung in the home or over doorways and above cradles, or scattered around the boundaries of a home, offer protection from all malevolence, especially envy.

Fenugreek	A few seeds of fenugreek should be placed in an open pot or jar on a kitchen shelf or in your hearth, beginning at the new Moon. Add a sprinkling of seeds each day until the jar is full. Then empty the jar and plant the seeds, to ensure that your money supply will continue to grow, and begin a new jar of seeds.
Garlic	Hung in kitchens on strings or ropes, garlic bulbs keep away all hostile influences. The string formation is especially potent. In a new home, garlic will remove sadness lingering from previous owners. Some magical authorities advise against using it for cooking as it has absorbed the bad vibes. I believe that as you use a garlic press you should visualise the bad vibes being squeezed out and clinging to the press, only to be washed down the drain when you wash the press.
Hyssop	Use infusions to lighten the atmosphere after quarrels or sorrow. Sprinkle the infusion over rooms and also over artefacts that are associated with unhappy times, rather than disposing of them.
Juniper	The berries are burned in homes in Scotland on New Year's morning to remove bad luck and the negative influences of the Old Year. Juniper, grown outside the front door, protects the home against all misfortune.
Kelp	An infusion of kelp for mopping floors will attract money to the home. Check tide tables for your nearest tidal water and wash the floors at high tide. Place a small piece of kelp or bladderwrack in a sealed jar of whisky on a window ledge, to draw in and then preserve money supplies.
Mustard	Seeds were traditionally buried under the doorstep or outside the front door in a pot to protect a home and its occupants.
Peppermint	Burned as incense or used as an infusion on floors, it will clean away negativity and illness.

Raspberries	Flowering branches bound in a hoop with red ribbon, hung at the entrance to homes, will offer protection. A raspberry bush grown near the door will tangle hostile vibes in its brambles.
Sage	Burn sage on an open fire or oil burner for harmony, health and protection. It is a good herb to grow in the kitchen or near the house to ensure long and happy lives for the family. An old saying is; Why should a man die while he has sage in his garden?

Protective and Luck-bringing Metals

Iron

The lucky horseshoe made of iron is said to be ten times more lucky if it is found rather than bought or given. It is associated with St Dunstan, patron saint of blacksmiths, who nailed the Devil to a smithy wall and refused to let him free until he promised never to enter a house or forge with a horseshoe nailed to the wall. Horseshoes should be placed over a main door or a fireplace, points upwards, to hold in the luck and protection of the dwelling.

The tradition of lucky horseshoes existed in Ancient Rome and in the northern magical tradition. The popular mixture of Christian and pagan beliefs that persisted for hundreds of years after the coming of Christianity is demonstrated in this protective and healing rhyme, spoken as three horseshoes were hammered with iron nails into either an external wall or, in times of sickness, to the foot of a bed:

One for God,
One for Wod
And one for Lok.

Our modern expression 'One for luck' is a corruption of this chant, said to appease Loki, god of mischief and change. Wod was short for Woden, the Anglo-Saxon Father God. Sometimes an iron hammer representing the hammer of Thor, the Norse god of thunder, would be nailed horizontally across the three horseshoes.

Iron gained its magical reputation as the metal of the gods, especially those of war, notably Mars, since it was first discovered in meteorites and so seen as a gift from the deities. Iron nails were driven into the walls of houses to protect the inhabitants against illness. A piece of iron, or an iron or steel object such as a pair of scissors, would be buried under the threshold of a new home to prevent negative influences entering. Alternatively, iron would be buried near the front door with just the tip showing, so that it would attract any unfriendly vibrations. These could pass into the Earth and be absorbed to regenerate as positive growth.

Brass

A symbol of prosperity, brass is also a protective metal. Horse brasses, worn to guard against evil, would be handed down by carters and farmers from father to son. They are often in the shape of moons, suns and stars, to invoke the brightness of the celestial spheres. Both these and the brass bells on the harness were a powerful deterrent against harm. Horse brasses can still be bought from antique shops or even car boot sales. Once they were a feature of many homes, but cleaning them has discouraged many people from following the old custom of displaying them above the fireplace, along with brass plates and warming pans which were once filled with hot coals and placed in beds in winter.

The brass bell was used long before protective wind chimes infiltrated from the East. Brass door stops and brass-edged steps to houses served the same purpose, as did polished white steps.

The Magical Garden

Protective Natural Boundaries

Open-plan housing and apartments with communal hallways make it much harder to mark our boundaries. Once even the humblest cottage had its patch of land around it, often essential for growing food. When industrialisation forced people into towns, the first terraced houses had their back yards, however small, with walls separating them from neighbours.

The custom of marking out boundaries came from a time before maps. Boundaries in the northern world were under the auspices of the Norse thunder god Thor, Holda, the crone version of the Mother Goddess Frigg and Freyja, goddess of fertility. They were marked with stones that were regarded as sacred, and the boundary itself, like all divisions, was a magical area.

In hotter climates a cactus of the same kind is planted outside a house at each of its four corners to protect the home from negative influences. In a colder place, you can keep the cacti indoors at the four outermost corners of your home.

Bay trees, palms, myrtle, juniper and rowan trees all form protective boundaries. If you do not have the room to plant these, bury an iron horseshoe, with its points upwards at the four corners. Alternatively insert nine bamboo canes into your perimeter fence, surrounding each with a clockwise circle drawn in the earth. Tie a scarlet cord from each of them, knotted nine times, and replace it when it rots.

Hawthorn hedges, among the most ancient boundaries for homes, are said to offer not only physical but psychic protection. For this reason solitary witches are called hedge witches, a reference to the hawthorn hedge they would erect around their home to keep out prying eyes.

If you do not have a garden, plant a protective window box with basil, cumin, wild garlic, parsley, rosemary, sage, thyme or vetivert.

A ritual to mark out your boundaries

Old ceremonies of marking out boundaries would involve walking round them and blessing them with sacred fire and water. Even if you have no land round your dwelling you can mark the outermost limits, which in an apartment might be the walls of several rooms without the room dividers. You can touch the four outermost corners of a house, or the two corners of your front and two of your back garden that mark out the limits of the area you own or rent.

- Begin in the corner nearest north.
- Place a large stone at the northern corner of the land or house if outdoors, or a rutilated quartz or tiger's eye in the corner of the room if indoors.
- Sprinkle this and the corner with salt and say: 'Guardians of the earth, keep my home safe from earthquake, subsidence and erosion.'

- Carry on walking in a clockwise direction to the next corner in the east. Mark this with a large stone if outdoors or a yellow jasper or citrine if indoors, and sprinkle this and the eastern corner with salt, repeating the call to the Earth guardians.
- At the southernmost corner place a stone or an amber or orange carnelian, repeating the salt ritual and words.
- At the western extremity, place a stone or moss agate or jade and repeat the ritual.
- Begin now in the eastern corner, using an incense stick of frankincense or citronella (you can buy special garden incense sticks). Waft the fragrance over the stone or crystal and the corner, saying: 'Guardians of the Air, keep my home safe from storms, hurricanes and whirlwinds.'
- Continue this ritual round the other three corners.
- Begin in the south with a pure white candle or torch. Pass the flame over the stone or crystal and corner, saying: 'Guardians of Fire, protect my home from lightning, and from destructive fires of natural and man-made origin.'
- Continue this ritual in the other three corners.
- Begin in the west, using water in which roses have been steeped or pure spring water. Sprinkle the stone or crystal and corner with water, saying words such as: 'Guardians of the Waters, protect my home from floods and lashing rain.
- If you live near the sea or a tidal river, you might ask for protection from the ocean's excesses.
- Repeat this ritual in the other three corners.
- Blow out the candle, but leave the incense to burn away. Dissolve your salt in the water and tip it down a drain, seeing any negative energies flowing away.
- Walk round your boundaries eight more times and then plant seedlings at any of the stone points, or place a small pot of protective herbs in each of the internal corners and plant the appropriate crystal in the soil.

Protection from Theft and Intruders

Rowan or mountain ash is especially good for protecting the home and outbuildings. Planted by the garden gate, it helps to keep out unwelcome visitors. Rowan crosses, tied in red twine with nine knots and made from branches that are not cut with a knife or any metal, have long been considered protective amulets for any outbuildings. Placed on the outside of a garage or bike shed, they will help to deter thieves.

I have already mentioned the practice of burying iron outside houses for protection. Iron is central to the ritual below that I know was still used in Wales when I went there on holidays as a child more than forty years ago, and may well be in use in other lands where descendants of the Celts dwell.

- Fill an old iron box from a junk shop or hardware store with iron nails and a key from the household – not a front or back door key, but one from a drawer or old cupboard.
- Sprinkle it with rosemary picked from the garden or a pot, and with rue and fennel, also freshly gathered.
- Tie the key with red wool or a natural fibre, knotted tightly with twine, and speak these words or similar ones:

Key of my home, of all I love,
Keep safe from all who lurk with dark intent,
From valleys, mountains, lakes of glass,
Lock fast what I do treasure most
Bind with iron chains my sacred hearth,
That those who come in greed
May find my door invincible
And those in need
Find welcome.

- Close the box and place an iron chain round it.
- Use an old padlock without a key, or with a cheap one, and as you close it throw away the key.
- When it is dark, on a night of the waning Moon, bury the box in your garden and tell no one where it is.
- Cover it over with earth and do not try to identify the place in the morning.
- If you do not have a garden, place the box in a basement, attic or storeroom on a high shelf.

7

Love Magic

We all need to be loved, to be special to someone, but often we may feel that we are not worthy of that love – that we are not sufficiently beautiful, witty, successful and so on – and so we may accept less than loving treatment. Or we may have suffered loss, or betrayal, compounded by perhaps unnecessary guilt and anger that we seek to repress. The media place the emphasis on youth and physical prowess in love and lovemaking, so we may long for an ideal that does not exist. If we seek only the outward veneer, we may miss out on potentially deep, meaningful, enduring relationships with people who, like ourselves, may be less than perfect, lacking confidence, and yet whose inner beauty will blossom in a true love match.

So love magic is complex, not in the rituals, (some, as old as time itself, that I described in Chapter 1) but because it involves focusing on what we really want and really need. It is very potent, and must not be used to bind people against their will or to make a person love you and leave someone else. But in its best form it can open you to love and attract the kind of person who will make you happy. It can add passion and encourage fidelity in an existing relationship, and can help you recover from a betrayal or even to walk away from a destructive relationship.

A Ritual to Increase Self-esteem and Inner Radiance

The most important love is that of yourself. This does not mean narcissistic vanity; but you must learn to value your strengths, your talents and your personal magnetism. Often the person that others are most drawn to is not the most glamorous or muscle-bound, but someone whose eyes glow with warmth, whose smile is genuine, whose voice is reassuring and who emits an aura of calm and welcome. If you are happy in yourself and your life is full, you can love others unconditionally and love will often come to you.

In Chapter 11 I explain how to make love sachets and love poppets, filled with herbs and tied together to attract a lover who would make you happy. But first you must be happy in yourself. In Chapter 14 I describe a salt and clay ritual for preserving fidelity, because clay does not have the negative connotations of wax images but enables us to mould what it is we most desire. This ritual involves making a clay image of yourself. It does not have to be a perfect replica – imperfections in the model are not reflections of imperfection in yourself – and in fact the image can be quite crude. The important thing is that, because you have made it rather than bought it, it holds something of your personality.

- Work in the garden at a small table placed on soil so that your feet connect with the land.
- If this is not possible, surround yourself by living growing greenery as you knead your clay.
- As you mould the clay in your hands, see light and love flowing into it from the cosmos and let all negativity flow away downwards to be reabsorbed by the earth.
- Sprinkle the clay with a little salt, pass over it a pine or cedar incense stick, hold your clay to the Sun or pass it through a golden candle flame, and finally sprinkle it with pure spring water, saying: 'Through earth, air, flame and water I cleanse and charge you that you will radiate only loveliness, optimism and joy.'
- Shape out a figure about the size of a small doll, saying: 'So am I freed from all criticism, all negative words, barbs and jibes that make me feel less than whole.'

- Scatter on to the earth or into the soil rosemary, the herb of love and remembrance, and let the voices from the past and present that have diminished your self-worth fall away, leaving you feeling new, ready to shape your own destiny.
- Now comes the hard part if you have come to undervalue yourself.
- Take a bag of tiny round quartz crystals (or clear glass nuggets if you do not have any crystals) and from the centre outwards press a crystal into the doll as you name each lovable, worthwhile quality you possess, emotional and spiritual as well as physical. Say words along these lines: 'I am worthy of love because [I am loyal, hard-working, have a lovely smile, am good in a crisis, tell brilliant jokes etc].'
- Even with an initial list, your doll of self-worth will be sparkling.
- Even if you do not feel attractive, pick out features on which people have complimented you. Ignore the old voices that try to creep back, which may have more to do with the inadequacies of your critics.
- Place your doll on a bedside table, wrapped in a bag of pure white velvet or linen, and repeat: 'I am special, I am unique and worthy of love and respect, not least from myself.'
- Try to add a crystal of worth every day by recalling some achievement until the doll is totally covered in crystals, and do something, however small, to make yourself happy every day.
- If your doll does crack or get broken, bury it in the bag with the crystals under a favourite tree. It is not you, only an image that helped you take back the love and radiance into yourself.
- You will find that people are more attentive to you, and if there is no one special in your life your inner radiance will ensure that soon there will be – if that is what you want.

The Flowers and Herbs of Love

You can use the herbs and flowers of love in a variety of ways that have come down to us through the ages, and are as potent today as they ever were. Many are not exotic blooms but humble wild flowers exchanged by lovers and, when given in love, are more precious than the most expensive bouquet.

Basil is for attracting and keeping love. Sprinkling powdered basil over a lover is said to prevent infidelity.
Caraway seeds can be pressed on to bread, cookies or cakes to act as an aphrodisiac. Or, if you are alone, they can attract a new love.
Cloves are a natural aphrodisiac, both attracting love and awakening sexual feelings. For those who have suffered loss, cloves offer solace.
Coriander is used in love sachets and the seeds added to mulled wine as an aphrodisiac. Traditionally pregnant women ate coriander to ensure their unborn children were quick-witted and creative.
Daisies were worn by medieval knights when they went into battle as a sign that they rode in the name of a lady whom they loved. A double-headed daisy showed the love was reciprocated. The daisy, a flower of Venus, is the most commonly used for love divination, as lovers pluck the petals chanting, 'He/she loves me, he/she loves me not.' It is said to be a talisman for all who are pure of heart and loyal in love. If placed under a pillow at night, a daisy root can bring back an absent lover.
Dandelions act as transmitters of love. Blow the seeds from a ripened dandelion head in the direction of a lover to carry your thoughts. The plant is used in country love divination, where petals are plucked to answer questions with alternative yes/no answers concerning a lover's fidelity and intentions.
Forget-me-nots are a symbol of undying love as well as lasting friendship. In Austrian legend, a man and his betrothed were walking hand in hand beside the Danube on the night before their wedding. A small blue flower was being carried away by the current and the woman began to weep that so lovely a flower should be lost forever. Her beloved, unable to bear her sorrow, leaped into the water to save the flower, but was swept away. In a last heroic gesture, he cast the flower on to the bank with the words: 'Forget me not, my love.' They are also good flowers for both men and women to send after a period apart, perhaps because of work commitments or a misunderstanding.
Lavender is the ultimate flower and herb of love. Lavender flowers or lavender water worn by women or placed in a clothes drawer attract love and deter potential cruelty.
Marigolds should be planted in a pot of earth imprinted with a lover's footstep. He or she will become more loving as the flowers grow, and will remain faithful.

Parsley encourages fertility, love and passion. A lover cutting parsley is said to cut through his or her love bond, so pull it up and shred by hand for cooking.
Rosemary or elf leaf is a herb of passion, love and healing. Poppets filled with rosemary attract lovers and bring healing. For this reason it can be a gentle herb in difficult periods in a relationship, encouraging fidelity and forgiveness, recalling happier times past and looking forward to those to come.
Roses are a herb of love and Venus's own flower. From the pink rosebud of first innocent attraction through the full red rose of passion and fidelity to the golden rose of mature love, they are used in love rituals of all kinds. Burning rose incense and putting rose petals in bathwater attracts love. The blood-red rose especially is a symbol of courage, which may be of special significance when a marriage or relationship runs into difficult times. You can also plant a rose on a special anniversary or on the birth of a child – red for a boy and white for a girl. As it blooms each year you can be reminded of the feelings of that first moment.
Sunflower seeds should be planted for unrequited love. If they grow, make some steps towards the person in mind, remembering that if your love is not reciprocated there are many other ways of making the Sun shine in your life – maybe by recognising someone close by who would make you happy. In Greek mythology the water nymph Clytie was so sad that her love for Helios, the Sun god, was not returned that she sat on the ground day and night, watching his fiery chariot pass across the sky as the Sun rose, reached its height and descended into the ocean. So long did she watch that her limbs became rooted in the Earth and she was transformed into a sunflower, symbol of constancy. Her gaze is forever fixed sunwards as she climbs towards her love. But she must die each year and let new seeds fall.
Vervain is a herb of fidelity and can be exchanged with a friend or lover as a promise of truth at all times – not always easy, but ultimately the only way to banish suspicion and the efforts of outsiders to sour love.
Witch hazel heals the pains of unrequited or faithless love and offers protection against all harm.
Yarrow is a herb of enduring love, said to keep a couple together for at least seven years and so given to newly-weds and used in love charms. Married couples keep the herb in a special sachet and

replace them just before seven years is over, continuing to do so throughout married life; this can be made into a ceremony of renewal. Alternatively, hang a ring of dried yarrow over the marital bed and replace when necessary.

See Chapter 11 for some further plants associated with love.

The Candle and Mirror Ritual to Attract or Strengthen Love

The ritual should be carried out on the three nights before the full Moon. Use a large oval mirror of the kind owned by all the best princesses in fairy stories.

- In a darkened room light a pink and green candle, the colour of Venus and of love. One is for you and one for your projected partner. Light the other person's candle first.
- Take a red rose for the male in the partnership and a white rose for the female, and place one in front of each candle so that the candlelight reflects on it.
- Look between the candles into the mirror and call softly the name of your love if you know him or her or the unknown person who is waiting for you. Say: 'I call you [name], my love, to come to me of your own free will, that I may see your image in this mirror and before long in reality, so that we may move ever closer together.'
- As you speak, move the candles slightly closer together, then the roses. As you do so, you may see in the mirror the image of the one you love.
- On the first night the image may be quite indistinct, perhaps no more than a shadow. But smile and murmur your private words of greeting. If you see nothing, wait until you have blown out the candle and you will see the other person in the after-image. Speak the words of love before blowing out the candles.
- Blow out the candles, first the other person's, then yours, sending the love to whoever is waiting, asking his or her light to return to you before the night is ended.
- Leave the candles, flowers and mirror in place.

- On the second night relight the candles, the other person's first. Repeat the ritual and words, bringing the candles and flowers even closer together.
- The image seen through the candle flame may be clearer now, and if you smile you may see the other person smiling too.
- Do not be surprised if you recognise the other person. We may work with someone or see them every day, then suddenly see them through the eyes of love as though it were the most natural thing in the world.
- Say softly the words you wish to share, and you may hear as a whisper or sigh words of love returning in your mind's ear.
- Once again blow out the candles, first yours and then that of the loved one. See the light in long thin rays bound off the mirror and go off into the darkness.
- You will see the person in the after-image, if not before.
- Once again leave the candles and flowers in place, but before you begin on the third night burn an oil or incense of love – jasmine, patchouli, neroil or lavender – and let the fragrance carry your thoughts as you sit in the darkness.
- This time, as you speak the words and light the candles, they will be touching, and if you place a tray beneath them their wax will mingle.
- Tie the roses together with red twine in nine knots, saying for each:

Knot one for love,
Knot two for joy,
Knot three for hope,
Knot four for passion,
Knot five for faithfulness,
Knot six for gentleness,
Knot seven for harmony,
Knot eight that we may grow old together,
Knot nine so be forever joined,
If it is the will of the other as it is mine.

- Only now look into the mirror over the candles, and see your face and that of the other person close in the two flames becoming one.
- Let the candles burn naturally, and in the mingled wax draw a

heart with your joint initials entwined (or yours and a question mark inside if the lover is as yet unknown).

- When the candles have burned out and the wax is cool, cut out the heart with a black-handled knife (see Chapter 3) and place the heart and the roses in a white silk scarf in a drawer.
- Do not actively seek your new relationship or put pressure on an existing one. Let nature take its course. Your loving rays have opened you to all kinds of happy possibilities, but as with those of any flower, the seeds of love must grow in their own time.
- Concentrate on making other aspects of your life happy, and love will come when the time is right.

Ritual for Consummating a Union or Making It Fruitful

There are many versions of this spell, sometimes called the knife and cup ritual, or the chalice and blade, because of its associations with the Grail legend. The chalice, cup, cauldron or bowl represents in many cultures the female principle, the nurturing womb, but also the hidden unconscious wisdom, the fierce, wild side of womanhood. The knife, blade or sword is the masculine, direct, forceful, but it also needs to submit to the waters of the cauldron or chalice to be complete. The cauldron or chalice represents the Water element in formal magic, just as the knife represents Air.

You can make this ritual as formal or informal as you wish. Obtain a small metal pot or cauldron with a handle and an athame if you like, but generally I find the chalice–knife combination is best. You can adapt as I do, using a stainless steel goblet and an ornate knife bought on holiday in Spain. I have seen the ritual carried out with a cup and paper knife (see Chapter 5). The magic is in those who practise it, not in the tools, but increasingly I am aware of the purpose of ceremony in reaching the deeper, more spiritual part of the psyche and marking this time as special, apart, important.

This ritual is meaningful if carried out by two people before lovemaking, especially if it is the first time they have made love or are marking a deeper commitment in the relationship. But if your partner would be worried or uneasy by such a ritual you can perform it alone and recall it during your lovemaking.

It is also very potent if you are trying to conceive a child. Perform this ritual as close to the full Moon as you can. The evening of the full Moon is perfect.

- Draw a circle in the air, using a clear crystal quartz or the index finger of your right hand with your arm outstretched.
- Begin either in the north or east, according to your preference, and create an unbroken clockwise invisible circle. Make it large enough for one or two to work in.
- Within the north of the circle, which you and/or your partner will face, place a semi-circle of six alternate green and purple candles on a low table. The table should be large enough to hold what you need for the ritual. If you have not carried out many formal rituals, practise how you will move naturally and check that everything you need is in reach.
- Place the chalice, and enough wine or black grape juice to fill it in a small bottle or phial, to the right of the candles and the knife or blade to the left.
- Light each candle clockwise in turn, saying: 'As the lance to the Grail cup, as the blade to the chalice, as the mighty sword to the cauldron, so do we join in loving union, never to be split asunder by the malice of others, faithful through sorrow and sickness, in riches or poverty, as one.'
- If you are working with a partner, light alternate candles, each speaking the words over the candles you light.
- In front of the candles, at right-angles to the central candles, place five sticks of incense (rose or jasmine for love) in holders on the floor, lighting the one nearest the candles first.
- If you are alone, kneel or sit and see your lover's face through the smoke, saying: 'Come to me through Fire, through Air, across Water, from lands far or near, but come to me.'
- If you are working with your lover, light alternate incense sticks from the altar down and kneel either side, saying the words one after the other. Then stand, joining hands over the incense.
- Place an incense stick between each of the candles, saying: 'Burn with love, burn with desire. Burn, true to me, true to you, burn that the light of love may never go out.'
- Take the chalice in your left hand if you are working alone, or between both hands if working with your love. Generally the female uses the chalice, although this is not a hard-and-fast rule.

- Fill the chalice with red wine or dark grape juice from the table and hold it over each candle in turn. Then move to the centre of the circle, holding it above your head and saying: 'May this union be fruitful as two become one. May the waters of the womb of the Mother welcome the other, that we may this night create great wisdom and joy.'
- Drink from the chalice.
- If you are working alone, pick up the knife in your right hand. Or your partner can pick up the knife and move to the centre of the circle where you will be waiting. You will then hold the chalice to his or her lips to drink.
- Hold the knife above the chalice and say: 'May this union be fruitful as we come together in love. May this blade be true, unflinching as it enters unknown realms, to bring forth new life and love.'
- Your partner can touch first your left breast, then your right, your stomach and your womb very gently with the flat side of the blade. If you are working alone, touch yourself with the knife.
- Finally you or your partner plunges the knife into the wine and you exchange words of love that are too personal for anyone else to utter.
- If you are alone, open your heart. You may find that you begin to speak the same words spontaneously during or after lovemaking and your lover finishes them.
- Place the cup with the blade still inside in front of the candles and leave them to burn.
- Whoever cast the circle, the other should close it, using the crystal or the index finger of the left hand with arm outstretched. You can make love within the circle, if that feels right, before closing it.
- As you climax, cry out your joint desire and let your hopes be carried to the cosmos on your love.

A Ritual for Ending a Relationship with Affection and Moving Forward

In the section on rain magic in Chapter 12, I describe a ritual for ending a destructive relationship or overcoming the pain of a faithless lover. This ritual is gentler and can be used when a love ends with regret, but there is still affection and a need for contact, perhaps because you work together or share children. It is also a good way of moving away from the regrets lingering from the end of an old relationship that are stopping you moving forward to seek new love. You can carry out the ritual on the waning Moon, but any time between dusk and midnight will work.

- Thread two silver lockets on a cord with a double knot, saying something like, 'This knot binds our hearts together, but no longer willingly and so we must part.'
- Untie the knot, slowly saying, 'Unravel gently, ties that link us, that we may go our separate ways with affection. Unravel slowly you that took so long to join, recalling only the happy moments, that we may remember our union with joy and each other with kindness, for we held the other's heart.'
- Slip the one heart off the knot, very slowly, taking care not to tug it, saying: 'I release you willingly, you who were once dear and are still for what was between us, friend, that we may meet with pleasure and not rancour.'
- Place the heart on a pink cord and tie it in a single knot, saying; 'You are now one no longer two. Go in peace.'
- Wrap the heart in dark silk or cotton, along with any photos and mementoes of the relationship. You may not wish to get rid of them, so after the ritual put them away in an attic.
- Retie your own cord and heart firmly and encircle the candle with it, saying: 'I am myself alone, but not lonely, wiser, more compassionate. I open my heart to new love when the time is right. Candle burn and when you are spent, it is done.'
- Sit quietly in the candlelight, letting thoughts come and go as they will. If you have a clear crystal ball or a chunk of amethyst or rose quartz, look into your crystal by candlelight and welcome the future.
- If the relationship lasted for many years, it may not be easy to let go, even if you have moved on physically. Repeat the ritual if you need to, opening the memory box, but keep the hearts on their separate cords and, holding them apart, say: 'The ties that link us have been unravelled that we may go our separate ways with affection. Now we recall only the happy moments. We remember our union with joy and each other with kindness, for we held the other's heart.'

8

Money Magic

After love magic spells, the most widely practised rituals are those to attract money. If I had a pound for every time I have been asked for methods to predict the National Lottery numbers, I would have no need to win the big prize. But real money magic is not about conjuring up a million pound's win out of thin air, nor about receiving out of the blue a huge cheque from the solicitors of a deceased unknown relative on the other side of the world. And it cannot be activated by a vague desire to be rich, for to bring a desire into reality in a practical area such as finance you need a specific focus and a plan for continuing success after the immediate impetus of the magical input. Logic and forward thinking do have a real place in magic, especially where money and careers are involved.

Real money magic has been practised by men and women for centuries to increase their resources at times of need, or for specific purposes and to develop their long-term money-making potential. There is nothing wrong in such rituals as long as they are based on realistic needs that cannot be met by the present situation or efforts; for example, you might desperately need £200 to have your car repaired so that you can drive to work or pick up the children from school.

Working on the magical principle of contagious magic and like attracting like, many money rituals involve either actual coins, metals from which coins are traditionally made, or richly coloured crystals. A silver, gold or bronze holed coin worn around the neck is said always to ensure that you will never be without money. The Spanish 25 peseta coin is ideal for this. It is gradually being replaced by the euro, but there are many of them still around so pick one up if you can. Chinese divinatory coins are also available from some shops.

Salt and Money Rituals

The oldest wealth-increasing rituals used salt as a focus (see also Chapter 14). The connection between salt and money dates back to Ancient Rome, when soldiers were sometimes paid in what was then a valuable commodity (hence the expression 'worth his salt'). Salt was traditionally traded for treasures, and the Celts would barter their salt for rich artefacts to put in their burial mounds.

The following ritual is also described in my book *The Complete Guide to Psychic Development*, but I am including it here because it is one that I have demonstrated many times and which seems very potent. Carry out the ritual when the crescent Moon is first visible in the sky.

- Heap up four or five tablespoons of salt into a cone shape on a table.
- Ring it with small shiny coins of your local currency, beginning at the twelve o'clock position and moving clockwise until you have completed the circle. Make sure each coin touches the ones on either side so that the circle is unbroken.
- Light golden candles outside the coins at the four compass points. Visualise the cone of salt being transformed into a heap of shining golden coins, rising higher and wider until it spills over the floor and covers it.
- Leaving the coins in a circle, spoon or scoop the salt into a clear glass container without a top.
- Let the candles burn away naturally. When they have gone out, remove your coins from the circle anti-clockwise, beginning at the eleven o'clock position so that the first coin you placed is the last to be removed. Put them in an uncovered box.
- Put both the glass container and box on a window ledge, and keep them uncovered until the full Moon first appears in the sky.

- At dawn, or when you wake the next morning, dissolve the salt in water in the glass container and pour it into a source of flowing water – your kitchen sink will do. As you do so, visualise your money-making plans flowing forward.
- Spend the coins on a present for someone who needs it, or give them to charity, or buy a small item to improve the house or garden.
- Use the rest of the month until the next crescent Moon putting your plans into practice. If necessary repeat the ritual, and keep the impetus in the real world going throughout the next month. If your plans are long-term you may need to carry out the ritual for several months and you will find that, if unbroken, your efforts in the real world will increasingly bear fruit.

Money Rituals and Candles

In the past I have used a gold or rich brown candle in money-making rituals. But recently I have tried, with some success, a popular North American tradition of using green candles and crystals. Green, a colour of growth and fertility, is effective especially if you need slow and steady financial growth. For the ritual below I have used undyed beeswax because of the associations between wealth and the honey bee.

Making a Coin Candle

Sheets of beeswax and wicks for candles can be obtained from craft shops. Oils for dressing the candles can be found at most chemists these days.

- Take a sheet of undyed yellow beeswax and a length of wick about ½ inch (1 cm) longer than the wax.
- Place the wick at the edge of the sheet, then roll the wax round it. As you do so, empower it with your need for money by repeating the word 'money' or your particular need, if you wish, in a chant.
- When you have formed the candle, press a coin into the soft wax near the base, if necessary gently warming the beeswax.

- Dress the candle with one of the oils of prosperity. You can use one of the special candle-anointing oils or a small quantity of virgin olive oil in which two or three drops of any of the following money oils are added: cinnamon, mint, patchouli, pine, cloves.
- Rub the candle in clockwise circles, first from the centre downwards and then from the centre upwards, ending at the place where you will light the candle.
- As you rub the oil in, visualise money flowing to you.
- Light your money candle, saying words such as: 'I draw to your light sufficient for my own needs, enough to fulfil my obligations to others and a little to spare, so may it be.'
- Let the candle burn to just above the coin and blow it out while saying:

East, south, west, north,
Money wishes, fly now forth.

- As the wax cools, press more coins into the top and sides until it is covered with coins.
- Keep your money candle in your kitchen.

A Mirror, Moon and Money Ritual

A large mirror on one wall of a small room can rid it of that cramped feeling by seeming to double the space. By association, in magic, mirrors are a vital feature of any spell to increase something. They have also long been associated with the Moon, and while old superstitions say that it is unlucky to see the Moon through glass, to hold the image of the Moon in a mirror is a potent form of magic.

Try to obtain an octagonal (eight-sided) mirror for money magic, as eight is the number of business acumen and in the Chinese tradition the octagonal bagua symbol is often placed on mirrors to attract good fortune. The following ritual is especially potent if money is needed urgently.

- On the night of the full Moon, hold the mirror so that you can catch the image of the Moon in it.

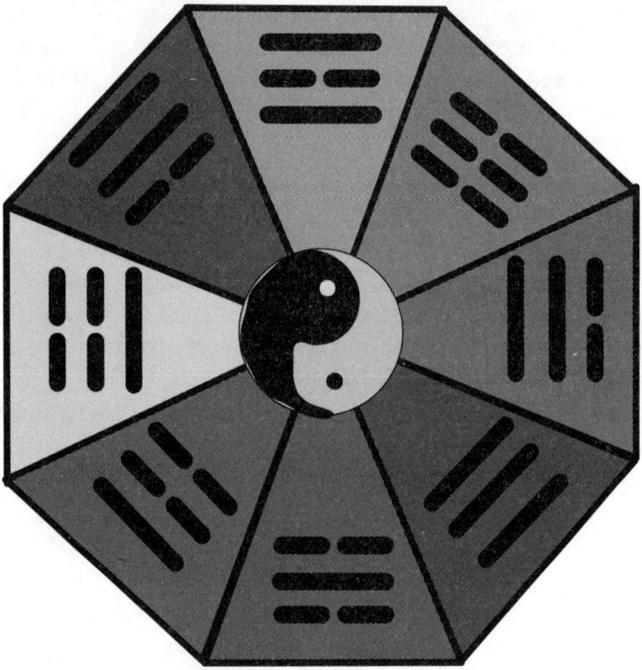

The Chinese bagua symbol

- In front of the Moon image hold a golden coin (preferably one with a hole), and let its golden reflected rays merge with the silver light of the moon while you say:

Full Moon,
Moon power,
Silver and gold,
I ask this hour,
Silver and gold,
On me shower,
Before this Moon is old.

Money-growing Rituals

Making a Money Tree

The old saying reminds us that money doesn't grow on trees. But by using a tree as a symbol we can focus our inner energies on money-making schemes. This ritual can be used either to meet immediate needs or to expand your long-term financial prospects.

- Take a small branch, if possible flowering or containing fruits, from one of the trees associated with prosperity (almond, ash, banana, horse chestnut, orange). Alternatively use a miniature orange tree or a bonsai, all kinds of which have associations with wealth.
- Plant it in a pot of rich brown soil with a moss agate, the crystal of natural growth.
- As you fill the pot, fill the soil with power and fertility by running it through your fingers as you say: 'I ask you with the warmth and radiance of the Sun, the fertility of gentle rain and your own life-giving, nourishing care, to make my own financial prospects grow that I may provide for myself/those who depend on me.'
- Take nine small gold or silver coins with holes in them. If you have none, substitute gold-coloured or brass discs (brass is a wealth-attracting metal and I will describe two brass rituals later).
- Tie these to the branches with silver or gold ribbons, saying as you attach each: 'As I bind you to the money tree, may you grow, multiply and bear fruit that my needs may be met and my money-making potential may grow.'
- Water your money tree, saying: 'Flow through my life energies, increase my power to generate money that I may be able to meet my financial obligations and more.'
- Every day water the tree, repeating all three of the affirmations above.
- If the tree appears to be dying, plant a second and transfer the coins, empowering the soil as before.

Herbs and Money

Herbs and spices traditionally associated with prosperity include allspice, basil, clover, dill, and ginger. It is said that carrying a basil leaf in a pocket or purse attracts money, and that a sachet of powdered ginger serves the same purpose. The elusive four-leaf clover will lead the finder to buried treasure or to an unexpected source of money, but the five-leaf clover is also a money-bringer.

A herb ritual to grow money

This works well for increasing long-term money prospects. If you need money in a hurry, plant a fast-growing herb such as mustard and cress.

- Take a large round earthenware pot. Fill it with soil which you run through your fingers to charge with power, as described above.
- Plant in the soil a circle of coins: brass for the power of the Sun, silver for the power of the Moon, copper for Venus, plus an old tin coin or circle of tin for Jupiter. If you wish, add an aluminium disc for Mercury, a steel or iron disc for Mars and a pewter or bronze coin or disc for Saturn for the seven-fold planetary energies.
- Sprinkle in the soil some dill or basil seeds, or, if the need is more urgent, seedlings of these herbs.
- As you plant the seeds or seedlings, gather the earth round them as you say: 'Grow strong, grow true, that I may increase my resources for the good of all.'
- Water the pot, saying: 'Grow tall, grow free, that I may increase my potential in every way.'
- As the seeds grow, you should find that your financial prospects improve. If they wither, do not despair. Add new seedlings to the pot and repeat the ritual. Success may be slower, but it will come with perseverance.

Magic Stones for Money

Round stones are especially good for money-making rituals, as this shape represents limitless possibility and the oval the celestial egg of creation.

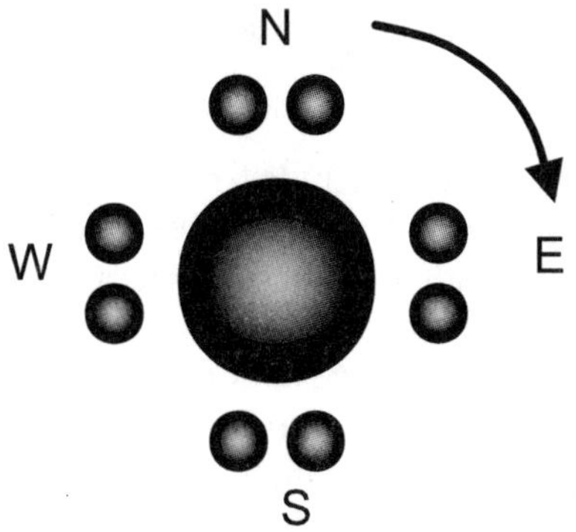

The central citrine with the jade around it

An instant crystal money spell

- Each morning, either on your desk at work or at home, surround a sparkling round yellow stone such as a citrine or yellow amber with small pieces of green olivine, peridot or jade in a square, two on each side to create eight, the number of financial gain. Some formal magical practitioners begin by setting the stones in the east position, the direction of the rising Sun, then moving clockwise round the circle. But I prefer to begin in the symbolic north, the place of rest, and then allow the energy to grow from there. The yellow stone makes nine, the number of perfection and completion. This will look to outsiders just like a small decorative display. Green crystals are used both in the USA and in Chinese tradition to create growth and fertility. Since adding them, I have found that crystal money spells not only work faster but tend to give more enduring growth.
- Try to place the crystals in sunlight or near a source of heat to incubate the wealth.
- Each evening – if at work, just before you go home – unmake the square from the west if you began from the north, or from the north if you began in the east, in both cases moving anti-clockwise.
- Place each stone in turn in a brown drawstring bag, ending with the yellow one, and leave it at night in what is your equivalent of a hearth – the symbolic centre of the home – surrounded by a ring of salt sprinkled clockwise.

- In the morning, re-create your square on your desk at work or at home.

Money-attracting crystals include:

Aventurine: A translucent dark or light green quartz, this is especially good when added to bathwater, as it promotes creative dreams for money-making inspiration and also reduces anxieties about money that can paralyse action and clear planning.

Bloodstone: Opaque mottled green and red chalcedony. This is a stone of courage, with sacred associations because, according to legend, the red spots were formed from the blood of Christ as it fell on green jasper at the crucifixion. Bloodstone is traditionally kept in a cash register to attract money but is equally effective if carried in a pocket or purse. Keeping one with credit cards can discourage impulse spending.

Cat's eye: This translucent gold or greeny brown quartz is often confused with the golden brown tiger's eye which is an excellent substitute in magic for the rarer cat's eye. The Asian form is a golden chrysoberyl. It is the money stone *par excellence*, for it is said a cat's eye will not only protect its owner's money but also increase it. A simple money-increasing ritual involves placing a cat's eye in a jar of gold-coloured coins. Cat's eyes are also said to restore a former state of prosperity.

Jade: Jadeite and nephrite, the two mineral forms of jade, come in many shades of green, opaque to translucent. Jade's use in magic dates back to Neolithic times, both in the Orient where it was sacred to the Mother Goddess and in Central and South America. A jade pendant, earrings or ring open the wearer to prosperity in many forms, especially in the long term.

Peridot/olivine: Olivine is an olive green translucent stone, while peridot is the transparent gem form. They are interchangeable for money-making magic. Olivine sand is quite hard to obtain, but is good for adding to purses or sprinkling on any official papers or money-seeking letters. It is especially potent for putting on bills and invoices that you send out for money you are owed, as it seems to clear blockages in money flow.

Pyrites/fool's gold: This dark, rock-like iron sulphide with gold inclusions is sometimes called the money magnet. Despite its name, it is a stone of the Sun and remarkably good for attracting money. It is especially good for guiding you away from seemingly

fail-safe offers – you will find that fool's gold becomes dull if held over contracts or offers that will prove a drain on money.
Opal: Comprising silica spheres, with water in its structure, this is one of the few gems that is non-crystalline or only poorly so. The fire opal, so-called because of its iridescent flashes of red and blue light, is good for financial gain and should be hidden on business premises or in the home to bring wealth.
Pearls: These iridescent organic gems, gifts of the sea, come in pale cream or white, gold, black, grey, pink and blue, although the gold and black varieties are especially associated with prosperity. Both opals and pearls are mistakenly regarded as unlucky. Pearls, especially, form a focus for powerful attracting rituals.
Tiger's eye: This yellow-gold and brown striped chalcedony is chatoyant, reflecting light in a wavy band, and is interchangeable with the cat's eye stone in rituals for promoting money. Used to circle a golden candle, tiger's eyes are excellent for helping the practical achievement of money-spinning ideas.
Topaz: This opaque, light blue/blue-green phosphate, mined by the Egyptians in Sinai more than six thousand years ago, is regarded as a sky stone, a manifestation of the Source of Creation, and is often called the lover of gold. It is most potent if given to you, rather than bought.

Metal Rituals

All metals can be used in money rituals, as suggested in the earlier herb coin ritual. Although gold is traditionally associated with wealth, brass is equally potent in money-attracting rituals.

Brass

Like gold, brass is sacred to all the solar gods: to Helios and Apollo in Classical tradition and to the Norse sun goddess Sol and Baldur, god of the growing light, in the northern tradition. Brass has the added bonus of being a protective metal. Many rituals can be centred around the brass ornaments that many of us have inherited from older relatives or which can be bought incredibly cheaply from car boot sales.

Brass bells are especially effective, because the bell is one of the ritual objects for the Earth element in Earth magic and also because by evoking sound it stirs up the energies that cause positive acquisition of resources. A brass bell rung in turn in the early morning and evening over each item in a circle of coins or golden crystals will awaken money-making potential and break through doubt and inertia.

A brass money ritual

This is a variation of another ritual I have used many times. I have modified it to incorporate the ideas of people who have tried my original form and contacted me with suggested improvements. Magic is living and growing. If we can share ideas and be prepared to make alterations it is like a casserole that becomes larger and richer as new ingredients are added and different methods of preparation attempted.

- Find a brass plate or dish and polish it in the noonday Sun until it gleams. As you work, see the sunbeams turning into coins.
- Collect a coin for every unit of money you need – these can be anything from five dollar units to a thousand pounds, if you need the deposit on a home or money to invest in a business.
- Polish each coin before you drop it in the dish, filling the coin with the power to increase and to become the basis for further expansion.
- Ring the dish with golden flowers – sunflowers, marigolds, chrysanthemums or even buttercups, the symbol of modest riches – which seem to work better than crystals in this case, though I am not sure why. Perhaps the living energies accelerate the growth.
- Between each flower place a circle of golden seeds, again a symbol of *prana* the life force. If you can obtain it, tie a circle of golden corn around the base of the dish. Golden fern seeds picked at midsummer are best of all (see Chapter 13).
- If the Sun is shining, place the dish in direct sunlight on an open window ledge. If it is a dull day use a brass lamp or one with a yellow lampshade and a yellow bulb.
- Visualise golden rays falling as coins into the dish. Watch them rise until the dish overflows in your mind's eye and cascades like a waterfall.
- Your dish may fill quickly or more gradually, but it will fill.

When it is overflowing in your mind's eye, which can take anything from five to fifteen minutes, cover the dish with a yellow or golden cloth or another brass plate or lid if you have one. Place the flowers and seeds inside the dish.

- Switch off the light and move the dish to the centre of a table where food is prepared or eaten.
- Each day add a coin or brass disc, a yellow flower and a few golden seeds until your bowl really does begin to overflow.
- As you add each coin, place the uncovered dish in the sunlight or under the yellow light bulb and re-create the golden waterfall of wealth for five minutes.
- If you can sit quietly, you will find that your mind begins spontaneously to generate money-making schemes.
- After five minutes or so cover your dish again and return to the table, where it will absorb abundance until the next day.
- If you begin to doubt, uncover your store of hidden wealth and leave it in the sunlight until your confidence returns.
- When the dish overflows, surround it with a circle of the surplus coins or discs and leave the lid off as a reminder of your own ability to generate wealth in whatever way.
- If the ritual has not worked within a month, take out all the coins and discs and place them in an open glass bottle on the table or near the place that serves as a hearth or focal point in your home.
- Collect all the seeds and dried flowers carefully into a box and bury them in a sunny place in the garden. You may see growth here as a reminder that all will be well.

Lodestones

These naturally occurring magnetic pieces of ore were once used as primitive compasses. Because of the way they would turn to point north when suspended from a string, they were regarded in ancient times as living spirits. Their magnetic power led them to be associated with spells for attracting money.

Traditionally they are soaked in water on a Friday morning until noon, left in sunlight to dry, sprinkled with iron filings and kept in a red bag when not in use. For attracting money, add to the red bag a silver coin, a gold ring or charm, and money-attracting herbs, such as ginger or allspice. Empower it with the words:

Lodestone, lodestone draw to me
What it takes to be
Happy, safe and without need.
Free from worry, without greed.

Carry your little bag with you whenever financial matters are concerned, for example visiting the bank for an interview concerning your account, applying for credit or when going for a job with a better salary.

Every Friday when you soak your lodestone, replace the herbs, wash the coin and ring and sprinkle them with salt before putting them back in the bag with your empowering chant.

Single large lodestones are used to draw money or success to a person, sometimes attached to a belt buckle.

Money Customs

Put the first coin you receive in a day into an empty pocket and it will attract more. In traditional English markets this custom is still followed and called Handsel. The first paper money received by a new shop or café is often framed. This operates on the sympathetic magic principle of like attracting like.

Collect all your debts by midnight on New Year's Eve and don't lend any money on New Year's Day to ensure that money comes in and does not go out during the following twelve months.

9

Defensive Magic

At some point we all feel threatened and afraid. In the night fears and worries can be magnified, causing nightmares or insomnia which blight the following day. If you are a sensitive person – and most people who develop their intuitive powers through magic or divination are – you will be more vulnerable than many other people to the pain of unfair criticism, petty spite and gossip.

Actual psychic attack is quite common but it is rarely from some dark spirit force, unless you have been dabbling with ouija boards or summoning up spirits in seances. But if someone is feeling hostile towards you and perhaps lying in bed fuming over some success of yours, or the fact that you are married to his or her ex-partner, you can feel the hostile waves quite tangibly. Something cold and slimy, like wet seaweed being dragged across your face, is one way I have heard this invasive darkness described. Such hostility strikes not only at night, but at any time when we are quiet and still and so more receptive to psychic discord.

I myself have been under psychic attack several times. In two cases I knew the source and was aware that the people concerned were not only unconsciously transmitting their own negative feelings, but actively causing trouble for me by vicious words and spiteful deeds.

At one point I became ill and everything I attempted went wrong. When I mentioned this to a medium I knew, she gave me a cross to put under my pillow and sent me protective light every night which helped. Ultimately I realised that, although I had previously considered psychic protection unnecessary, there are times when it is important to close your personal doors just as you do your household ones, especially at night when your bodily and mental defences are down and your more vulnerable unconscious mind and spirit are closer to the surface.

For you can, as I did, become so overwhelmed by negativity pouring towards you that you start to give off bad luck signals to the cosmos and to people around. Suddenly you find that a cold or cough will linger for weeks, you are constantly losing your car keys or wallet, and suffer a series of minor accidents to yourself and your property.

The hostility is not always deliberate, nor is it necessarily always from someone who has cause to hate us, but the draining effects are the same. At my local supermarket one of the checkout assistants radiates hatred whenever I use her till. I have no idea why, as I am always especially courteous to her and try to engage her in friendly conversation. But she cannot even bear to look at me or touch my hand as I offer her my money. When she has served me I sometimes feel quite shaken at the intensity of her dislike, especially if I am feeling vulnerable or off-colour, but I suspect that she is not deliberately spooking me and may even be unaware of what is happening.

Good and bad vibes attract similar rays. If you are confident, all goes well. Conversely, if things are going really badly, you become nervous and accident-prone and give off victim vibes. Of course illness or misfortune are often not our fault, but if we can protect ourselves from accumulating negativity we have more chance of fighting back, using our natural protective shield. So defensive magic is at the root of positive responses to life, and to improving our fortunes.

Banishing Personal Negativity

Negative feelings can act like a magnet, attracting more hostility, so dealing with our own negative feelings first is a bedrock of protection. Also, our own anger can wear down our natural protective shield, making us particularly susceptible to the hostility of others.

This method can be used by the whole family, who can create a domestic anger knot pot to leave the troubles of the day at the door on returning home. The knot pot is equally effective as a personal filter of bad feeling at work. It is based on a very ancient ceremony of plaiting dead grasses and flowers to represent lost causes and leaving them in a high place or burying them. Over the centuries, perhaps under the influence of weaving communities, it has become associated with tying wool or thread.

Basically, when you find yourself in a situation where your anger is about to spill out and create a conflict which will leave you more battered and bruised than your opponent, instead of firing off a harsh word or a nasty memo you tie up your fury in a piece of thread or wool and deposit it safely in the anger pot. This will give you a chance to compose yourself and decide on the course of action which will offer protection to yourself and the ones you love most.

- You need a wide-necked dark glass bottle – one that has contained bath oils is fine. There are an amazing array of glass bottles on sale in almost every homeware shop.
- Keep a bottle at home by the front door and also at work in a drawer if you have a stressful job or work in a potentially confrontational or authoritarian atmosphere.
- Get together a variety of threads, silks and wools of varying thicknesses, and a pair of scissors.
- According to the source of the irritation, you can vary the colours using the meanings explained in Chapter 4. For example, if you are annoyed about a financial matter – perhaps the bank has suddenly imposed heavy charges for an unpaid cheque – you would use brown thread. If it was a travel irritant – your train might be late for the fifth time in a week – you would use yellow thread.
- Anything that invokes bad feelings in you, or makes you angry or tense, can be bound in the wool.
- When an injustice or a flash of anger occurs, stop and file it in a section of your mind for later. Revenge, it is said, is a dish best eaten cold, and though I do not think that revenge is helpful in making us feel better, the principle that you file away a sarcastic reply or put-down is a good one. Ten minutes along the line, you may decide it is not necessary. If it is, you can

make a considered response rather than an outburst in which the justice of your claim can get overlooked by the vehemence of the delivery.
- When you have a free moment, contemplate what action you can take to right the matter. Some cannot be resolved, and so must either be consigned to the cosmos or Earth or fester inside you.
- Whether or not justice is possible, choose one of your threads, thick for a major annoyance, thin for a petty irritation.
- Cut the length of thread according to the degree of stress caused to you, seeing the scissors severing once and for all the link between you and the aggression or annoyance.
- Momentarily relive your feelings as you tie and tangle the thread.
- When it is knotted tightly and all the bad feeling enclosed in it, place it in your bottle, saying:

Tangle the anger,
Tangle the pain
By this knot
Make me free again.

- Cork the bottle to keep in the threads of negativity, and only open it to add another knot.
- When the bottle is full, dispose of it in an environmentally-friendly way and start another.
- You can also use your bottle to bind your fears and worries.
- If you continue this ritual over a period of months you will find it takes longer to fill a bottle as your resistance to stress increases.

Creating a Protective Shell or Shield of Crystal

When you come under attack at work, socially or at home, the simplest and most effective form of protection is to create a pillar of brilliant crystal to enclose you. There are countless similar rituals, using towers, castles, an iridescent mother of pearl shell, cones of light, ellipses or shields of radiance, and pyramids of colour.

By focusing on a sparkling crystal you can initially create your defensive pillar of radiance that will afterwards be hovering in the background ready to be activated. The crystal will also renew your natural protective energies if you repeat the ritual at times when you have been subject to a great deal of stress.

You can visualise this protection in any way that feels right for you. This crystalline shield is actively brilliant and very hard, reflecting and therefore repelling all who would attack you mentally or psychically or intrude on your private space. There are many ways of creating this safe space around yourself. This method works well for me:

- Use a crystal that is full of light. A clear crystal quartz is perfect, as is a crystal ball or sphere.
- Begin on a sunny day and position the crystal so that it is filled with natural light.
- Sit at a table facing the crystal and begin breathing in slowly and deeply through your nose, absorbing the crystalline brilliance around you.
- When you exhale, breathe out any darkness, doubts and negative feelings.
- As you continue to breathe, visualise the crystal rising up around you from beneath your feet so that it becomes higher with each inhalation.
- When it is high enough to cover your head, visualise it closing over you to form a shape that feels comfortable – a pyramid, a cone, a dome or an ellipse in the shape of the cosmic egg.
- Allow your senses to stretch out so that you can feel the smooth crystal beneath your feet. Extend your arms and feel yourself safe within this sparking cocoon. Look upwards and see that you are enclosed and inviolable.
- Visualise golden sparks emanating outwards from the edges. These are not intended to harm anyone, but to fend off any hostility, whether intentioned or otherwise.
- Decide upon a power word, a mantra you can utter silently or an action that will serve as a short cut at times when you need instant protection. An example might be: 'When I cup my fingers in the shape of a tower, I will feel my protective shield instantly around me.'
- At other times you can visualise the crystalline sides rising upwards more gradually.
- When you are ready, let the radiant pillar slowly fade until it

becomes a faint glowing outline. It is there to be activated whenever you need it.

- Top up your protective energies regularly, perhaps keeping a sparkling crystal in your workplace as well as at home.

The Cloak of Invisibility or Greyness

The second kind of personal protection has more in common with the shadowy protection of the Earth guardians described in Chapter 14. It has been described variously as a cloak of invisibility or greyness cast around your form, and is much softer and more fluid than the tower of crystal light.

This cloak cannot make you physically invisible, but can help you to merge into the background when you are in a dangerous situation – either physically or emotionally. It can also be invoked when you are feeling your way in a new environment and do not wish to stand out.

- As before use a crystal, this time a smoky quartz or obsidian (apache tear), in the same way as the clear crystal.
- Instead of a tower of light, visualise a dark, swirling mist rising out of the crystal and enveloping you in a soft, enfolding, igloo-shaped tent or a cloak that pulls over your head. Now it is as though you are looking through smoked glass, able to see out while no one can see in.
- Allow the tent of grey mist to fade into the background until you sense rather than see a faint grey mist around you. This is your shield, ready to be activated when necessary by your personal words of power, for example: 'When I touch my fingertips, my Cloak of Grey will cover me.'

A powerful alternative is the Native American smudge stick. These can be bought from some New Age stores, but are easy to make.

- Use sprigs of fresh herbs, about 9 inches (15 cm) long, about six or seven sprigs in total. Sage, sweet grass and cedar are traditional and have innate protective properties, but you can also use thyme or dill.

- Hold the herbs tightly together and bind them with cotton thread every ½ inch (1 cm) along the stick.
- Leave the herbs to dry for two to three weeks.
- Light a candle of green or brown for Mother Earth and hold the smudge stick about 3 inches (10 cm) above the flame until it glows and smoulders, releasing a thin trail of smoke.
- Hold the smudge stick a few centimetres away from your body and, working from bottom to top, circle yourself, moving clockwise with the smudge stick so that you are literally being wrapped in mist.
- Cast an anti-clockwise circle above your head to remove negative influences.
- As with the clear crystal pillar, you need a power word or action to raise your curtain of greyness instantly. Try: 'When I put my hands over my eyes, I will be cloaked in grey and fade from the consciousness of others.'
- When you are ready let your cloak slowly disappear, but be aware that it is still in the background whenever you need it.
- Carry out a smudge stick ritual if you have experienced a prolonged period when tensions around you have been running high.

Diverting Your Foes

Another creative, non-harmful form of psychic self-defence is to divert anyone who is gossiping about you. This may be a jealous colleague, a sour ex-lover who will not leave you alone or an official who is intruding unnecessarily into your affairs. It can also be used for someone who wishes you no harm but is undermining you by constantly interfering – perhaps a relative, friend or neighbour who has become over-dependent on your company. Diversion is also effective with colleagues at work whose chatter affects your concentration.

I have modified a method taught to me by Lilian, a friend and wise clairvoyant who believed that a period in the sea of tranquillity and contemplation would calm down the most persistent of persecutors. At the time I was unconvinced, but I was then still relatively naive about the havoc that the malicious intentions of others could wreak.

- When you are alone, visualise the intrusive person. If you have a photograph or some item that he or she gave you, it can help to serve as a focus.
- Use a large uncut piece of calcite, rose quartz or amethyst – these crystals are widely obtainable and quite cheap.
- Place the crystal on the symbol if you have one, or write the name of the intrusive person on a piece of paper and place it beneath the crystal.
- Imagine the potential trouble-maker approaching you. Say softly: 'I am sorry but I am really busy right now and so I cannot give you the attention you need.'
- Very gently visualise a soft healing blanket rising from the crystal and enveloping the source of irritation.
- In your mind's eye, move the figure wrapped in the blanket towards an unspecified, shadowy figure who will make the intrusive person happy and welcome such attention. If the source of interference was malevolent, Lilian would visualise him or her, still in the blanket, floating in the warm, healing sea of tranquillity for a while, until the urge to interfere had diminished. She would then repeat the ritual to offer them an alternative focus for their attentions.
- Once you have established the ritual, choose a word or action that will instantly activate the process. If there are several people who are irritants or unfriendly, develop a different power word for each and keep your uncut crystal between you and the door.

Putting an Aggressor on the Karmic Wheel

People who are unpleasant usually carry the seeds of their own destruction. The concept of karma and the cosmic wheel is not only for Buddhists and Hindus but one that people of different faiths find helpful for coping with injustice and hostility.

- When you are subject to a barrage of sarcasm or criticism or someone seems to single you out for unfair treatment, so that you are unable to follow your life path in your own way, visualise a huge Ferris wheel covered with golden lights and soft, rich velvet seats.
- Visualise yourself gently leading the perpetrator of the pain to

one of the seats. Wish them well, but ask that their adverse influence on your life may be transformed in love by the cosmos and that he or she may follow their own destiny and not intrude on yours.

- Let the wheel rise slowly to flowing, life-enhancing music and turn away, seeking positive people who will boost your self-esteem.
- This can be very effective if someone is haranguing you. As you watch the figure rise, he or she will stop mid-sentence, look puzzled and wander off.

Sending Back the Pain

Occasionally we cannot just write off an injustice or put up psychic barriers, because harm has been done in a material or physical sense or the pain is so great that even the most tolerant among us feels outraged. An unfair sacking or redundancy after years of loyal service, betrayal by a partner, someone who is bullying one of our children, a vicious threat or an unprovoked attack, lies that damage our reputation – any of these can make us physically ill as well as desperately unhappy.

I do not think that it is ever justifiable to curse or hex someone, whatever they have done, because bad vibes rebound upon the sender of negative magic. But therein lies the solution: return the pain to the perpetrator. This ritual is especially effective when carried out at the time of the waning Moon, or on any moonless light.

- Take nine iron nails (iron is a protective, defensive metal), and place them in a dark glass bottle with sprigs of rosemary, milk that is beginning to curdle and a very cheap red wine that has gone sour.
- Cork the bottle and shake it, saying: 'May venom and viciousness coil like poisonous snakes and bottle up the evil that is done to me.'
- Purify a sink or drain with a few drops of fenugreek or pine dissolved in warm water with a sprinkling of salt.
- Shake the bottle well and tip the contents down the drain or sink, saying words such as:

Pain, misery flow from me,
Flow not to the sea,
Flow back to he or she
Inflicter of disharmony.
Wheresover you may be.

- You can use this ritual also for anonymous letters, phone calls or unidentifiable malice.
- Rinse out the bottle with very hot water and tip any remnants away, rinsing until the water from the bottle runs clear.
- When the bottle is empty, say:

I have returned the pain,
Send it not again.

- Purify the bottle by placing a clear crystal quartz in it with pure spring water and leave it uncorked for a Sun-and-Moon cycle.

Protective Crystals

These traditionally include black agate, amethysts, bloodstones, carnelians, garnets, black and red jasper, lapis lazuli, rose and smoky quartz, tiger's eye, topaz and turquoise.

- Carry one or more in a dark silk purse when you are entering a potentially hostile situation.
- You can use protective crystals on a desk or table between you and potential sources of negativity or between you and someone who unintentionally drains your energy by regularly off-loading woes and problems on you.
- Keep a chunk of unpolished amethyst or rose quartz near your bed to offer protection while you sleep.
- Frequently wash your protective crystals in running water to cleanse them. If you have been in touch with a particularly negative influence, after you have washed the stones sprinkle them with salt, pass over them an incense stick or oil burner in a fragrance such as lavender, pine or rose and the flame of a purple, silver or pink candle. Finally wrap them for a few days in a dark cloth to rest.

Section Three

Magical Beings

10

Witches and Earth Guardians

In the *Sathya Sai Baba* magazine in autumn 1998 Paul Buro wrote:

I always make a habit of greeting the guardian of a place. There is a small river that runs through Cemaes [in Anglesey], to the sea with bridges and walkways. The guardian's name is Seedor. He told me that no one had greeted him for centuries. He isn't very tall. He has a broad and bearded face and a wonderful smile and wears an off-white robe with a hood and a girdle made of the same material that accents his pot belly. He is a Druid – he told me he would give me healing.

It is traditionally believed that every place on Earth has a sacred guardian. If you approach even an ordinary place such as a park or city square with reverence, and ask silently to be allowed to receive what you need to know, you may find that you quite naturally see these sacred guardians. Some are, like Seedor, wise souls who have become protectors of a place that they loved centuries before; others are more elemental, part of the land itself, and came into being when the land took form.

Guardians of the Stones

Stand in the midst of any stone circle on a misty day, and if you are sensitive or lucky you may see the misty outlines of the tall, grey guardians of the site. Where do they come from? From the stones, from the clay of the earth, born from the marriage of the sacred site, the trees and huge slabs of rock sometimes transported thousands of miles to create mighty megaliths. Ask any sculptor who hews a piece of rock and he or she will tell you that a statue already exists within, waiting to be released.

So it is with the sacred guardians. They wait to be recognised by those who can see with the inner eye, witnessing the cosmic changes of the millennia under the stars, the Moon, the Sun that existed long before the first visitors came with their radios and foil-wrapped picnics. These silent watchers absorb the pain caused by those who have broken, taken, and vandalised the stones or consecrated land over the centuries, though you may hear them sighing in the wind, their tears mingling with the raindrops, their smiles reflected in sunbeams glinting suddenly on half-hidden quartz shards.

One of the most remarkable prehistoric monuments to time is at Newgrange in County Meath, Eire, once called Grian Uaigh or the Cave of the Sun. Created near the end of the fourth millennium BC, Newgrange consists of a mound containing a passage to a burial chamber, surrounded by an almost complete circle of twelve giant stones. It is close to Tara, the sacred hill and former palace of the Tuatha de Danaan, the Celtic hero gods and later home of the high kings of Ireland. These stones have symbols inscribed on them, recording movements of the Sun, Moon and planets, that reveal highly accurate ancient astronomical calculations. Newgrange is aligned to the midwinter sunrise so that the beam of the rising Sun falls directly into the main chamber. Knowth and Dowth, its sister sites, make up the main spokes of the wheel of the year. Knowth is aligned to the spring and autumnal equinoxes, while Dowth is aligned to the midsummer sunrise. The twelve stones surrounding the Newgrange mound themselves point to the sunrises and sunsets of the solstices and equinoxes, also aligning to Knowth and Dowth.

How to Meet Guardians of the Stones

- Stand alone near any old stone circle or medicine wheel – for example the Moose Mountain Medicine Wheel in Saskatchewan, Canada – that is aligned to the solstices. In fact you can visit any stone ancient monument or temple in the world when it is silent and misty, for these guardians know no cultural barriers.
- Extend your arms as high and wide as you can until you encounter a slight resistance in the air. You are moving into the aura of one of the great stone giants, so do not advance any further.
- Place your hands on one of the stones and wait. You can sit if you wish, or stand, but do not develop any conscious thoughts or dialogue.
- Before long you may feel a slight pressure on your hand or head or a sudden breeze or shiver up your spine, and you will know that the presence is making contact with you. Normal sounds and senses will retreat.
- Speak a few words either silently or out loud, asking the great guardian to impart some of the timeless wisdom of the stones. Thank the guardian for allowing you to feel his presence.
- You may hear words or see images in your mind's eye, perhaps visions of the old ceremonies.
- Gradually you will feel the presence withdraw, and when you are ready you should leave.
- Do not attempt to leave a gift, not even a crystal. Do not light candles or incense, and do not take any stones. It is fine to take a stone from an adjoining field, for that will be imbued with the same energies, but the actual site should not be disturbed.
- View the place now from a distance, and you may be rewarded with a final glimpse of the tall grey sentinel.
- Spend a quiet evening alone or with someone who will not want to dissect your experience or fill your mind with their needs, perhaps at a small hotel or camp site near the monument. This is the simplest and purest form of sacred space, and will do more for your spiritual development than a dozen expensive courses.
- You may dream of the old circle, perhaps seeing it as it was thousands of years ago, and the wisdom will permeate your consciousness over the ensuing days.

Guardians of the Leys

These sacred guardians are tall and brown and merge into the tree line or the distant markers on a muddy brown track. Sometimes called landwights when they oversee a whole area, they patrol and protect the fairy paths and leys, old straight tracks between aligned energy points, beacons, sacred wells, clumps of hawthorn, churches built on the sites of temples to the old deities, rocks and standing stones. They are also found at earth sites, chalk figures, grassed over Iron Age forts, and spots where you can see the aligned marker points stretching in front and behind you; there should be five to meet the technical criteria of a ley, but then Earth Powers don't count in man measures.

The Ridgeway, a haven from the noise and fumes of the M4, is an ancient way that once carried the hopes and prayers of pilgrims as they travelled to the sacred cluster of Wilshire sites – Avebury Rings, Silbury Hill, womb of the Goddess and West Kennet Long Barrow. Close to the Ridgeway, on Uffington Down, is the figure of a huge chalk horse. The White Horse, one of the ancient chalk representations of fertility, was dedicated to the old gods more than two thousand years ago. It is more dragon than horse, as the hill in front of it bears witness: Dragon Hill was associated with St George, who in turn was linked with the old Celtic Sun God Og.

As well as these shadowy forms who imbue the old tracks with psychic energy, we may also see on the leys or close to earth sites spirits like Seedor the Druid. Other presences that may be detected are the spirits of the earthly guardians who keep the chalk figures clean and tend the hawthorns, a task handed down from father to son and often kept secret. Though the traditional, often ribald, public festivities centred around scouring the chalk figures have been replaced by more subdued renovation work by government employees, I am convinced that many of these places are still tended privately by descendants of the earlier earthly caretakers.

How to Meet the Guardians of the Leys

- Make your starting point one of the old chalk figures, such as the Cerne Abbas Giant in Dorset or the Long Man of Wilmington in East Sussex. Alternatively begin at one of the sacred rock paintings of Australia situated along the old Aboriginal song-

lines, or at a site on one of the energy lines that have been identified throughout Europe, Scandinavia, India and the United States.
- Look around you until you can see an aligned marker point on a distant hill in front and behind you; alternatively you can use a map to identify these in advance (see the section on measuring leys by expert mathematician and dowser John Plowman in my book *Ghost Encounters* [Blandford, 1997]).
- Ignore the experts who tell you that you cannot find leys without years of expertise and training. Do what the ancients did – follow your feet and your intuition.
- As you walk you will hear faint voices and the rustle of leaves behind you, and sense a benign presence. Slow down and you may see beside you very faintly or in your mind's eye the guardian who has chosen to reveal himself or herself – perhaps a Druid, a Native American or an Aborigine with an intricate shield marking out the thousand tracks he knows through song and story.
- Greet the guardian and ask that your feet be guided to the place you need to visit. Like Paul Buro (quoted at the beginning of the chapter) you may be offered healing, whether for a physical or spiritual ill, and as you look towards the next marker point you may glimpse one of the tall brown guardians.
- Unlike the stone guardians they rarely contact mankind, but you may receive a sign of their benevolence: a butterfly which appears in winter, a wild bird which settles by the path, the first flower of spring, a jewelled spider's web glistening between two trees, or a blossoming tree on a waste site.
- Ask your questions and let the answers unfold over the ensuing weeks; these brown earth giants work slowly, but their wisdom is rooted in firm foundations. Again you should take nothing, especially from one of the earth sites, nor leave offerings.

Guardians of the Sacred Waters

The spirit of the waters is usually seen as white mist rising from the surface of the water, and especially from sacred wells in the early morning. Many of the old sacred wells, dedicated to the Mother Goddess, were rededicated in Christian times to a saint. Where the

Christian association was female the ancient tradition of a female guardian or white lady who gave healing continued.

Even today ghosts of white ladies are consistently reported around ancient wells throughout Europe, especially those formerly dedicated to Brigid, the Celtic Triple Goddess who latterly became St Bride, the midwife of Christ. The place name Ladywell offers a clue that a well there was once dedicated to the White Goddess of the Celts, Goddess of the Moon, wisdom and healing, who in Christian times took on the mantle of the Virgin Mary. So the misty form tends to be of human adult female size, although her face may be veiled and her clothes ethereal.

The well was viewed as the entrance to the womb of the Earth Mother herself, hence the presence near these wells of the ancient stone fertility figures called Sheela-na-gig, especially in Ireland. These stone carvings of the archetypal female fertility figure in the process of giving birth, date back thousands of years.

In Cornwall traces of a well priestess tradition survived later than elsewhere. In the seventeenth century, Gulval Well was tended by an old woman who made prophecies to strangers, and revealed the whereabouts of lost and stolen objects including local cattle. She was said to be the last of the well priestesses, the manifest form of the sacred water guardian who was linked with the Earth Mother herself.

In Scotland and Ireland old women have been reported appearing mysteriously at sacred wells, teaching the old healing ways.

How to Meet the Guardians of the Sacred Waters

Some better-known wells have become so commercialised that you may find it hard to tune into the spirit of the water. If you can find a lesser-known well, or even one that is no longer used, you may connect more easily with the spirit or guardian of the well, who may be one and the same.

In the UK, the Ordnance Survey 1:25,000 Pathfinder series includes many of the old wells and springs. Or you can search out old guides to local history and folklore. Nowadays these are often reproduced cheaply since the original material, often collected by intrepid explorers and historians of the late eighteenth and nineteenth centuries, is long out of copyright.

Unlike those to the Stone and Earth guardians, offerings to Water guardians are encouraged. Indeed, the origin of modern wishing wells lies in the ancient practice of casting coins in the water to pay for healing. At the springs in Bath you can see examples of prayers engraved on pieces of lead which were cast into the waters.

Check in local legend if there are any special times of the day or dates that are associated with the well, perhaps the saint's own day. For example, St Colman's Day, 7 June, would be a good time to visit his well on the shores of Lough Neagh in Northern Ireland. The well contains gypsum crystals known as Cranfield Pebbles, and legend says that anyone who finds one will be protected from drowning and painful childbirth.

If not, visit a well at early morning and you may be rewarded by a glimpse of the misty form of the White Lady rising from the water.

- Begin by making an offering.
- You should not take water from the well, except any being given or sold by the modern-day custodians.
- Nor should you leave any offerings that are likely to pollute the water. Although treasure hoards that date back to the Bronze Age have been retrieved from the holy wells, it is better not to cast anything into a well unless it is a designated wishing well. Modern coins lack the purity of those of our forebears.
- The most acceptable offering is to tie a biodegradable ribbon to a nearby tree or to place flowers around the base of the well.
- Better still, bring seeds or tiny flowering shrubs and clear away a little of the undergrowth if the well has fallen into disrepair.
- As you make your offering do not make specific requests, but open yourself to the healing wisdom of the Lady of the Well.
- If you do obtain any holy water, sprinkle a few drops into your bath before bedtime and keep the rest for healing purposes.

How to Invoke the Guardians of Your Home

The ward sprites are the natural guardians of settlements. They are said to assemble each evening at a crossroads near the centre of a village or town, and then pass along the old fairy paths warding hills or watch posts where they stand sentinel against all that is malevolent, earthly or otherwise. Wherever we live we are under the protection of one of these sprites. In earlier times people would ask to be kept safe, but this practice has now fallen into disuse. Though we surround our homes with high fences and burglar alarms, we often still feel vulnerable.

- As dusk falls, light a scarlet candle in the downstairs or main window facing the road.
- As you light the candle encircle it with a protective herb – dill or vervain are best – and recite the age-old rhyme used for protection, both at the old festivals and by families as a nightly ritual:

Trefoil, vervain, John's wort, dill,
Guardians protect us, by your will.

- Take the candle to the front door, open the door and blow out the candle.
- The light will be carried into the darkness and reach the Earth Guardians, who will respond by watching over your home and family.
- If you or your children see large dark shadows outside the window, do not be afraid – it is your sentinels keeping you safe while you sleep (see also Chapter 9).

Witches

Unlike Earth guardians, witches are very definitely mortals and come from all walks of life – people like you, me or the couple next door. No pointed hats, not a broomstick in sight, no human sacrifice on the back patio – although my black cat often insists on walking to the local shops with me.

The Origins and History of Witchcraft

Witches have long had a bad press – think of the secret, black and midnight hags in *Macbeth*. But the positive side of witchcraft, a religion which regards the Earth as sacred, is becoming more accepted. One theory says that the word 'witch' is from the Old

English word *wita*, meaning wise; the Wicca were the wise ones. It is said that witchcraft goes back more than twenty thousand years to Paleolithic times; though we no longer celebrate the cutting down of the corn god who sacrificed himself each year that the crops might grow, or the rebirth of the Sun at the midwinter solstice or shortest day, the parallels are there in the modern Easter and Christmas festivals (see also Chapter 13).

After the formation of the Christian Church, the worship of the old gods and old ways was banned and the nature festivals supplanted by religious ones, although Pope Gregory, who sent St Augustine to England in 597, acknowledged that it was better to try to graft the new festivals on to the existing solstices and equinoxes, for example Easter instead of the spring equinox. Churches and abbeys were erected on the sites of the old pagan temples, which were rededicated with holy water. Sometimes local standing stones or stone circles were torn up to use as the fabric of the new edifices. The builders of the new shrines were of course the creators of the old, so not only the magical stones but also images of the green man, the early god of vegetation, as well as fauns and satyrs, were introduced into many of the early cathedral and church buildings.

The worst period for witch burnings and hangings in Europe was between the mid-fifteenth and early eighteenth centuries. In Britain Matthew Hopkins, who died in 1647, brought about the executions of at least 236 accused witches. He dubbed himself Witchfinder General and hired four assistants, instigating a reign of torture and terror especially in the eastern counties of England. Charging between £4 and £26 for each witch found, at a time when a man's wage was typically sixpence a day, encouraged many people to accuse their neighbours.

In the colonies of America, where witches were hanged, the most notorious trials were those at Salem in Massachusetts in 1692–3. During this mass hysteria, 141 people from the town and immediate area were arrested, 19 were hanged and a landowner, Giles Corey, apparently originally an innocent watcher of the trials, was pressed to death, an execution which took three days. Even a dog was hanged. The hysteria began with accusations by teenage girls who had been dabbling with the occult and whose experiments went wrong. A four-year-old child, Dorcas Good, was the youngest victim to be accused of witchcraft and imprisoned. Dorcas was released on bail after her mother was hanged, but her younger sibling died in prison. Dorcas was driven insane by her experience.

Although the last execution for witchcraft in England was that of Alice Molland at Exeter in 1712, it was not until 1951 that the Witchcraft Act of 1736 was repealed and replaced with the Fraudulent Mediums Act.

The numbers judicially executed as witches between the mid-fifteenth and early eighteenth centuries is generally accepted as about a quarter of a million, although many more were lynched or hanged by mobs eager to blame bad harvests or dying cattle on a scapegoat.

About three-quarter of all those killed as witches were women, mainly lower-class older women, also healers and village herbalists and 'wise women' and midwives. The latter were especially vulnerable at times of high mortality, especially since it was believed that witches needed unbaptised babies to sacrifice to the Devil.

But anyone who was different, eccentric, senile or physically deformed could be accused. High magicians who included popes and royalty who attempted to conjure demons usually escaped censure. The folk religion of the countryside was an easier target.

With the death of so many experienced healers and wise women, much knowledge was lost forever. For a time infant mortality increased as male physicians increasingly took over the role of the midwife and more women were forced to give birth unassisted.

Wicca

This is not modern witchcraft *per se*, but a contemporary neo-pagan religion. Neo-paganism regards the divine life source as a part of nature, not a force beyond creation. *Paganus* is the Latin word for country-dweller, and so *neo* or new paganism looks back to the old nature religions and many deities that embodied different aspects of the natural world. This divine source of life is manifest as the God and Goddess within us all, male and female, animal, bird, tree and flower.

Most Wiccans worship some form of the Goddess and her consort, the Horned God. Along with other earlier deities, the Horned God became demonised with the advent of Christianity and was associated with the forces of darkness.

Wiccans do not, however, recognise any demonic figures in their religion. Rather, the Horned God and the Goddess are the creative male and female principles, not in opposition to each other but complementary and necessary parts of the whole. There are variations within Wicca: some traditions emphasise the Goddess, while others regard them as equal, assuming different aspects according to the season and ritual, the Goddess as the Earth or Moon deity, the God of the Sun or corn.

Wiccan Rituals and Ethics

The chief moral codes are the Wiccan Rede and the three-fold law. The Rede states: 'An [If] it harm none, do what you will.' This deceptively simple statement refers to self as well as others. Its positive intent, the threefold law, states that whatever you do or send to others will be returned threefold, a great incentive to positive thought and action.

Rituals are held at Wiccan sabbats and esbats. The eight sabbats, described in Chapter 13, celebrate the Celtic eightfold year on the solstices, the equinoxes and the old fire festivals, to mark the coming of spring at the end of January/beginning of February, the start of the Celtic summer on May Eve/Day, the first corn harvest at the end of July/beginning of August, and the Celtic winter/New Year which began on Hallowe'en. Esbats are ceremonies traditionally held at the full Moon, but can mark any coming together for meeting or celebration. There are also many lovely ceremonies to mark the transitions in the life cycle, such as handfasting or weddings and rites of passage to welcome a recently deceased Wiccan to the familiar circle whenever he or she wishes to draw near.

On p. 255 you will find a list of books and ways to find out more about the different Wiccan traditions. There are many, including the Gardnerian (Gerald Gardner is often called the founding father of modern Wicca), the Alexandrian, (established by Alex Sanders, and another major branch), Seax or Saxon Wicca, Faery Wicca, the feminist Dianic Wicca, as well as those that identify with other allied traditions, for example Druidism and shamanism.

Wiccan covens or groups, which can be of any number and do not have to be the mythical thirteen, vary in organisation and formality. Dedication, usually ceremonial, marks the beginning of the path to learning about Wicca. Initiation, perhaps after a year and a day or a similar recognised magical period, confers formal entry into a coven/tradition, or may refer to different levels of knowledge and responsibility, for example elevation to a second or third degree. Chapter 3 describes some of the more formal rituals and tools used.

How to Find a Coven

The coven is the basic, cellular congregation. It generally does not permit onlookers and may have quite stringent criteria for membership because of the very deep nature of the links between members, which rely on mutual love, and trust and respect.

Because of prejudice, such organisations tend to be kept very private. However there are many natural, less formal entry points to Wiccan practice that give you an opportunity to meet people involved and to learn something about the ideas. Many Green organisations have Wiccan connections, and pagan magazines advertise festivals, public rituals, classes and open circles. You can also make connection on the Internet through the Pagan Federation (address on p. 254) and on the noticeboards of New Age bookstores.

If these initial explorations make you want to go further, opportunities will arise naturally through friends you make at these events. This method may seem slow, but it does have its own inbuilt safety net. Wiccan groups are expert at shielding themselves from curious teenagers or adults eager for what they imagine as an opportunity for free love and a good time. This caution itself protects genuine seekers from more dubious practices masquerading under the guise of Wicca or witchcraft.

Answering adverts in newspapers can be risky: you should only ever meet people you do not know in a public place, and even then offer no personal information. I myself have come across people claiming to be Wiccans who instantly steer the conversation round to weird sexual practices and sexual demons. This is the point to back off, for no genuine witch would behave this way.

Beware also of strangers or acquaintances who regale you with supposed Wiccan practices or offer to do spells for you, usually for money. True Wiccans are among the most tolerant of folk, would never seek to impose their beliefs on others, and are usually incredibly reticent with people they do not know. Indeed, some branches of Wicca do not carry out magical rituals at all, though the majority practice healing rituals and have ceremonies to tune into the divinity of their life source.

Being a Hedge Witch or Solitary Practitioner

The term 'hedge witch' comes from the old practice of a witch planting hawthorns round her home as a sacred boundary. Many Wiccans begin as solitary practitioners, and a number prefer to continue in that fashion. Other people who follow the old ways do not subscribe to any tradition but use herbs and divination in a way often passed down by older family members. Indeed, many of our grandmothers and great-grandmothers, who possessed remarkable intuition, read tea leaves and made herbal concoctions, were jokingly called witches by their own families – and were just that!

If you want to carry out regular rituals alone, perhaps on the new and full Moon and the old festivals, you are among countless ordinary men and women who tap into their own powers and those of the natural world to heal, protect and help themselves and those they love. This folk magic I have described in Chapters 5, 6 and 9.

Satanism and Black Magic

Magic is said to be neutral, although, as I acknowledged at the beginning of the book, there are people who use it for evil, just as in many other walks of life people use power and knowledge for unworthy aims. Where the problem arises is that it is still, in practice, very hard to acknowledge openly that one is a Wiccan, certainly in the UK; therefore it is easy for evil and perverted people to use the pretext of magic and nature religions as a front for child abuse and drug peddling, as well as attempts to control the minds of others.

Incredible films about black magic and religious extremists, and blinkered social workers who see normal psychic instincts and the celebration of the seasons in the same light as sacrificing babies and upside-down crosses, fuel media hysteria. The problem is that sex, drugs and alcohol are discussed openly with even quite young children, whereas anything to do with the psychic is taboo in schools and regarded as something weird, thus increasing the potential for false mystique and sensationalism bred of secrecy.

Wiccan children grow up to be kind, learn a wealth of mythology, respect animals and the planet and can share in many joyous celebrations on the old agricultural festivals. No responsible Wiccan parent – indeed no responsible parent of any kind – introduces a child to ideas or experiences before they are ready, or acts in a way that might lower their children's respect. So the children of so-called witches are in no danger, although some professionals unfairly view Wiccan families with suspicion.

At the end of the day we need to leave behind the images created centuries ago and the stuff of Gothic horror movies and apply the same common sense to magic as we do to other important areas of our lives.

Section Four

Magic of the Natural World

11

Natural Magic

The natural world was once the source of rituals performed both by the village wise women and by ordinary men and women seeking love, happiness and good fortune. Herbal pillows brought divinatory dreams, while poppets or dolls filled with herbs might be used to attract love or to restore health. The cauldron, beloved in portrayals of witches from Shakespeare's *Macbeth* to Bette Midler's role in the film *Hocus Pocus*, started life as the iron pot that hung over the family hearth from the Iron Age onwards.

The formal witches' esbats at the full Moon stem from gatherings of village folk in woodland at a time when it was light enough to connect with the trees and fields from which positive energies came. Hugging trees is no New Age concept; in medieval times and until quite recently young children who were ill would be passed through a split ash nine times, and the ash then bound so that as it healed so would the child. As we have become urbanised and reliant on technology, so we have lost touch with our instinctive connection with flowers, trees and herbs and the old love and luck rhymes and chants, learned in childhood, that by their repetitive simplicity gave power to the spells of the countryside.

Herb Rituals

You can use herbs in many ways: in sachets, poppets or dolls, in incense (see Chapter 14) and in baths, potions and brews. Check carefully before taking any herb internally, whether as a tea or in food, that it is not harmful, however little the amounts you propose using. If you are giving them to children reduce the potency, and in all cases consult a good herbal book.

The following herbs should not be taken internally during pregnancy (if in doubt check, as this is not an exhaustive list but only includes those in popular use). In the first three months of pregnancy, all remedies should be checked before use.

Avoid during pregnancy

angelica	golden seal	marjoram	tansy
basil	juniper	pennyroyal	thyme
cedarwood	male fern	rue	wormwood
fennel	mandrake	sage	yarrow

Herbs for Empowerment and Protection

Herb	*Power*
Acacia	Money, love, protection, psychic powers, herb of Lammas (beginning of August, first harvest)
Aconite	Healing, invisibility to those who would harm
Adder's tongue	All forms of healing, dream and Moon magic
Agaric	Fertility, both physical and of ideas
Agrimony	Protection, peaceful sleep

Herb	*Power*
Alfalfa	Prosperity, abundance, money
Allspice	Money, luck, healing
Aloe	Protection, luck
Aloes, wood	Love, spirituality
Althea	Protects against negativity, draws spirit guides closer
Alyssum	Protection, moderating anger in self and others
Angelica	Banishes hostility from others, protection, healing, visions. Herb of Candlemas (beginning of February), and Beltane (May Day, the start of the old Celtic summer)
Balm, lemon	Love, success, healing
Balm of Gilead	Love (carried as love amulet), manifestations of other dimensions, protection, healing
Basil	Love, exorcism, wealth. Conquers fear of flying in the real world. One of the traditional herbs of Candlemas
Bay	Protection, psychic powers, healing, purification, strength and endurance. One of the traditional herbs of Candlemas and midwinter solstice
Benzoin	Purification, prosperity
Bergamot, orange	Money, property
Betony, wood	Protection, purification, love

Herb	*Power*
Bladderwrack	Protection against accidents or illness, especially at sea, sea rituals, wind rituals, action, money, psychic powers
Bodhi	Fertility, protection, wisdom, meditation
Borage	Courage, psychic awareness
Bracken/broom	Healing, divination, especially runes, prophetic dreams, female fertility, rainmaking among Native Americans
Briony	Image magic, visualisation, money, protection
Buchu	Psychic powers, prophetic dreams
Buckthorn	Protection, exorcism, wishes, legal matters
Burdock	Protection against negativity, healing. Love and sex magic, magical cure for coughs, hung around necks of babies in southern USA
Cactus	Protection, purity
Camphor	Purity, fidelity, health, divination
Caraway	Protection, passion, health, anti-theft, mental powers
Carob	Protection, health
Cascara sagrada	Legal matters, money, protection
Catnip	Cat magic, love, beauty, happiness in home, fertility charm
Cedarwood	Healing, purification, money, protection

Herb	*Power*
Chamomile	Money, quiet sleep, affection and family
Chicory	Removing obstacles, invisibility in hostile situations, receiving favours, melts frigidity both physical and mental
Cinnamon	Spirituality, success, healing powers, psychic powers, money, love and passion
Cinquefoil	Money, protection, prophetic dreams especially about love, peaceful sleep, good health
Cloth of gold	Telepathic communication with animals
Clove	Protection, banishing negativity, love, money
Clover	Protection, money, love, fidelity, banishing negativity, success
Cohosh, black	Love, courage, protection, potency
Coltsfoot	Love, visions, peace and tranquillity, protects horses
Columbine	Courage, love, the lion's herb, retrieves lost love
Comfrey	Safety during travel, money
Coriander	Love, health, healing
Cotton	Luck, healing, protection, rainmaking, fishing magic
Cumin	Protection, fidelity, exorcism
Curry	Protection
Deerstongue	Passion, psychic powers

Herb	*Power*
Devil's shoestring	Protection, gambling, luck, power, employment
Dill	Protection, keeping home safe from enemies and those who have envy in their hearts. Also for money, passion, luck
Dittany of Crete	Contact with other dimensions
Dock	Healing, fertility, money
Dodder	Love, divination, knot divination
Dogwood	Wishes, protection
Dragon's blood	Love magic, protection, dispels negativity, increases male potency
Dulse	Passion, harmony and reconciliation
Echinacea	Strengthening rituals, personal intuitive powers
Endive	Passion, love
Eryngo	Travelling luck and safety, peace, passion, love
Evening primrose	Finding what is lost
Eyebright	Improves mental powers, psychic awareness, increased perception
Fennel	Protection, healing, purification
Fern	Rainmaking, protection, luck, riches, finding hidden treasure, youthfulness, good health
Feverfew	Protection

Herb	*Power*
Flax	Money, protection, beauty, psychic powers, healing
Fleabane	Banishing negativity, protection, purity
Galangal	Protection, passion, health, money, psychic powers, dispelling hostility
Garlic	Protection, healing, banishing negativity, passion, security from thieves
Gentian	Love, power
Ginger	Love, passion, money, success, power
Ginseng	Love, wishes, healing, beauty, protection, passion, increases male sexual potency. Often used as a substitute for mandrake root, which is difficult to obtain
Goldenrod	Money, divination, finding buried treasure, charm against rheumatism
Golden seal	Healing, money
Gotu kola	Meditation
Grass, sweet	Protection, wisdom, purification, psychic awareness
Groundsel	Health, healing
Gum Arabic	Purifies negativity and evil
Heliotrope	Banishing negativity, prophetic dreams, healing, wealth, invisibility in potentially threatening situations

Herb	*Power*
Hibiscus	Passion, love, divination
Honesty	Money, banishing dark fears
Hops	Healing, peaceful sleep
Horseradish	Purification, banishing negativity
Horsetail	Fertility, repels spite, protection against snakes
Hyssop	Purification, protection
Irish moss	Money, luck, protection
Ivy	Protection, healing
Juniper	Protection, anti-theft, love, banishing negativity, health, protects against accidents; increases male potency
Kava-kave	Psychic visions, protection, luck, magical powers, especially highly regarded as magical token in its native Hawaii and Polynesia
Knotweed	Binding lovers or friends, for keeping promises, health
Lavender	Love, protection especially of children, quiet sleep, long life, purification, happiness, peace
Lemongrass	Repels spite, protection against snakes, passion, increases psychic awareness
Lemon verbena	Purification, love
Lettuce	Purity, protection, love, divination, sleep
Licorice	Love, passion, fidelity

Herb	*Power*
Liverwort	Protection, love
Lovage	Love
Lucky hand root	Employment, luck, protection, money, safe travel
Mace	Increases psychic awareness and mental powers
Mahogany, mountain	Anti-lightning, anti-shock
Maidenhair	Beauty, love
Male fern	Luck, love
Mallow	Love, protection, exorcism
Mandrake	Protection, love, money, fertility, health
Marigold	Protection, prophetic dreams, legal matters, increases psychic powers
Marjoram	Protection, love, happiness, health, money
Master wort	Strength, courage, protection
Mastic	Increases psychic awareness, visions of other dimensions, passion
Meadowsweet	Love, divination, peace, happiness, gathered at midsummer and associated with summer solstice
Mesquite	Healing
Mimosa	Protection, love, prophetic dreams, purification
Mint	Money, love, increasing sexual desire, healing, banishing malevolence, protection especially while travelling

Herb	*Power*
Moonwort	Money, love, associated with phases of the Moon
Mugwort	Strength, psychic powers, protection, prophetic dreams, healing
Mulberry	Protection, strength
Mullein	Courage, protection, health, love and love divination, banishes nightmares and malevolence, especially popular in India and parts of the USA
Mustard	Fertility, protection, increases mental powers
Myrrh	Protection, banishing negativity, for charging magical tools, healing, spirituality
Myrtle	Love, fertility, preserving youthfulness, peace, money
Nettle	Banishing negativity, protection, healing, passion
Oats	Money
Oregon grape	Money, prosperity
Orris	Love, protection, divination
Parsley	Love, protection, divination, passion, purification
Pennyroyal	Strength, protection, peace
Pepper	Protection, banishing malevolence, overcomes inertia and gives focus, positive anger for change
Peppermint	Purification, energy, love, healing, increases psychic powers
Pimpernel	Protection, maintains good health

Herb	*Power*
Pine	Healing, fertility, purification, protection, money. A herb of midwinter solstice, although its powers against negativity are strongest when its needles and cones are gathered at midsummer. Returns hostility to sender
Purslane	Sleep, love, luck, protection, happiness
Quassia	Love
Quince	Protection, love, happiness
Ragweed	Courage
Ragwort	Protection, fairy magic and the ability to see fairies
Rattlesnake root	Protection, money
Rose	Love, enchantment, increases psychic powers, healing, love and love divination, luck, protection, associated with spring and autumn equinoxes
Rosemary	Love, passion, increases mental powers, banishes negativity and depression, banishes nightmares. Also for purification, healing, quiet sleep, preserves youthfulness
Rue	Healing, protects against illnesses of all kinds and speeds recovery from surgery or wounds, increases mental powers, love enchantment; banishes regrets and redundant guilt or anger
Rye	Love, fidelity
Saffron	Love, healing, happiness, raising the winds, passion, strength, increases psychic powers and offers second sight

Herb	*Power*
Sage	Long life, wisdom, protection, grants wishes, improves memory. A Hallowe'en herb (Samhain, beginning of the Celtic winter)
Sagebrush	Purification, banishing negativity
St John's wort	Health, power, protection, strength, love and fertility, love divination, happiness (gathered on Midsummer Eve)
Sandalwood	Protection, healing, banishes negativity, spirituality, contact with guardian angels, higher self. A herb for Lammas (festival at beginning of August celebrating the first corn harvest)
Sarsaparilla	Love, money
Sassafras	Health, money
Savory	Increases mental abilities, passion
Skullcap	Love, fidelity, peace
Sesame	Money, passion
Slippery elm	Prevents gossip and malice
Snakeroot	Luck, money
Snakeroot, black	Love, passion, money
Solomon's seal	Protection, banishes all negativity and hostility
Sorrel, wood	Healing, preserves good health
Spanish moss	Protection
Spearmint	Healing, love, mental powers

Herb	*Power*
Spider wort	Love
Star anise	Increases psychic awareness, luck
Tansy	Health, long life, conception and pregnancy, invisibility against potential danger. A herb of the spring equinox
Thistle	Strength, protection against thieves, prolonged sadness and active hostility of thought or deed, speeds healing
Thistle, holy	Purification, protection against all danger
Thyme	Health, healing, prophetic dreams, increases psychic powers; improves memory, love and love divination, purification, courage
Toadflax	Protection, banishes negativity and active hostility
Turmeric	Purification
Turnip	Protection, eases natural endings; promotes harmonious relationships
Uva ursa	Psychic rituals, divination
Valerian	Love and love divination, quiet sleep, purification, protection against outer hostility, inner fears and despair
Vanilla	Love, passion, increases mental powers
Vervain	Love, protection, transforms enemies into friends. Purification, peace, money, prophecy, preserves youthfulness, peaceful sleep, healing. Gathered at midsummer or when Sirius is in the ascendant

Herb	*Power*
Vetivert	Love, breaks a run of bad luck, money, anti-theft, protects against all negativity
Wintergreen	Protection, healing, deflects hostility
Winter's bark	Success
Witch grass	Happiness, passion, love, protects against negativity
Witch hazel	Mends broken hearts and relationships, finds buried treasure and underground streams, protection
Wolf's bane	Protection, invisibility against hostility
Woodruff	Victory, protection, money
Wormwood	Promoting psychic awareness, love, visions of dimensions
Yarrow	Courage, love, psychic powers, divination, banishes negativity. Brought into house at midsummer for protection against illness and domestic strife
Yerba mate	Fidelity, love, passion
Yerba santa	Beauty, healing, increasing psychic awareness, protection
Yohimbe	Love, passion
Yucca	Transformation, change, protection, purification

Herb Sachets for Health, Happiness, Harmony and Prosperity

Herbs can be placed in sachets around the home, carried or worn pinned to undergarments for confidence or protection, to attract love, money and success and to preserve good health. Herb sachets are very easy to make, and at their simplest need be no more than a piece of cloth or small porous bag in which the herbs are tied.

You can make herb sachets for almost any positive magical use by referring to the list above. Concentrate the energies by combining two or three herbs with the same magical strengths. For example, a love sachet might contain equal amounts of coriander, lavender and lemon verbena. You could perhaps add a few drops of geranium oil, an oil of love, to make the sachet even more fragrant, and rose petals, a flower of love and romance, (see the list of essential oils in Chapter 14 and the list of flowers on p. 162).

Be as inventive as you like, but keep a note in your magic journal of combinations that are especially effective, plus any particular proportions you used. You may want to include a herb of protection in sachets for other purposes, although some herbs do have a protective property along with their main magical use. You can increase the strength of a sachet by using two related herbs. For example, if you were studying for an exam you could use rosemary to increase mental powers plus sage and thyme which specifically improve memory. Finally add lemon balm for success.

Making a Herb Sachet

- Whether you use ready dried and powdered herbs or chop your own and grind them in a mortar and pestle, place the herbs in a small ceramic or glass bowl and empower them by running them through your fingers repeating, for example, 'Lavender, lavender bring me love', until you can feel their power rising.
- Chant for each herb in turn in this way as you add it to the mix.
- To make the sachet, use a piece of fabric about 4 × 10 inches (10 × 25 cm) in a natural fabric such as felt, wool or cotton. You can vary the size depending on whether you want to wear it or use it in the home, but the colour should be appropriate to the spell you are about to use:

Red for passion, change, courage or action
Orange for harmony, fertility and identity
Yellow for communication, learning, business acumen, travel and logic
Green for love and emotions, healing and the natural world
Blue for power, justice and idealism
Purple for wisdom and spirituality, also psychic development and inner harmony
White for new beginnings and energy, happiness and fulfilment
Pink for reconciliation, friendship, children and animals
Grey for compromise, keeping secrets and older people, who are also under the auspices of brown
Brown for home and money, security and possessions, and older people
Black for sleep and endings and banishing negative feelings (see Chapter 4 for more about the magical significance of colour)

- Place about a tablespoon of the herb or herbs in the centre of the cloth (more if you are making a larger sachet). As you fill the sachet, repeat your chant about the energies you are calling in the herbs, for instance, 'Sage, sage bring me wisdom.'
- Again list each property in turn, not forgetting that of the essential oil if you are adding it.
- Tie the material in three consecutive knots using a natural twine of the same colour as the bag, seeing your energy and hopes bound in the knots. As you tie your bag, visualise yourself after your wish has been realised. If the ritual is urgent or vital, add words such as 'Rue, rue, speed my healing/grant my wish.'
- Carry the sachet until it loses its fragrance. Alternatively, if it represents a long-term objective, open it and replace the herbs with fresh ones, following the same ritual described above.
- Scatter some of the old herbs to the four winds, burn a few, bury some and dissolve the rest in water.

Herbal Poppets or Dolls for Healing

The modern world associates the creating of images and dolls with voodoo and sensationalist films of witches pricking waxen images of enemies or love rivals with pins. This is a pity, as creating dolls or poppets and filling them with herbs is a powerful form of healing, energising and attracting love or good fortune. In fact cloth poppets, rough featureless images in green or blue cloth for healing and pink or red for love, have been used from early times in the northern magical tradition in a positive way.

Because I am aware of this more negative association, I never use poppets or representations for any form of banishing magic or getting rid of negative feelings. In such cases, I find that stones or sticks are best. Nor would I ever add hair or any other personal symbol of another person to their poppet, as that seems to intrude on their privacy.

I believe we can and should do magic and send healing for others, as long as we do not seek to influence the individual on a course that might not be right for him or her and ultimately not right for you. Therefore in poppet magic for love, if I was focusing on a particular person I knew, I would always ask that he might see me though the eyes of love, if it was right for his personal path. Equally, I would specify that there might be healing in whatever way would be of benefit to that person I was trying to help.

You can make poppets to represent yourself and a lover or an unknown love yet to come into your life; to represent you in a new job or home; or to represent a sick person well and strong again. You can also create a poppet filled with protective herbs for a child or yourself if you feel vulnerable and keep it under your pillow. My youngest son has a lavender bear that sleeps with him when he is away from home.

Animal poppets filled with the appropriate herbs form powerful talismans, for example a lion of yarrow and borage for courage. It is possible to buy ready-prepared fabric herb dolls and animals – I have used lavender bears for friendship and family magic many times. But if you can make your own – and they require minimal skill in needlework and can be sewn together with a rough running stitch – you endow them as you work with your own hopes, desires and positive feelings.

Whether making poppets for yourself or for others, use the colours listed above for the doll and the thread. You can combine more than one wish, for example, by using a green doll for healing sewn with white thread for energy, if the person is exhausted. Or you could use purple or pink for tranquillity or healing if troubled emotions are making the condition worse.

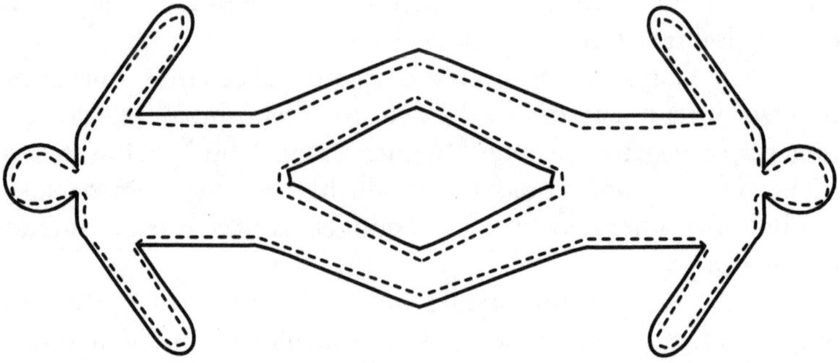

Pattern for a simple poppet: the dotted line shows where it should be stitched

- Just before sunset cut out the front and back of the doll, seeing yourself or the person you are representing well or happy as you work.
- As you sew the doll, see each stitch filled with healing, energising or calming light.
- Leave the head open to be filled with the herbs.
- When the poppet is ready prepare your herbs as for sachets, mixing them in a ceramic bowl or mortar and chanting, for example, as you make a protective doll, 'Vervain, vervain, turn my enemies' wrath from me.'
- See the herbs filling with light of a colour appropriate to the need and with your own love and optimism.
- As with the sachets you can use a combination of herbs, either to strengthen a single need or to combine different qualities.
- As you place the herbs inside the doll or animal say: 'May only love and light fill this image and bring an increase of [what you are wishing for] if it is right to do so.'
- Finally sew the head, saying: 'As I have created this image of myself [or whoever you are making the poppet for] in love, may I and/or he/she be filled with the healing wisdom of gentle

Mother Earth, by the creative light of Father Sky, the fertile waters of well, river and sacred spring and the warming fires of the Sun'.

- Sprinkle the doll or dolls with salt for health.
- Circle over it anti-clockwise a healing incense stick of frankincense or myrrh to remove all negativity.
- Pass the doll clockwise around a candle of the appropriate colour.
- Sprinkle over it a few drops in which rose petals or lavender flowers have soaked for twenty-four hours, or pure spring water left in a glass or crystal container for a full twenty-four-hour Sun-and-Moon cycle.
- Let the candle burn out naturally in a safe place.
- If the doll or dolls are for healing, place it/them in white linen, cotton or silk in a high place where the air will circulate and Moon, Sun and starlight can penetrate.
- If they are for love, bind them together face to face with red ribbon or thread tied in nine knots. Place them next to your bed during the day and under your pillow at night.
- In both love and healing, keep the doll or dolls until the purpose is achieved or the herbs lose their fragrance, in which case you can refill them in the same way.
- If the doll or dolls are for money or success, surround them with a circle of salt and a ring of coins and leave from the crescent Moon to the full Moon. After the full Moon, dissolve the salt in water and let it flow away to speed the flow of money. Wrap the money and dolls in dark silk and keep them covered until the new Moon cycle or the aim is achieved. As before, replace the herbs when they are no longer fragrant (see also Chapter 8).

Tree Magic

My husband and I took our two younger children into the local forest for a Sunday walk and found evidence of tree magic close to the path. Against one mighty oak a pentagram (see p. 64), a magical symbol of power, had been made from branches, while five trees had been joined with wool in an intricate pattern. There was no sense of evil or foreboding, only a strong sense of people who had come to this natural church to celebrate the benign forces of nature.

Before long the children indulged in that true innocent magic of childhood that we adults spend our lives trying to recapture. They found a log that looked like a wooden pig and created for him a shelter of wood, adorning the door with woven fronds and creepers. My daughter demonstrated her skill at dowsing for hidden objects using a forked branch, and as the wind blew we listened for messages in the leaves. We could have been a family in any age, for the magic of the forest is timeless. It is easy, seeing the intricate designs carved by time on the tree trunks, to recognise the faces of the tree spirits worshipped by the Druids and still recalled every time we touch wood for luck.

Trees have been regarded as sacred in almost every culture and time, and many early peoples thought that the spirits of their ancestors and the souls of unborn babies lived in trees until birth. The natural affinity between mankind and trees is symbolised by the number of myths in which the first people were created from trees. For example, in Indonesia, two deities were said to have hewed vertical logs from a fig tree to bring forth man and horizontal sections of the same tree for woman.

Gradually associations grew up between the physical and spiritual or magical properties of trees. The aspen and white poplar are both known as the shiver-tree and were believed to have the power to cure fevers and agues. This was because their leaves shook even when there was apparently no breeze: sympathetic magic held that 'like cures like'. An old rhyme would request: 'Aspen tree, Aspen tree, I pray thee shiver instead of me.' One explanation for the aspen tree shivering is that it was the wood used in the crucifixion, and thereafter it has shaken at the thought of the agony it caused.

Below I have listed some of these associations, taken from a variety of sources.

Tree Symbolism

Tree	*Quality*
Alder	Called the tree of fire, it symbolises firm foundations and power to control the external forces, symbolised by the four winds
Almond	Abundance, prosperity and love without limits
Apple	Fertility, health, love and long life
Ash	Expansion of horizons, travel especially by sea, healing and strength, prosperity
Aspen	Communication, eloquence, protection against theft, healing
Avocado	Desire, increase of beauty in self or environment
Bamboo	Protection, especially of household boundaries and against the negative thoughts of others
Banana	Fertility, male potency, prosperity
Banyan	Luck
Bay	Preservation of family, home, pleasant dreams
Beech	Knowledge, formal learning
Birch	Cleansing, health, wisdom, new beginnings, lunar workings, protection of the young
Boxwood	Hidden treasure, buried talents, the unexpected
Cedar	Good fortune, faithful lovers
Cherry	New love, divinatory abilities

Tree	*Quality*
Chestnut	Abundance
Chestnut, horse	Money, healing
Coconut	Fertility and motherhood (the shell representing the womb and the milk the flow of new life and energies), gives protection against all negativity, especially psychic attack
Cypress	Long life, healing and comfort in sorrow
Dogwood	Clear focus
Elder	Tree of the White (Moon) Goddess of the Celts and of protective female household gods; gives ability to see other dimensions, increases clairvoyance. A fairy tree, it absorbs personal negativity
Elm	Tree of sleep, love and giving
Fig	Tree of wisdom, of creativity and creation, fertility, harmony and balance
Fir	The Christmas tree and so a tree of birth, the return of light and new beginnings, the life cycle
Hawthorn	Courage, marking boundaries, the coming of summer; purification, male potency, cleansing and endurance; a fairy tree
Hazel	Wisdom, luck, fertility, knowledge and inspiration, justice and divination, especially dowsing for water and treasure
Holly	Protection, especially of the home, against all negativity; king of the waning year. Its name means holy and it is associated with spirituality. Also a tree for money and material gain

Tree	*Quality*
Ivy	Fidelity, married love, relationships, constancy
Juniper	Protection against all negative forces, purification
Larch	Protection, especially against thieves; optimism
Laurel	Protection from illness; success and ambition; winning through in spite of difficulty
Lime linden	Justice, cooperation with others, partnerships of all kinds, officialdom
Mango	Health, permanence
Maple	Long life, health of children, money
Mistletoe	Known to the Druids as the all-healer; peace, love and purity, fertility and sexual potency, protection and good health
Myrtle	Stable relationships, married love, fertility, youth, peace, money
Norfolk Island pine	Ensures that you and your family will never go without the necessities of life
Oak	King of the waxing year and sacred tree of the Druids, supreme tree of knowledge, power and independence, confidence, prosperity and potency
Olive	Peace and reconciliation, forgiveness, abundance, nourishment, healing, fertility
Orange	Love, abundance, luck, money
Palm, date	Fertility, potency, self-renewal, rejuvenation, the life cycle

Tree	*Quality*
Peach	Marriage and birth, abundance, happiness, fertility, wishes, long life
Pear	New life, health, women, fertility
Pine	Fire and illumination, cleansing, balance, friendship in adversity, knowledge, protection from all negativity
Poplar, black	Endings.
Poplar, white	Money, astral projection, hope, rebirth, divination.
Rowan/mountain ash	A tree of the White Goddess of the Celts; domestic protection, psychic powers, healing, metal dowsing, astral projection
Sycamore	Protection, granting of wishes, increasing influence
Tamarind	Love, especially new love, and the rebuilding of trust
Vine	Rebirth and renewal, joy, ecstasy, fairy magic
Walnut	Tree of prophecy, traditionally a tree where witches meet; health, increase of mental powers, fertility, granting of wishes
Willow	A Moon tree, intuition, Moon magic, healing, making wishes come true, increasing psychic energies, understanding emotions of others
Yew	Tree of endings, of new coming out of the old, of permanence, aims that are slow to come to fruition but which endure, of union between two people after difficulty

Connecting with Trees

Before you begin tree rituals, or if you want to connect with tree energies either to empower or to calm yourself, sit at the foot of your chosen tree facing the direction of the sun with your back against the trunk.

- Let the energies of the tree enter you via the base of your spine.
- You may feel the sap rising, warming you as it flows upwards and around your body. This simple connection with a tree is one that can be practised unobtrusively. If you need power, sit against a tree of strength or one of the Sun trees; if you need calm, choose a tree with gentle healing energies; and for inspiration, choose one of the fertility trees. If you cannot find a particular tree listed, choose one indigenous to your region that shares similar qualities.

Tree Divination

This is a very ancient form of getting in touch with answers that lie just beyond consciousness and over the horizon. There are two main methods:

Listening to the leaves

Oak groves and pine forests are said to have the clearest voices, but you can stand in any grove of trees on a windy day and receive answers to your questions. This is especially potent at a transition time such as sunrise or sunset, or you can choose an hour from the table on pp. 229–30 that is appropriate for your current concern.

- Face the direction of the Sun and ask your question while the trees are still, making it as specific as possible. Alternatively, carve its initials or the first word on a fallen twig and cast it towards the Sun just as the leaves begin to move.
- Let the leaves speak the words. Do not try to interpret them, but continue listening until the wind is silent.
- When the trees stop talking, write down the messages and draw any patterns you see in the leaves above you.
- The answer will become clear as you walk.

Making a decision

If you have a yes/no question that circles your mind without resolution, go to a grove or forest early in the morning and find thirty twigs of similar size and texture made from the same wood. Oak and ash are especially good for divination.

- On one side of each carve away the bark and mark it as the positive side, with a Sun symbol.

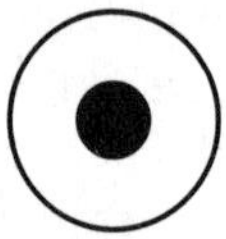

- With a stick draw a clockwise circle about 2 feet (60 cm) in diameter between two trees.
- Hold your sticks between your two hands.
- Ask a question that will elicit a yes or no response, and cast your sticks towards the circle.
- Ignore any that land outside the circle, and count whether there are more positive or negative responses.
- If you get an equal number, you may need to ask the question in a different way – the new question will be the one you need to ask.

Trees and Healing

Many trees were used for healing rituals, not only for physical healing but for the ending of quarrels. Maple and ash, as mentioned earlier, were the focus for healing children, who would be passed nine times through a specially split large branch. The tree would then be bound, and as it grew together so would the illness heal. In Poland and other Eastern European countries, objects symbolising sins and anger were buried beneath an elder tree.

A tree ritual for mending a quarrel or estrangement

Choose one of the trees of healing listed above and find one with a natural cleft that reaches to the base of the trunk so that you can easily climb through.

- Take a long scarf or length of cord long enough to pass round the two branches with ease.
- Holding the scarf or cord in your power or writing hand, pass nine times through the tree anti-clockwise, reciting:

Untangle the anger,
That makes us a stranger
Untie the pain,
Bring love back again.

- Now repeat the movements nine times clockwise, reciting:

Oh, tree heal the pain,
Bring love back again
Let harsh words soon mend,
And bitterness end.

- Loop the scarf around the tree so that you are holding both ends and chant as you bind the tree with three knots:

Knot one be for peace,
Knot two sorrow cease,
Knot three bind the pain
Bring love back again.

- Make a non-confrontational, low-key gesture of reconciliation towards the estranged person, and then allow the other person to respond or not. Either way, you have mended the quarrel and can walk free.

The Symbolism of Flowers

Although traditionally, the language of flowers is associated with sending messages of love, a practice that reached its height of popularity in Victorian times, flower symbolism formed the basis for many countryside spells and divination. Even today children and young lovers still pluck daisy petals or blow dandelion clocks and recite, 'He/she loves me/not.'

Flower rituals were frequently connected with love and fertility, but also focused on the desire for health, wealth and happiness. Modern air freight and hothouses mean that flowers are no longer confined to their own seasons or regions. However, there is something very special about using seasonal flowers that grow in the area in which the ritual is carried out, and it is quite acceptable to use substitutes of the same colour and similar size.

The list below links different flowers with particular areas of experience. As with herbs, you can combine two or three with the same meaning to add to the potency, or use different flower symbols to bring two or three related needs together. You may wish to add a flower of protection to your rituals.

Flower	*Quality*
Acacia	Hidden emotions, secrets
African violet	Spirituality, protection
Anemone	Honesty, health, healing protection
Aster	Love, inner worth
Azalea	Caution, harmony, vulnerability
Bluebell	Faithfulness, luck, modesty, truth
Buttercup	Riches, self-esteem
Cactus	Endurance
Carnation	Strength, healing, family devotion
Celandine	Protection, escape from sorrow and worry, happiness, justice and legal matters
Chrysanthemum	Protection, riches, truth, peace of mind
Cowslip	The fairy cup, for healing, youthfulness, finding treasure or lost objects, protects houses against intruders

Flower	*Quality*
Crocus	New hope, positive attitudes, visions
Cuckoo flower	Fertility, attracting new love
Cyclamen	Fertility, protection, desire, partings
Daffodil	Love, luck, fidelity, increasing self-esteem
Daisy	Idealistic love, devotion, luck
Dandelion	Divination, wishes, increasing clairvoyant powers
Edelweiss	Invisibility, protection from sudden attack
Forget-me-not	Memories, all matters concerned with the past
Foxglove	Protection, fairy magic.
Freesia	For increasing trust
Heather	Passion, loyalty, rainmaking, luck
Honeysuckle	Money, psychic powers, protection
Hyacinth	Happiness, desire for reconciliation
Hydrangea	Repels negativity and sends it back to its source
Gardenia	Peace, healing, spirituality
Geranium	Fertility, health, love, protection
Iris	Courage, faith, optimism, harmony, intuitive wisdom
Jasmine	Passion, Moon magic, money, prophetic dreams
Jonquil	To seek and increase mutual love and affection

Flower	*Quality*
Larkspur	Health, protection, gifts
Lilac	Cleansing negativity, domestic happiness, nostalgia
Lily	Purity, breaking negative influences in love
Lily, tiger	Wealth, confidence
Lily of the valley	Increases mental abilities, happiness, restoration of joy
Lotus	Protection, reveals secrets
Magnolia	Fidelity, idealism, strong principles
Marigold	Attraction, to increase love, prophetic dreams
Mimosa	Protection, love, prophetic dreams, purification
Myrtle	Marriage, fidelity, permanence
Nasturtium	Success after a struggle, triumph through effort
Oleander	Caution
Orchid	Spirituality, unique worth, grace, many blessings
Pansy	Affection, rain magic, divination, affection
Passion flower	Sacrifice, peace, quiet sleep, friendship
Peony	Protection, banishing negativity
Periwinkle	Passion, increases mental powers, money
Pimpernel	Good health, forgiveness
Poppy	Fertility, sleep, money, luck, invisibility

Flower	*Quality*
Primrose	New beginnings, reconciliation
Rose	Love, psychic powers, healing, divination
Snapdragon	Keeping secrets, finding what is lost
Sunflower	Developing potential, fertility, confidence, self-esteem
Sweet pea	Friendship, purity, courage, strength
Tulip	Desire for fame
Violet	Modesty, secrecy, uncovering hidden talents

A Flower Ritual to Increase Confidence and to Restore Self-esteem

This is an excellent ritual if you have been betrayed or unfairly treated and are doubting your own self-worth.

- Go to a patch of rich golden soil when the sun is high in the sky, and if necessary moisten it so that you leave a series of footprints.
- Step five times, making each imprint slowly and deliberately, and saying one line for each step:

I am [stamp here] myself,
I am [stamp here] of worth,
I do [stamp here] exist.
I will [stamp here] survive,
I will [stamp here] succeed.

- Carefully scoop up the soil in which you have made your footprints and place it in an earthenware pot.
- In the pot, plant five sunflower seeds one at a time, as you do so repeating a single line for the first, the first two lines for the second, the first three lines for the third and so on, until with the last seed you repeat the whole chant.

- Buy yourself any golden or yellow flowers you can find, or a pot plant with yellow flowers, and place them where you can see them as a reminder of your own emerging Sun. When they die replace them, until your seeds begin to grow. Even dandelions or buttercups are symbols of sunshine and hope.
- Tend your seeds every day, and after you have done so carry out a small action to make yourself happy.

Astrological Associations

Each birth sign has its associated herb, tree and flower that you can use during your Sun sign period as a symbol of your unique strength and worth. You can also add the leaves, bark, flowers and herbs of the appropriate Sun sign to any sachets or poppets representing yourself and other people. A third use is to incorporate an astrological herb, leaf or flower to add a quality you might need, for example rosemary for the determination of Aries. The qualities are listed next to the Sun sign.

You can use astrological flowers, herbs and leaves to strengthen any ritual in which you need enhanced energy or confidence, or to strengthen your own identity where this may be undermined by others or by events.

	Herbs	*Trees*	*Flowers*
Aries 21 March–20 April	Peppermint, thyme	Holly, pine	Carnation, honeysuckle
Taurus 21 April–21 May	Thyme, vervain	Apple, ash	Lilac, rose
Gemini 22 May–21 June	Lemongrass, parsley	Almond, hazel	Lavender, lily of the valley
Cancer 22 June–22 July	Lemon balm, moonwort	Eucalyptus, willow	Gardenia, jasmine
Leo 23 July–23 August	Cinnamon, rue	Laurel, palm	Marigold, sunflower

	Herbs	*Trees*	*Flowers*
Virgo 24 August– 22 September	Dill, fennel	Cypress, walnut	Lavender, lily
Libra 23 September– 23 October	Marjoram, vanilla	Olive, vine	Hydrangea, primrose
Scorpio 24 October– 22 November	Basil, cumin	Blackthorn, rowan	Geranium, poinsettia
Sagittarius 23 November– 21 December	Feverfew, sage	Birch, oak	Dandelion, tulip
Capricorn 22 December– 20 January	Comfrey, vetivert	Poplar, yew	Magnolia, pansy
Aquarius 21 January– 20 February	Anise, frankincense	Pear tree, cherry tree	Acacia, orchid
Pisces 21 February– 20 March	Catnip, bladderwrack (seaweed)	Alder, lemon tree	Sweet pea, water lily

There are variations in associations, and also varying dates for the Sun sign periods according to the system you use. If your birthday is on the cusp, you can use the trees, herbs and flowers of the overlapping sign. This is the version that I find useful, but if you feel that other herbs work better for you, especially for your own Sun sign, substitute them and note these in your magical journal or let me know so I can try them.

If your astrological plant or tree does not grow in your region, choose a similar one or one that fits with the characteristics of your sign. Take, for example, an orange tree for golden Leo, which is ruled by the Sun; or you could use cactus as a plant that retains water as a substitute for the watery willow. As long as you are consistent about substitutions, let your intuition guide you.

12

Weather Magic

Weather magic uses the forces of nature – the clouds, dew, wind, rain and storms – for both divination and rituals of change, success and empowerment. It is one of the oldest forms of magic practised by people worldwide. Weather omens are universal, and especially important in places where many people have open-air occupations. For this reason fishermen, shepherds and farmers have become noted weather prophets by making links between observed phenomena and typical results. Many have proved startlingly accurate. The shepherd who linked the sight of a red sky at sunset with fine weather to come and an angry sky in the morning with forthcoming squalls was the first meteorologist.

Dew

Long regarded as a mystical manifestation, dew appears even on clear nights, only to disappear in the early morning light. It has been called fairy pearls, cosmic semen and Lady Moon's promise, the transformation of the previous night's discarded dreams and failed hopes transformed by gentle lunar power into the seeds of new hope. Its connection with the Moon inspired the French writer and soldier Cyrano de Bergerac when he produced his romance *A Trip to the Moon* published in 1657. He claimed to have fastened small bottles filled with dew to his body, to have been sucked up by the Sun and to have landed on the Moon. I cannot promise you a lunar holiday with dew magic, but we can still use the magic of dew to lift our spirits and to raise our dreams to reality.

Dew has also been used for healing and countryside spells. It is said to soothe and heal sore eyes, skin diseases, gout, vertigo and children with delicate health. Collected from fennel leaves, it was said to improve the eyesight.

We do not know when the ancient tradition began of maidens bathing their faces in the May morn dew, preferably gathered from beneath an oak tree, the Druidic tree of wisdom, to enhance their beauty. Certainly the Druids regarded dew as a powerful fertility symbol, and the Celtic festival of Beltane or Beltain to mark the coming of summer began on May Eve.

May dew was also said to be endowed with the power to enhance fertility and to offer protection against malice. It promised luck throughout the year to all who rolled or washed in it, especially as the Sun rose.

A Dew Ritual for Fertility and Abundance

This is best carried out as the first dawn light floods the sky (particularly on May morning). Use it to focus on any aspect of your life which is in need of fertility or abundance. This can range from the desire for a child to a new project or job; from love to prosperity.

- Go out into the open air as early as possible. Ideally it should be somewhere you can be alone and feel relaxed and confident.
- Take with you a symbol of whatever it is you want to increase: a tiny doll to represent a baby, a pair of china figures for reviving an ailing love match, a silver heart for attracting new love, a coin for money or an apple for health.
- Collect nine drops of dew with an eye dropper in a clear glass phial or small bottle with a stopper. The dew should be on a flower or plant rather than on the ground.
- Using the eye dropper, allow a single drop at a time to fall on the symbol, saying something like,

Dew of the Moon,
Dew of the dawn,
Bring health – wealth – love [name whatever you need]
To me this morn.

- Repeat the chant for each drop until all nine have fallen on the symbol.
- Leave the symbol to dry naturally on a pure white cloth in the sunlight. When the Sun sets, cover the symbol with a dark scarf until the next dawn.
- If the matter is an urgent or major one, repeat the ritual each morning at dawn for three days.

Cloud Divination

To the experienced eye, cloud formations can reveal the forthcoming weather for up to twenty-four hours. For example, red clouds round the rising Sun indicate that rain will fall in the next four hours.

But clouds can also be used for another type of forecasting. Their ever-changing patterns can stimulate our innate powers of intuition to guide us through the storm and calm of life. The practice dates back to the Druids, and lives on in the heart of every child who points out pictures in the clouds.

Cloud divination operates through the visual imaging system that underpins many folk magical practices, such as interpreting tea leaf images, light flickering on water or pictures in the fire. It is one of the oldest and most potent forms of divination.

- Take time over a few days to identify images in the sky, whether fluffy white cumulus or wispy grey streaks. Study the changing patterns as the rising and setting Sun stains them with scarlet. Take your time and relax. Let the sky slowly reveal its secrets to you.
- When you have reactivated your ability to read clouds, ask a question or focus on an issue about your future. This may involve your career, a relationship or any changes you may be planning.

- Choose a broad expanse of sky and identify what seems to be the clearest image on the left of your field of vision. Sketch the image and scribble a few words about your immediate and intuitive reaction to what you see in the sky.
- Ask next about the course of action. This may be the one you are already following, or an alternative course that may be suggested by the clouds in the centre of your field of vision.
- Finally, ask about the possible outcome of following the path suggested by the second cloud. The answer will be found in one of the clouds to the right of your field of vision.
- Sit quietly and examine the three images, which may be read as a story. If they do not make sense, sleep with your notes under your pillow after looking at the sketched images and your notes immediately before you fall asleep. The answer may come in your dreams.

Sam's Cloud Divination

Sam, who had worked at the same administrative job for twenty years, was offered the chance of early retirement. Shona, his wife, was a reflexologist and healer and Sam had read several of her course books with growing interest. But he had lived so long by the clock that he was not sure what he would or could do if he left his job now and was considering staying on for another five years, even though he admitted to feeling stifled by the office. He had always lived by logic, but he felt for the first time that it had failed him. Eventually, at his wife's prompting, he agreed to try to awaken his intuitive side through cloud divination. He went out on a bright spring day and saw the following images.

Cloud 1: The issue or choices

Sam saw the image as a pit pony on a railway line, a memory from his childhood in Yorkshire. This, he felt, reflected his dilemma: being trapped in a routine as though trudging through a long, dark tunnel. He had always worked with numbers since leaving school and, though he felt increasingly dissatisfied with his life, he was afraid of facing a vast expanse of empty time. Like the pit pony, when brought into the light of day he had forgotten how to kick up his heels.

Cloud 2: A possible course of action

The image was of a pair of hands reaching outwards, as if cupped round a sphere. To some it might have suggested a ball being caught. Should Sam take up cricket again? But his sporting days were long past and this thought did not even occur to him. Instead, his first thoughts were of healing hands. Sam admitted that he was drawn to healing and several times he had been aware of energies in his fingertips. But he had dismissed this as just imagination.

Cloud 3: Possible outcome of following the suggested action

The third image was of a big house. Sam told me that he and Shona had talked about one day opening a centre for alternative healing methods. Could this be the big house? Their current house was quite small.

The cloud divination did not change Sam overnight. But it did plant a seed which began to grow. To the surprise – and pleasure – of his wife, Sam decided to begin training as a healer and to think seriously about early retirement.

His cloud divination did not predict a fixed future. This is not surprising, since the images seen in the clouds reflected Sam's own deep unconscious wisdom, exploring avenues that his conscious thought processes had dismissed as unrealistic, and suggested ways of moving forward.

We see the images in the clouds that mirror our own internal world. Cloud divination, like all Druidic magic and indeed the prophecies of all wise people, prompts questions rather than answers. The answers must come from the seeker.

Magic and the Winds

Fisher folk once recited the following rhyme

When the wind is in the East,
'Tis neither good for man nor beast,
When the wind is the North
The skilful fisher goes not forth.
When the wind is in the South,
The hungry fish opens its mouth,
When the wind is in the West
It's then the fishing's at its best.

Wind magic represents the stirring of energies that can act as a catalyst for change and overcome stagnation. According to the folklore of the northern tradition, witches and women who had just given birth had the power to control winds. Sailors used to undo knotted cords to release winds. In East Anglia, where there were many windmills, offerings of milk to encourage the wind to blow were placed in 'dobbie stones' – stones with natural or artificial hollows. These can still be seen near farmhouse doors, stiles and where paths intersect. Honey was sometimes added to the milk.

Depending on the prevailing wind – whether east, south, north or west – you can perform different rituals. In the Native American tradition each wind had its particular quality and totem animal, although this varied from tribe to tribe. The winds represented the four cardinal points on the Medicine or Power Wheel that was central to many rituals; see my book *The Mammoth Book of Ancient Wisdom* (Robinson, 1997) for further details of Medicine Wheel Magic.

The power of the wind, which also appears in other magical traditions, can be effectively adapted for modern rituals that work as well in an urban development as on the open plains.

Finding Your Wind Direction

The wind is named after the direction from which it comes, so that a pennant being blown towards the east is being driven by the west wind. You can buy weathercocks quite cheaply or improvise with a long, heavy strip of fabric about 3 feet (1 metre) long, tied to a tall post in the garden where it can blow freely unhampered by buildings.

Alternatively, since in Oriental lore winds, rain and storms were caused by dragons fighting, you can create a Chinese-style banner (see diagram) on thick card or thin plywood, covering it with water-resistant plastic. Paint your dragon according to the season. The Chinese Dragon of the East is blue. He is the predominant spirit of rain and rules the spring. In the south were two dragon gods, the red and the yellow. The Red God ruled all the summer season except for the last month, when the Yellow Dragon held sway. In the west was the White Dragon of autumn. The northern dragon was black, presiding over the winter. All the weather dragons offer protection and bring good fortune.

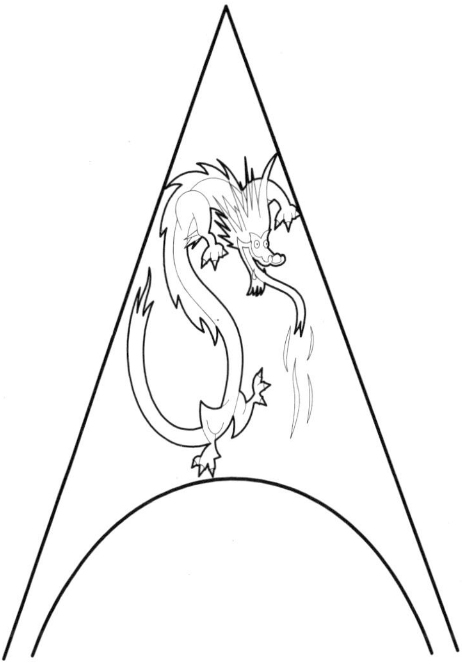

It is rare that winds blow exactly from the north, south, east or west. Their positions can be determined from this chart.

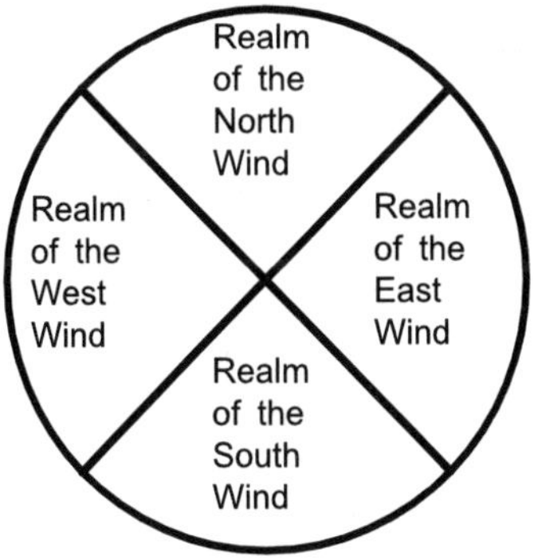

The East Winds for New Beginnings

The influence of the east winds begins at the spring equinox on 21 March in the north-east. Its influence continues until 20 June, the summer solstice, in the south-east. It therefore covers the compass position north-east/south-east.

The east winds herald spring. They are associated with new beginnings and a fresh approach to old problems, with clear communication, change, logic and open-mindedness.

East wind magic is good for rituals for learning, for changes, especially dramatic or sudden ones, for travel and health and for divination of all kinds.

The South Winds for Power and Achievement

The influence of the south winds extends from 21 June to 21 September, from the summer solstice to the autumn equinox. It spans the south-east to south-west compass points.

The south winds herald the summer and talk of abundance, of growth and giving oneself wholeheartedly to whatever needs to be done. At a time requiring great personal effort and input, they offer the power to put the new east wind ideas into practice. They relate to rapid growth and to blossoming and development.

The south winds are good for rituals involving action, attracting money, justice, careers and ambitions, and for clairvoyance.

The West Winds for Love and Reconciliation

The influence of the west winds extends from 22 September to 20 December, from the autumn equinox to the midwinter solstice. They blow from the south-west to the north-west.

The west winds herald autumn and talk of fruition, of gathering the fruits of summer's labours and preparing for winter, whether physically or emotionally. It is time for resolving issues and also for accepting what cannot be resolved.

The west winds are good for rituals involving love, friendship, children and animals, healing quarrels, healing of all kinds and for seeing ghosts.

The North Winds for Endings and Development of the Inner World

The influence of the north winds extends from 22 December to 20 March, from the midwinter solstice to the spring equinox that completes the cycle of the year.

The north winds herald the winter, representing the period of the inner world, of growing strong by rest and withdrawal from the colds of winter, whether physical or emotional. This time of creative withdrawal to explore dreams and intuition has become lost in modern life, where unremitting action is the root cause of many stress illnesses.

The north winds are good for banishing rituals, for example giving up a bad habit or destructive relationship, for exploring the inner world, for renewing depleted energies and for past-life work and psychometry (the psychic art of gaining information about people or places by touching objects which have some history attached to them).

Wind Rituals

Here are some sample rituals that harness the winds, but devise your own for any needs that come under the auspices of each wind. If you need to do a ritual and the wind is in the wrong direction, follow the modern practice and use an electric fan to help things along (see Chapter 5).

An east wind balloon ritual for changing the direction of your life

This ritual is especially good after a period of stagnation, or if you need the impetus for a desired change. Substitute your own words if you wish. Those given below are ones that work for me.

- Wait until the wind is blowing keenly from the east.
- Go to a high, open place and let the wind blow all around you, so that it fills your clothes.
- Take three silver helium balloons, and tie to the string of each one some strips of paper on which you have written your hopes for the following three months – one month for each balloon.

- Hold the balloons in your power hand, the one you write with, and feel them tugging eagerly to leave your thoughts and move into reality.
- As you resist the pull, recite:

Wishes fly free,
Go from me,
Into the world
Where you can be
Free.
Wishes now free
Gone from me
Into the sky,
So I can be
Me

- Release your first month's balloon, watching it soar.
- As it flies away repeat:

Be free
Free be
Free me

- When it is out of sight release your second month's balloon.
- As it flies away repeat:

Wishes fly free
Go from me
Where you can
Be free

- Release your third balloon, as you do so repeating the whole rhyme.
- Run as fast as you can down the hill, feeling the wind carrying you forward.

A south wind smoke ritual for improving your luck

Wait until the south wind is blowing. If you have the space in your garden, or an open space, create a small fire in a fireproof container or dig a small pit within a structure of bricks, making sure there are no overhanging trees.

- When the fire is burning, cast into it first pine needles, then cedar twigs and leaves, mint or sweet grass, and finally sage.
- As the fragrant smoke rises and drifts northwards on the wind, draw smoke circles around your head and body, enveloping yourself in good fortune of every kind.
- Let the bonfire die down naturally and make sure it is out, burying the ashes.
- If you cannot light a fire, use pine, cedar, mint or sweet grass and sage incense sticks. Light one after the other and let the fragrance of each in turn waft around your head.

A west wind bubble ritual for sending love

This ritual is particularly good for sending friendly feelings towards someone from whom you are estranged.

- Use a large bubble blower and soapy water.
- Take a symbol linking you to the person from whom you are estranged – a photograph of you together, a card or small gift he or she sent you, a dried flower from a bouquet, a CD of music you both loved.
- Hold the symbol and visualise the shared happy occasion that it encapsulates, re-creating especially the loving words and feelings.
- Go to an open window or door facing the direction in which the person lives, and as you blow your first rainbow bubble enclose in it all the love and regrets.
- As it floats away, ring a tiny bell or wind chime and whisper a phrase you shared.
- Send six bubbles one after the other, waiting until one has dispersed before sensing the next, and seeing the former loving feelings growing with each bubble and each sound of your chime. Six was the number of days it took to create the Earth, according to the Old Testament, and so is an appropriate number to use in rituals which involve rebuilding love.
- After six days have elapsed, make a simple gesture of friendship towards the estranged person – a card, a brief phone call.
- Repeat the ritual on the east wind if necessary. Sending out love is always a positive act and will attract back love threefold, although not always from the object of your ritual.

A north wind banishing ritual

This is useful for dispersing guilt and unnecessary regrets. It is a rather slow-acting but nevertheless effective ritual for guilt that may have taken years to accumulate.

- Write down what makes you feel guilty or consumes you with regret.
- Find a branch with the number of leaves corresponding to your specific guilts or regrets.
- Identify each leaf, name each guilt or sorrow, and leave it in the north wind. It does not matter if the wind changes in the following days as long as you begin on the north wind.
- As the branch is stripped bare, so will you be able to start anew.

Rain

There is a great deal of folklore connected with rain. Rainwater that falls on Ascension Day or on any day during June is believed to have healing properties. The water should be collected in a clear glass or crystal bowl as it falls from the sky. In Wales, babies who are bathed in rainwater are said to talk at an earlier age. It is generally believed that money washed in rainwater is safe from thieves.

The most famous piece of rain weather lore concerns St Swithin, whose Day is 15 July:

St Swithin's day if thou be fair,
For forty days, 'twill rain nae mair.
St Swithin's day if thou bring rain,
For forty days it will remain.

This tradition began after St Swithin, Bishop of Winchester, was buried in 862 in a simple grave outside the west door of the old cathedral, situated to the north of the Norman building we know today. It is said he desired this spot so that the sweet rain of heaven might fall on him. Various reasons are suggested for the attempt to move his bones on 15 July 971; one of these was that, because he had been canonised, the monks believed a shrine in the cathedral would honour him. It rained on that day and for the following forty days and nights, delaying the proceedings. This was said to be a sign of the saint's disapproval of his new shrine within the cathedral.

A Rainy Day Ritual

This is a useful way to end a destructive relationship or forget a faithless lover.

- Choose a day when the rain is falling steadily and looks set to continue for much of the day. If possible work at dusk, during the waning half of the Moon cycle.
- On a circle of green paper draw two images or symbols to represent the relationship. Draw one in black washable marker on one half of the circle to represent the other person in the relationship, and on the other half of the paper draw in white the image to represent yourself. Do not write the name of the other person. You should not attempt banishing magic against people, merely against the ties that bind you, because the other person, however objectionably he or she is acting, must have the choice. Therefore you are severing their link with you rather than the actual person.
- Between the two halves draw a jagged line in permanent pen and cut along it accurately.
- Place the half representing the relationship from which you want to be severed in the rain until the image has disappeared.
- Cut the remaining half representing your separate self into a new smaller but intact oval to represent the cosmic egg and new birth, and ring it with tiny rose quartz crystals for healing. Leave it on the window ledge until the rain ceases, and then place it in a drawer until new love comes.

Rainbow Magic

Rainbows are incredibly lucky and in almost all cultures have magical associations. The crock of gold at the end of the rainbow belongs to the fairy folk, and if you can find it before the rainbow fades it is yours. Rainbows are seen as bridges between the heavens and the Earth; *bifrost*, the rainbow bridge in Norse tradition, was the bridge over which the gods travelled between the realms. In the biblical tradition the rainbow was set in the sky as God's pledge that there would never again be separation of man from God. In this way it became a token of reconciliation.

Among the Maoris rainbows, which are frequent in New Zealand, were a vital source of divine counsel. A low rainbow directly ahead would indicate that a projected journey might be difficult. A high-arched rainbow promised favour on any enterprise; and one forming a circle assured total success and happiness.

A Rainbow Ritual for Happiness

Because rainbows are associated with good fortune and the fairy folk, most rainbow rituals centre around finding your personal crock of gold.

- Focus on a single wish or desire. However, if you see a double rainbow or one that forms a complete circle if reflected in water you can have two wishes, as the power is doubled.
- Go out of doors, as you cannot work rainbow magic effectively through glass.
- Mark with a stick or chalk a point that corresponds with the centre of the rainbow as viewed from the spot where you are working.
- Walk nine foot lengths below the point, then nine foot lengths to the left. Turn and walk eighteen foot lengths to the right to mark your symbolic rainbow's beginning and end.
- Stand at the beginning of the rainbow and, using tiny white stones or small crystals in rainbow colours, mark out the curve of the rainbow. As you do so focus on your need and the steps you can take to fulfilling it. As you place each stone chant:

Rainbow, rainbow,
Magic measure
On the path I wend,
Let me find the treasure,
At the rainbow's end.

- When you reach the rainbow's end place a tiny golden symbol, whether real gold or a circle of golden foil, in exchange for the granting of your wish.

• Leave your rainbow in place until the rainbow in the sky has faded.

Storms

Traditionally storms have been regarded as an omen of divine wrath or due to malign influence, such as witchcraft against a neighbour's property. In medieval times many an unfortunate old woman was blamed for the uncontrolled forces of nature. Yet storms can be a very positive and potent force for change, and for energising any magic where instant energy is needed to overcome opposition or attain a goal that is fraught with difficulty.

An old rhyme speaks of which tree is least likely to attract a lightning strike, and therefore should be sheltered under if you are caught outside during a storm:

Beware of the oak, it draws the stroke,
Avoid the ash, it courts the flash,
Creep under a thorn, it will save you from harm.

Electrical storms are especially powerful, but you need to take precautions since lightning seeks out the highest object – tall and exposed trees, telegraph poles and even hilltops. It is sensible to avoid all metal objects, whether indoors or out, and not to run in a storm, although some research suggests that lightning passes more easily through walls than through air.

Among the Maori people of New Zealand, if lightning flashed vertically towards the home village this was seen as inauspicious for the tribe, and so ceremonies had to be held to propitiate the gods. Lightning flashing away from the village indicated that the tribe was protected. Sheet lightning indicated war or problems stemming from human rather than divine error.

Lightning Magic for Overcoming Obstacles or Achieving a Difficult Goal

• Obtain a branch from an oak or ash which, because they attract lightning, were regarded as protective against a home or person being struck – unless you were, in defiance of the old rhyme quoted above, sheltering under one.

- Split the branch almost through and fix it securely upright in the garden or in an open space away from the house or overhanging buildings or trees. Position it so that it is visible from the house or a sheltered place.
- Plant a circle of protective seeds or stones around it so that it is completely enclosed and therefore a source of concentrated power.
- When a storm begins, wait until the sky is full of light but the storm is still far away.
- Stand so that you are facing your storm tree and, with a similar piece of oak, begin to split it with a wooden mallet, hammer or non-metallic tool, with each lightning flash saying:

Oak [or ash] cleave,
Path leave,
Clear for me,
Mighty tree,
Split for me,
Cleave.

- As the light surrounds the oak in the garden, see it clearing a path for you towards your goal.
- As the storm gets nearer and the lightning more frequent increase the speed of the chant and the vigour of your blows until the branch is cut clean through.
- Carve an image from each side to make a protective amulet, and if you can obtain a piece of oak charred by lightning you can use it both for healing and as a source of power.

Weather Protection

For protecting your home and those you love from storms there are many rituals that invoke natural substances and date back hundreds of years. One of the most effective methods involves burning at dusk on the eve of the spring equinox a branch from each of the four sacred trees of the Celts – oak, ash, hazel and yew.

- Collect the ash and scatter this around the boundary of your home, or if you live in an apartment keep it in an earthenware dish near the door. Some people keep a small portion of the charred branches in the hearth or in a central place in the home until the following spring equinox.

- If you cannot find the woods, light four candles: gold for oak, blue for ash, purple for hazel and deep green for yew. Place the yew candle in the north of your home, the hazel candle in the east, the oak candle in the south and the ash candle in the west. Light the northern candle first and end with ash.
- As the wax melts, drip some of each on to a bowl of cold water.
- When the shape sets, carve on it a protective sign such as the Anglo-Saxon runic Viking Ing that used to appear on old houses on the east coast of England, and after whom the inglenook fireplace is named.

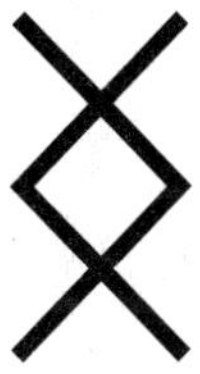

Ing

Alternatively you could carve

This is the rune of hail, and as the Mother Rune a very protective sign in the northern world, especially against inclement weather.

- Place your wax amulet in the hearth or a central place until the following spring equinox eve, when you should replace it.

13

Seasonal Magic

In the modern Western world, where no food is ever out of season, it can be hard to keep track of the passing year. Artificial lighting and central heating have flattened out the contrasts between winter and summer and the natural connection with the changing energies of the year. Yet out in the open air there is still a time of new life, the birth of young creatures, the appearance of the first shoots in the soil or the return of the herds of animals or shoals of fish, a time of plenty and a time of dearth when the soil bursts into life or lies resting beneath the snow.

These underlying seasonal energies of the land are reflected in the cycles of human life, beginnings, coming to fruition, fading away and regeneration time and time again as we complete one phase and move on to the next. Each involves a small death and the birth of the next stage. Ignoring the natural cycles of existence and trying to keep up a constant intense pace may account for the sense of alienation, irritability and exhaustion in daily life.

The Solar Tides and Seasons

The four solar tides and seasons of the year are marked by the equinoxes and solstices. Seasonal influences are especially powerful for major life changes, long-term plans or gains that may take many months to reach fruition. The predominant energies of the seasons also offer a recipe for harmonious living.

Few people can actually withdraw from life for the winter. But it may be worthwhile trying to slow down and using the long winter evenings for quiet contemplation. Avoid major change where possible during the winter months and develop the domestic aspects of your world; if you do, when it is cold and wet outside you may suffer less from anxiety and constant tiredness than if your pace never varies.

If you do need to initiate a new project in the autumn, you can harness the energies of spring by focusing on the symbols of that season. The seasons given below refer to the northern hemisphere. If you live in the southern hemisphere, substitute the relevant dates by counting on six months. Similarly people in the southern hemisphere can reverse the magical associations so that midwinter will fall in mid-June rather than December.

Because the solstices and equinoxes are astronomical measures the date may vary by a few days depending on the year, although certain festival days associated with the symbolic date of the birth of Christ and various saints' days have, over the centuries, been set as a focal point for these celebrations.

Spring

Lasts from 21 March to 20 June in the northern hemisphere, from the spring equinox to the summer solstice. It is the time of sowing. Its direction is east and its colour is yellow. This is the quadrant of Air, which promises the impetus for change and growth.

The vernal equinox or Ostara time, 21–23 March (for the northern hemisphere), marks the transition point between the dark and light halves of the year. At the spring equinox, the Sun rises due east and sets due west, giving exactly twelve hours of daylight. The first eggs of spring were painted and offered on the shrine of the Anglo-Saxon goddess Eostre (Norse Ostara), to whom the hare was sacred (this is the origin of the Easter rabbit). Long before the days of intensive farming methods turned natural cycles on their head, the festival of Eostre was the time when hens began to lay eggs after the winter.

At the spring equinox bonfires were lit and the corn dolly of the previous harvest (or in Christian times a Judas figure) was burned on the Easter fires. The ashes were scattered on the field for fertility. It is said that if you wake at dawn on Easter Sunday you will see the Sun dance in the water and the angels playing. Easter is regulated by the paschal Moon or first full Moon between the vernal equinox and fourteen days afterwards.

Spring Rituals

These rituals for new hopes, new beginnings, new relationships, fertility and life changes, and anything to do with fertility, pregnancy, babies, children and new-flowering love, are especially potent at the spring equinox as light supersedes darkness from this point.

To harness spring energies during this season or at any time of the year when you need a new beginning, use as a focus for your own spiralling energies eggs, any spring flowers or leaves in bud, a sprouting pot of seeds, pottery or china rabbits, birds or feathers. Carry as your spring talisman sparkling yellow crystals such as citrine, the strengthening stone; yellow beryl, the energiser; or a yellow rutilated quartz with streaks of gold, the regenerator.

Special flowers and herbs of the spring equinox are celandine, cinquefoil, crocus, daffodil, honeysuckle, primrose, sage, tansy, thyme and violet.

A spring ritual for new hope and beginnings

This is an early morning ritual, and if you can collect or buy your eggs from a market as the sun rises the ritual will be even more potent. Eating the magic object is a very ancient way of absorbing magical energies, and in pagan times hot cross buns were believed to endow the protection of the Earth to the eater. This belief transferred in Christian times, so that hot cross buns made on Good Friday are believed to protect sailors from drowning – the fossilised remains of buns can be seen on the rafters of churches in parishes by the sea.

- Take some eggs as newly laid as you can obtain, and very gently boil them in a vegetable dye in shades of pale pink, blue and green.

- Decorate the eggs with flower and leaf motifs and place them in a basket lined with spring flowers and leaves, if possible collected in the early morning when the dew is still on them.
- In the centre of the basket place a single agate egg in a pale cream, or, if you cannot obtain one, a sparkling yellow sun crystal.
- If the weather is dry carry out the rest of the ritual outdoors. If not, perform it near a window with an open view.
- Choose one egg to be yours and endow it with a single wish for a new beginning or hope for the spring by holding it between your cupped hands and whispering in a low voice, so that no one can hear except the breeze:

Egg of spring,
New life, new hope
Bring me [whatever]
And this wish.

- Return the egg to the basket.
- Name each of the other eggs for a friend or family member and name a secret wish for each of them, adapting the words above.
- When you have filled each egg with wishes, make a cross like that on a hot cross bun (originally the old astrological sign of the Earth), with two tiny branches from a birch tree, the tree of regeneration, or from any early-budding tree.
- Eat your egg at noon or, if you cannot eat eggs, give it to an animal of which you are very fond.
- Give each of the other eggs to the appropriate friend or family member, remembering that gifts come back threefold (see Chapter 2).
- Leave your agate egg with the flowers and leaves as an offering to new hope, and each day add fresh flowers and leaves to replace dying ones, which should be buried.

Summer

Lasts from 21 June to 21 September in the northern hemisphere, from the summer solstice to the autumn equinox. Its direction is south and its colour is red. This is the quadrant of Fire, which promises dynamic results, inspiration and success for any venture when the sun is at its height.

The summer solstice or the time of nurturing marks the high point of the year, the longest day, and is the zenith of its light and of magic. It is a time for full power and for putting in hard work that it is hoped will bear fruit in autumn. Modern Druids still celebrate this festival of light with ceremonies at midnight on solstice eve, dawn and noon. Great fire wheels used to be rolled down the hillsides in honour of the triumph of Baldur, the Sun God, over death.

Summer Rituals

Rituals for success, happiness, strength, identity, wealth, fertility, adolescents and young adults, career and travel are especially potent during the summer, and are most effective of all on the longest day.

For summer energies, or when you need confidence and power at any time during the year, use brightly coloured flowers; oak boughs; golden fern pollen, which is said to reveal buried treasure wherever it falls; scarlet, orange and yellow ribbons; gold-coloured coins; or orange or red candles to evoke the power of the Sun and your own strength and potential, even in dark times. Carry as your summer talisman brilliant red or orange crystals, stones of the Sun, such as amber, carnelian or jasper. The herbs and incense of the summer solstice include chamomile, elder, fennel, lavender, St John's wort and verbena.

A summer ritual for success

This ritual must be carried out on high ground – a hilltop or at least a high building – near noon.

- Light a large golden candle or, better still, if possible make a small fire in a safe spot where it will not spread to foliage or grass.
- As you light it say:

Summer Sun bright,
At your full height,
With your great power
This noonday hour
Sun of true might
Fill me with light,
Fill me with joy
Let me achieve
All in my sight.

- Take in turn five golden-coloured metal objects: a key; a ring; a small jug filled with mead, nectar or orange juice; a small golden dish containing some of the herbs of summer; and a paper knife.
- In front of the fire or candle draw in the Earth the shape of an attracting pentagram (see Chapter 5).
- Place each of the objects in order on the five points as you draw them. You can be specific about your aims in the words you use. I have suggested some general ones.
- Pick up the key and hold it skywards in the direction of the Sun if it is shining. Pass it through the golden candle nine times, or circle the fire nine times holding it between your hands, saying: 'Key of the Sun, open the door to my golden future.'
- Lift the ring, and put the key down in the place where the ring was.
- Hold the ring skywards towards the Sun, again circling the candle or fire as you say: 'Ring of sparkling solar orb, may my endeavours encircle me with success and roll on without cease to their completion.'
- Take up the jug filled with golden liquid, and put the ring down in the place where the jug was.
- Lift the jug towards the Sun, passing it through the candle flame or circling the fire, saying as you drink from it: 'Jug of the golden Sun, fill me with fire and joy and unceasing enthusiasm for my endeavour.'
- Lift the golden dish of herbs and put the jug down where it was.
- Scatter the herbs in the fire or the candle flame, saying, 'Fragrances of the Sun, on your aromatic skyward trail, carry my plans to the cosmos that they may bear fruit.'
- Lift the golden knife and put the dish down where it was.
- With the knife, draw a clockwise circle in the air around either

the candle flame or the fire, saying, 'Golden blade of the Sun, cut through my doubts, inertia and any obstacles I may encounter on my path to fulfilment.'

- Put the knife down in the position originally occupied by the key.
- Extinguish the candle or fire, saying: 'Golden flames give power to the Sun that it may ever shine, warm and illumine my way and nourish all nature.'

Autumn

Lasts from 22 September to 20 December, from the autumn equinox to the midwinter solstice. Its direction is west and its colour is blue. This is the quadrant of Water, and augurs well for rituals of reconciliation and harmony both within and with others.

The autumn equinox or time of gathering was traditionally celebrated as the second 'wild or green harvest', a time of celebration for the fruits and vegetables of the Earth and the Earth Mother. This is the time of the second harvest of vegetables and fruit and of the remaining crops, the harvest home. The harvest supper predates Christianity. On the day when equal night and day heralded winter, the feast, by displaying and consuming the finest of the harvest, formed a sympathetic magical gesture to ensure that there would be enough food during the winter.

It is also a time when the sky and animal god is said to retreat for the long winter. Druids climb to the top of a hill to take leave of the summer Sun as the nights will get longer.

Michaelmas, the day of St Michael, the Archangel of the Sun, was celebrated on 29 September with a feast centred around a goose. Since St Michael was patron saint of high places and replaced the pagan Sun deities, he was an apt symbol for the last days of the summer Sun.

The herbs and incense of the autumn equinox include ferns, geranium, myrrh, pine and Solomon's seal.

Autumn Rituals

These are for the fruition of long-term goals, for reaping the benefits of earlier input, for love and relationships, especially concerning the family, adult children, brothers and sisters, friendships and for material security in the months ahead.

For autumn energies, or whenever you need to mend quarrels or seek harmony in your life, choose coppery, yellow or orange leaves; willow boughs; harvest fruits such as apples; and pottery or china geese. Use also as a focus knots of corn, wheat or barley from the earlier harvest, and copper or bronze coins to ensure enough money and happy family relationships. Choose soft blue crystals, such as blue lace agate, blue beryl or azurite, as a talisman of autumn.

An autumn ritual for a happy family

This is especially potent if carried out at the autumn equinox, but is good whenever there is a new addition to the family or after a period of domestic unrest.

- Place on the altar a dish piled high with autumn harvest fruits such as apples, pears and plums.
- Surround it with a circle of family photos and mementoes.
- Ring these objects with plaited ears of corn or dried grasses.
- Finally make a square enclosing the circle with tiny blue crystals, blue glass nuggets and blue-tinged pebbles. This marks the limits of any negative influences from the outside world.
- At each of the four corners, place on fireproof trays or dishes deep blue candles, the colour of the Water quadrant, and light first the one in the north-east corner, saying: 'I enclose my beloved family in the light of love and mature wisdom, that they may increasingly recognise the unique contribution of each part to the whole, grow closer every day with humour and compassion, compensating for the others' weaknesses and reaping the benefits of mutual love.'
- If there is a new member of the family add his or her image to the inner circle and dedicate a white candle. As you light it, saying something like: 'I welcome [name the person] to the midst of this family, asking him/her to value what we are, to accept our vulnerabilities and blind spots, and to change us with his/her special gifts that we may be enriched and strengthened by his/her presence.'
- Place the new candle in the centre at the top of the square.
- Take an autumn leaf and burn it in the first candle you lit, saying; 'With this dying leaf I banish all rancour from within the

family, all unprovoked jealousy, unwarranted resentment and misunderstandings.'

- Take another autumn leaf and burn it in the second candle, saying, 'With this dying leaf I banish all external malice, interference and cold indifference that may wound any member of our family or threaten loyalty and unity.'
- Take a third leaf and burn it in the next candle, saying, 'With this dying leaf I banish all unfair actions, unkind or thoughtless words, coldness and confrontations between the members of our kin, that the family may be a sanctuary and a starting place for positive relationships beyond.'
- Take a fourth leaf and burn it in the final candle, saying, 'With this dying leaf I banish all possessiveness, over-sentimentality guilt, and stifling love that holds family members from finding love, fulfilment and independence in the world, letting go willingly so that each person will return willingly and in love.'
- Let the candles burn down naturally so that the light and protection will fall on the images and symbols of each member and the whole, as symbolised by the fruit.
- The next day place the fruit on the kitchen table, to be taken when wanted by the family and all who are welcomed into the home over the ensuing days.

Winter

Lasts from 21 December to 20 March, from the midwinter solstice or shortest day to the spring equinox. The direction is north and its colour is green. The quadrant of Earth promises rest, regeneration, wisdom and psychic awareness, especially when rituals are carried out on the eve or day of the midwinter solstice.

The midwinter solstice or the time of waiting predates organised religion. When early man saw the Sun at its lowest point and the vegetation dead or dying, he feared that light and life would never return. So he lit great bonfires from yule logs, hung torches from trees and decorated his home with evergreens to persuade the other greenery to grow again. This midwinter magic forms the origins of Christmas festivals throughout the globe. The Mithraic birth of the unconquered Sun in Persia was just one pre-Christian festival that was celebrated on 25 December.

Winter Rituals

These are for removing unwanted influences and redundant phases, for home and long-term money plans and for older members of the family.

For winter energies, or when you feel pressurised or tired, or face hostility, choose evergreen boughs, especially pine or fir; a circle of red and green candles; and small logs of wood, especially oak and ash, found naturally as a focus for faith that tomorrow is another day and for inner vision. Choose deep green stones such as aventurine, bloodstone or amazonite as your winter talisman.

The herbs and incense for winter include bay, cedar, feverfew, holly, juniper, pine and rosemary.

A winter ritual to ensure abundance

This is a lovely evening ritual when carried out in a candlelit room using alternate red and green candles, and can be enjoyed with friends or family. Share out the actions so that everyone participates.

- Before you begin, leave simmering in the oven a casserole of root vegetables and, if you eat meat, one of turkey or pork.
- Make bread to eat with it, stirring the dough thirteen times clockwise in the old tradition. As you knead the dough, endow the bread with all your wishes for increase, your specific needs for abundance, your hopes for the future, and your plans for personal and professional growth. Leave it to rise naturally before decorating it with holly leaves made out of dough.
- Decorate an evergreen bough with pine cones painted gold for the Sun, and with tiny red and green garlands in shiny paper or foil. Hang from it small pieces of jewellery as a symbol of future prosperity.
- Buy or make a large yule candle in scarlet, and decorate it with holly, ivy and mistletoe berries for abundance and fertility even in winter.
- Place around the candle nine hazelnuts, traditional Celtic symbol of knowledge; raisins to symbolise the fruits of the Earth; seeds to symbolise the grains of the Earth; and silver coins to symbolise the metals of the Earth.
- Blow out the candles one by one, welcoming the growing

darkness that will soon be overcome by light, saying, 'Darkness increase, that I become still, gestating within the womb of the Earth Mother whose fruits and grains surround the yuletide candle, accepting the cycle of endings and beginnings, death and rebirth, for everything has a time and season, decrease before increase, loss before gain, dearth before abundance.'

- Sit quietly in the darkness, letting the ideas, the seeds of the future germinate in your mind, the shadows offering insights into your own self and soul.
- When you are ready, say, 'The light is returning and with it life. The Sun did not die but only slumbered, and now is reborn to the Earth Mother as I kindle this flame.'
- Light your yule candle and from it take a taper to relight the other candles in turn, saying, 'Light from light, life from life, so abundance grows.'
- Eat now a few nuts, seeds and raisins, for each one naming a need of growth and expansion in your life, and saying for each, 'As I take in the power of the growing light and the Earth, so my own abundance grows.'
- Sit in the light of the candles, letting growing optimism flow through you. Trust in the future and in your own survival, just as ancient man in the depths of midwinter trusted that the Sun would return.
- Eat your casserole and warm bread by the light of the candles, letting thoughts or conversation, if with others, gently ebb and flow.
- Leave the yule candle in a safe place near an uncurtained window, so that it may light travellers on their way – as does the Christmas candle that is still lit on Christmas Eve, in places where people of Celtic origins live, to light the Virgin Mary on her way.

The Eightfold Year

The eightfold year or wheel is an ancient division that goes back to the first agricultural societies, though it was formalised by the Celts. It incorporates the four solar festivals described briefly above that fall on the solstices and the equinoxes, the astronomical marker points. But where these solar markers dominate the pattern of the seasons in the older eightfold division of the year, they are the minor festivals or sabbats in the calendars of modern witches and pagans. The four greater sabbats were the old fire or lunar festivals and, though their dates originally also varied slightly according to astronomical observations, they became associated with fixed celebrations that underpin modern festivals. So festivals fall every six weeks, the greatest being the beginning of summer on what we now call May Eve and Day, and the beginning of winter on what is now called Hallowe'en. The following diagram may help.

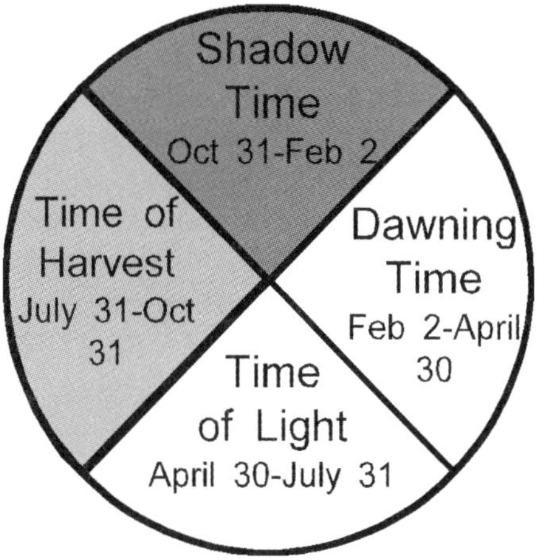

The transition point of the Celtic day was at sunset, so the time when two periods meet is very magical. Each of the major festivals ran for three days from sunset to sunset, hence it is Hallowe'en itself that has retained its prominence, while the significance of this sacred period as a celebration of the dead has been lost except in some Catholic countries.

The wheel of the year tells the story of the battle between darkness and light and the sacred marriage between the Earth Mother and her son/consort, the Sun/corn God, who originally was the Horned God of vegetation and animals and who appears in this guise around May Day as Jack o' the Green. The god of light is born at the winter solstice. His power increases as the days grow longer until his zenith on the summer solstice, the longest day. The god of darkness, born at the summer solstice, grows with the lengthening nights until he triumphs at the winter solstice, the longest night, only to be defeated by the rebirth of the light.

Shadow Time: 31 October to 2 February

This runs from Samhain, our Hallowe'en, the beginning of the Celtic winter and new year, when the cattle were brought from the hills by the herdsmen and it was believed that the family ghosts also came shivering home from the fields to be welcomed by their families. In the middle of this period, about 21 December, falls the midwinter solstice, the shortest day.

After this turning point, the days slowly became longer until the season ended at Imbolc, the festival of the maiden aspect of the Goddess Bride when the first ewe's milk was available. This was the festival of early spring, when snowdrops were pushing through the frozen earth and life was stirring again.

This period is naturally a time for domestic concerns, older family members and issues of mortality, natural cycles, endings that clear the way for beginnings, tradition and secrets.

Dawning Time: 2 February (Imbolc) to 30 April (Beltain or Beltane)

In the middle of this period falls the spring equinox, equal day and night. May Eve, 30 April, was the beginning of the Celtic summer when the great twin fires burned and the cattle were driven between them to purify them after the winter, when young couples gathered hawthorn blossoms and coupled in the fields to make the crops grow. New projects, travel, house moves, matters concerning babies, animals and children, friendships and changes of any kind can be undertaken with confidence, although the results may not be immediate.

Time of Light: 30 April (Beltain or Beltane) to 31 July (Lughnasadh or Lammas)

In the middle of this segment, around 21 June, falls the summer solstice or longest day. At Lughnasadh the corn God was symbolically sacrificed in the last sheaf or corn cut, that the seeds might be scattered for the next year's growth. A loaf was made with the last sheaf as a symbol of abundance.

Matters concerning young people, love and partnerships are especially favoured, as are health issues. It is a period for maximising existing opportunities. However, some people believed that this was the time of the funerary games for the God of light, and that he was not in fact cut down until the second harvest at the autumn equinox. There are legends for both, but my own research and many country practices favour the corn God falling at Lammas.

Time of Harvest: 31 July (Lughnasadh or Lammas) to 31 October (Samhain)

In the middle of this period, about 22 September, falls the autumn equinox.

The Festivals

Imbolc, Oilmec or Brigantia

This ran from sunset on 31 January to sunset on 2 February and was a festival of candles. The Christian Candlemas on 2 February continues the custom of lighting candles to welcome the spring and the lambing season. Household candles were blessed, for the end of the long nights was at hand. Candlemakers took a holiday, and modern witches and pagans still sometimes follow the custom of placing a lighted candle in every window from sunset to sunrise (safely, of course) to welcome Bride's Eve. In some traditions this is done on the night of 1 February.

The festival is in honour of the Celtic Brigit, the Triple Goddess, patron of smiths, poets and healers, who has the longest-enduring cult in Ireland – it merged into that of St Brigit of Kildare. Her name means 'high one' and she is sometimes seen as three sisters, daughters of the god Dagda, the Divine Father, or as maiden, mother and crone. At Imbolc, Oilmec or Brigantia, as the festival was also called, the maiden aspect of the Goddess, and her first mating with the god of light, are celebrated.

This is one of the major sabbats or fire festivals, when sacred fires were lit on hilltops to welcome and encourage the growing light and warmth. In the USA even today Groundhog Day recalls the ancient weather prophecies of whether it would be a good or hard spring.

On Bride's Eve, 31 January, a Bride's bed made from a sheaf of corn, sometimes with corn preserved from the last corn cut down at the first harvest at Lammas (end of July), would be decorated with ribbons to represent the Earth Goddess. It would also be adorned with any early spring flowers. The bed was made in front of the fire, and the inhabitants would shout: 'Bride, come in, your bed is ready.' The symbolic Bride maiden would leave her cows and a cauldron at the door, bringing in peace, fertility and plenty. From this we get the term 'bride' for a woman who is about to be married. Milk and honey were poured over the Bride bed by the women of the household. Originally the bed was laid in the home of the chief of the village, but in later times it was made in the main farm of an area. The menfolk were summoned and, having paid with a coin, a flower posy or a kiss, would enter the circle of firelight and ask for help with their craft or agriculture and make a wish on the Bride bed. Brigit crosses were woven from straw or wheat to hang around the house for protection.

The festival of Imbolc is a time to carry out spells for new love, fertility and for any projects that start in a small way, using a circle of candles and a container of fresh milk. Choose candles in pastel colours such as pale pink, green, blue and white, dark gemstones such as garnet and bloodstone, but also amethysts and rose quartz and gentle moonstones for fertility and awakening feelings. Use the very first snowdrops or other very early budding leaves or flowers, milk and seeds. The incenses and herbs of Brigantia include angelica, basil, benzoin, celandine, heather and myrrh.

You can carry out Imbolc rituals whenever you are beginning something with uncertainty or need fertility in your life (see Chapter 12).

An Imbolc ritual for the beginning of trust

We all get hurt at some time, whether it is a betrayal in love, by a family member or at work. Even the smallest barb may wound deeply, so this ritual is one for slow rebuilding – whether of trust with the betrayer or in a new situation. If possible, begin this ritual in the early morning as it is just getting light.

- Take a container of ice or snow – ice cubes are fine if you need to carry out the ritual in midsummer or in a warm climate.
- Place a few small moonstones or amethysts in a clear glass or crystal bowl, cover them with ice and put it in a cool place.

- Go out and search for any signs of rebirth, perhaps a budding twig or a straw dropped by a bird on its way to build its nest – anything that to you is a suggestion of renewal – and bring it back to surround the bowl.
- Light an Imbolc candle in a pale colour – blue is good for a worldly betrayal, pink for the family, green for love – and say: 'Burn, candle, burn. Melt the ice that has grown around my heart and let new life flow.'
- Plant a basil seedling or some seeds for new life in a ceramic pot, and as you pat down the earth say: 'I bury the pain, the anger, the betrayal and plant the seeds of hope.'
- As the ice melts and the first water appears, stir it, saying: 'Flow, waters, flow, to new life, trust and joy.'
- Leave the ice until it has melted, occupying yourself with positive tasks – answering correspondence, sorting financial affairs, clearing out a cluttered drawer or corner.
- Once the water has appeared, pour a little on to your seedling or seeds, saying: 'Grow, hope, grow, that my trust may bear fruit.'
- Tip the rest of the water on to the garden and extinguish your Imbolc candle, sending the light to anyone who has hurt you.

The Vernal or Spring Equinox

Six weeks later, around 21 March, comes the vernal equinox. At this time light and darkness are equal, but now light triumphs over darkness and the light year begins. It is now that the Mother Goddess conceives a child, to be born at the next winter solstice. This links with the Christian Annunciation of the Blessed Virgin Mary, the day on which the Angel Gabriel told Mary she was to conceive a son. This forms one of the lesser sabbats in modern Wiccan celebrations.

Beltane or Beltain

This runs from sunset on 30 April to sunset on 2 May, and is the second major festival or sabbat of the year. It is named after the Irish Bealtaine meaning 'Bel-fire', the fire of the Celtic God of light, known as Bel, Beli or Belinus. Also known as May Eve, May Day and Walpurgis Night, it celebrates the coming of the old summer and the flowering of life. The Goddess manifests as the May Queen and Flora, goddess of flowers, whose festival was celebrated in Ancient Rome in early May.

Sunset on May Eve was the signal for Druids to kindle the great Bel-fires from nine different kinds of wood. They did so by turning an oak spindle in an oak socket on top of the nearest beacon hill, for example on Tara Hill, Co. Meath, in Ireland, former home of the Dagda, the hero gods of old Ireland. As time went on every village had its Beltane fires, to which were attributed both fertility and healing powers.

Young couples leaped over the twin Beltane fires, ran between them or danced clockwise. Cattle released from the barns after the long winter were driven between the two fires to cleanse them of disease and to ensure their continuing fertility and rich milk yield for the coming months.

But the chief feature of the festival was a custom that dates back to the first farming communities and finds echoes worldwide. Young couples went into the woods and fields to make love and bring back the first May or hawthorn blossoms to decorate homes and barns. May Day is the only time of year, according to tradition, that hawthorn may be brought indoors. May baskets filled with the first flowers of summer were left on the doorsteps of friends, family, lovers and the elderly and infirm, a custom worthy of revival in every community and home.

Beltane is therefore a festival potent for fertility magic of all kinds, whether conceiving a child or financial or business ventures bearing fruit, for an improvement in health and an increase in energy as the light and warmth move into summer.

As a focus gather fresh greenery, especially hawthorn (indoors only on 1 May), and any flowers that are native to your region, and place them in baskets. Dew gathered on the morning of 1 May is especially potent, and girls would bathe their faces in it (see p. 172), or use pure spring water left for a full Sun-and-Moon cycle in a crystal or glass container.

Light dark green, scarlet and silver candles and use sparkling citrines, clear crystal quartz, golden tiger's eyes, amber and topaz.

The incenses and herbs of Beltane include almond, angelica, ash, cowslip, frankincense, hawthorn, lilac, marigold and roses for love.

A Beltane fertility ritual

This can be carried at any time when you need fertility, at any new Moon or on Beltane Eve.

- Take a tiny doll and make for it a cradle of flowers and greenery.
- Place in the cradle symbols of increase: golden coins, sparkling crystals, ears of corn, nuts and seeds.
- Loop over the cradle nine ribbons: red, yellow, green and blue for the four seasons, silver for the Moon, gold for the Sun, white for the Earth Mother, purple for the Sky Father and pink for new life.
- As you bind each ribbon clockwise say,

> *Grow strong in love,*
> *Bear fruit and multiply,*
> *Child of mine [or whatever it is you wish to increase]*
> *From seed to fruition,*
> *Be safe from all harm, all fear.*
> *You whom I bind close with hope,*
> *All the spiralling energies of Earth, Air, Fire,*
> *Water, Moon, sky and Mother Earth*
> *Who gives life to all,*
> *Aid me.*

- Tie the ribbons loosely in threes, saying:

> *As one becomes two, becomes three,*
> *So three to six to nine,*
> *Winding, binding,*
> *Babe of mine [or other appropriate words if it is*
> *another fertility matter]*

- Go into the open air and make love in a private place, or if this is not possible go outdoors immediately afterwards and gather greenery to bring indoors. This is effective for the fertility of joint ventures as well as for conceiving an infant.
- If you do not have a partner, gather greenery and flowers (even from a balcony or window box) and encircle yourself with them before you go to sleep.
- In either case, have the cradle close to you while you sleep.
- In the morning, sprinkle salt nine times clockwise over the cradle, then nine drops of water or dew (May dew is most potent of all). Burn a silver candle, a colour especially associated with fertility, and pass it clockwise over the cradle, being careful not to let any wax fall.

- Finally waft the smoke of frankincense or rose incense clockwise.
- Leave the cradle by your bed either until the full Moon or for fourteen days after Beltane Eve, replacing any wilting greenery or flowers with fresh ones.
- After this period bury all the greenery in the earth, and cover over the cradle.
- Repeat monthly if necessary.

I have a knitted cradle that folds like a bag over the doll within, which is very useful for this ritual. Or you can buy large pottery or wooden hens used for holding eggs. Any lid will do – even the lid of a silver-coloured wok. Magic is all about adapting the available tools rather than not carrying out a ritual because you don't have the precise ones. Our ancestors managed remarkably well with the hedgerows and fields as source material, and much of today's most potent magic has a simple countryside origin.

The Summer Solstice

Just as the midwinter solstice became Christmas with the spread of Christianity, so was the summer solstice, around 21 June, linked with the feast of John the Baptist on 24 June. In medieval times on St John the Baptist's day bonfires were lit on the highest points to mark the highest position of the Sun.

If the golden herb of midsummer and symbol of the summer solstice, St John's wort, is picked on the Eve of St John, 23 June, at midnight or on the actual solstice eve, and then carried or placed under a pillow, it confers fertility and powers to attract love.

However you can go to any stone circle, medicine wheel, rock carving or hilltop barrow at noon to feel the full power of the Sun before its decline on the actual longest day. If you follow the old custom and it is safe to do so, you can keep vigil on a hilltop from sunset on the solstice eve through to noon the next day, an exhausting experience but one worth doing at least once in a lifetime.

If you find a dark glassy stone on the solstice day you have discovered a Druid's egg, said to be formed when snakes roll themselves into hissing balls on the solstice eve because they fear the dawn of the day of pure light. It will endow you with incredible good fortune, wisdom and second sight – so use your gifts wisely.

Lughnasadh or Lammas

Lasting from sunset on 31 July to sunset on 2 August, this is the feast of Lugh, Celtic god of light and son of the Sun. It was the first harvest festival, to give thanks to the Earth for her bounty. In Irish Gaelic the feast was referred to as Lugnasadh, a feast to commemorate the funeral games of Lugh. As mentioned earlier, some people argue that these were held to anticipate the death of the Sun God at the second harvest, the autumn equinox. If you wish to follow this tradition, simply transfer the material concerning the ritual cutting down of the last sheaf of corn to the next festival. However, it would seem that this was the first grain harvest in many areas and so the symbolic slaying of the corn god seems more natural here. Certainly the Christianised version, Lammas, which is derived from 'loaf-mass', was the medieval Christian name for the day on which loaves of bread were baked from the first grain harvest and placed on the altar to symbolise the first fruits.

It was considered unlucky to cut down the last sheaf of corn, as it was thought to represent the corn god who was willingly offering his life in sacrifice so that the cycle of life, death and rebirth, planting, growth and harvesting might continue. Harvesters would all hurl their sickles at the last sheaf so that no one knew who had killed the corn god. It has been suggested that the death of William Rufus while hunting on 31 July 1100 was a ritual one engineered by himself because he was infertile.

This last sheaf was made into a corn dolly, symbol of the Earth Mother, and decorated with the scarlet ribbons of Cerridwen, the Celtic Mother Goddess. It would be hung over the hearth throughout the winter.

As Lammas was a time for feasting and meeting for distant members of the tribe, it was a natural occasion for arranging marriages. Trial marriages for a year and a day were frequently set up at Lammas. The young couple would thrust their hands through a holed stone and agree to stay together for a year and a day. The following Lammas they could renew the arrangement or stand back to back and walk away from one another, bringing the marriage to a formal close.

Contracts were fixed at this time, and an old name for the month was claim-time. Roads were sufficiently dry for travelling during this period, and courts of justice would travel round settling disputes and ordering the payment of debts.

Lammas rituals therefore focus on justice, rights, partnerships both personal and legal, promotion and career advancement and the regularising of personal finances. Since corn and corn dollies are a feature of this time fertility is also favoured, perhaps preparing for future ventures or getting healthy in order to have a child.

Use as your focus a straw object such as a corn dolly, a corn knot or a straw hat, perhaps decorated with poppies or cornflowers or a container of mixed cereals. Circle this with crystals of Lammas which include tiger's eye, fossilised woods, amber, rutilated quartz or any dark yellow and brown stones. Light golden brown or dark yellow candles and use herbs and incense such as cedarwood, cinnamon, fenugreek, ginger, heather, myrtle and sunflowers.

A Lammas ritual for resolving injustice

The injustice may involve official, business, domestic or personal issues. This ritual can also be used for overcoming official inertia in a matter of importance.

- Take a sharp pair of golden-coloured scissors or a sharp knife with a golden handle.
- On a piece of yellow paper write down the matter with which you are concerned, together with your frustrations and the main obstacles in the path to justice.
- Roll the paper into a scroll and tie it loosely with long grasses or ears of corn, wheat or barley, wrapping in them the desire for a swift and positive ending to the matter.
- Finally tie the bundle with a scarlet ribbon, colour of the Norse Mother Goddess Frigg, who like Cerridwen rules corn dollies, binding in it any residual negativity or doubts concerning the matter.
- With your knife or scissors, cut through the ribbon, saying: 'Let the matter proceed with all swiftness to a positive conclusion that I may be free of its cords.'
- You can be as specific or general as you wish about the nature of the problem.
- Catch the corn and paper on a large tray and continue to cut or shred the paper and corn until you have a pile of small pieces.
- Throw the pieces on to a bonfire or fire in a domestic hearth and look into the embers to see pictures of a brighter tomorrow.

The Autumn Equinox

The autumnal equinox falls around 22 September, when the Sun crosses the equator on its apparent journey southward. Day and night are of equal length and so it is one of the balance days, the other being the spring or vernal equinox six months away. In the story of the year the god of light is defeated by his twin and alter-ego, the god of darkness, but with the fruits of the second harvest gathered in. The harvest suppers are themselves a magical ritual to ensure that the table will never be empty during the ensuing months.

But the simplest custom, and my favourite, is followed on the equinox eve or Michaelmas Eve – whichever you prefer. Scatter seeds for the wild birds and they will bring you fortune throughout the winter (see also Chapter 2).

Samhain or Hallowe'en

This festival runs roughly from sunset on 31 October to sunset on 2 November and means 'summer's end'. It marked the beginning of the Celtic New Year. The Celts believed that at this festival, especially on the evening that we now celebrate as Hallowe'en, the family dead could be welcomed back for this special night. It was also a time for looking into the future, especially for matters of love.

The burial mounds of Ireland and other lands where Celtic influence held sway, such as Wales and Brittany, were opened and lighted torches placed on the walls, so that the dead could find their way. Food would be laid on the hearth for these ghosts and from that day a fire was kept burning continuously until the first day of the true spring, marked by the spring equinox around 21 March, for both dead and living.

In Catholic countries today the Days of the Dead, 1 and 2 November, are a time of joy and family remembrance. In my book *Ghost Encounters* (Blandford, 1997) I describe a visit on 1 November to Mont St Michel in northern France, where it was said in legend that dead souls gathered at what was believed to be the Celtic Isle of the Blessed.

On All Hallows' Eve masks and disguises were worn, especially by those returning from huts in the hills to the family home for the winter, so that evil spirits would not recognise them and spirit them away. Faces were blacked with soot and clothes worn inside out or back to front as a disguise. Turnip heads holding a lighted candle were placed in windows to frighten off evil spirits (in America the pumpkin took over this role).

The lighted candle inside the turnip or pumpkin is a reminder of the Hallowe'en fires. In Britain Bonfire Night on 5 November, has replaced the Hallowe'en fires that still burn brightly on this night in Ireland and parts of northern Europe. Formerly in Ireland, all fires were extinguished on All Hallows' Eve and could be rekindled only from a ceremonial fire lit by the Druids on Tlachtga, now the Hill of Ward.

Samhain rituals are potent for protection; overcoming fears; laying old ghosts, psychological as well as psychic; and for marking the natural transition between one stage of life and the next.

Light golden or huge orange candles and put them in a safe place, facing a window to protect your home and to light the way of absent loved ones. Burn them from dusk until midnight on Hallowe'en and at any time when you feel under threat. Use deep blue, purple, brown and black crystals such as sodalite, dark amethyst, smoky quartz, deep brown jasper, jet and obsidian (apache tear). Hold your apache tear up to the light of the candle and see the light shine through, promising that winter – and sorrows or setbacks – will not last forever. Use as a focus apples, which are a symbol of health and feature in Hallowe'en love divination, a custom dating from Druidic times, pumpkins, nuts and autumn leaves, mingled with evergreens as a promise that life continues.

Herbs and incense of Samhain include cypress, dittany, ferns, nutmeg, sage and pine.

A Samhain ritual for banishing fear

Begin work as dusk falls on Hallowe'en, or whenever old fears and voices from the past come to haunt you.

- Use a turnip or large golden swede, the forerunner of the Hallowe'en pumpkin, and hollow out the inside, placing the discarded vegetable in a bowl.
- As you work name your fears, saying between each scoop words such as: 'Out fear, out doubt, out pain, out phantoms from my past who seek to haunt me, out old voices that hold me back

when I would go forward, out old faces that paralyse me with uncertainty and needless guilt.'

- When the shell is quite empty form eyes, nose and mouth, saying: 'Enter light and hope and new life.'
- Light an orange candle and place it in the turnip or swede, letting it fill the growing darkness and banish the shadow.
- Let the candle burn away naturally in a safe place, preferably near a window.
- Sprinkle the discarded part of the vegetable with sea salt, season with sage and a pinch of nutmeg, cook and eat as a symbol of new coming from old and hope out of fear.

The Midwinter Solstice

The winter solstice marks the longest night and shortest day. As well as being the moment for lighting your yule log and Christmas candle to welcome light back in the world, the eve of the Solstice or Christmas Eve itself is an excellent time for following the old custom of making the crib.

The crib was introduced in 1224 by St Francis of Assisi, who was trying to remind people of the religious meaning of Christmas. He led the local people up the hills to a cave where he had created a scene complete with animals. In parts of France *santons*, clay figures, are made for the nativity scene and include models of local village characters and dignitaries.

Whether you are Christian, pagan or of a different religion or none at all, creating *santons* from clay to represent those whom you love encapsulates love in its widest and purest sense. As well as a Christ or Sun figure, a Holy Father and Mother or the Earth Mother and Sky Father, a crib or a cave from which the Unconquerable Sun was said by the Egyptians to be born each year at this time, animals and wise men and women, you can fashion rough images of all those whom you love, endowing each with wishes for a special secret Christmas gift that they most need – confidence, health, joy, a child.

As you work by candlelight or firelight enfold yourself in love; or, if you are lonely, draw to yourself in the image of the unknown person or potential family figures you create out of clay to stand round the manger, your future source of strength and affection. The magic of love is the most powerful of all, at any season.

14

Earth, Air, Fire and Water Magic

Plato, the Greek philosopher who lived around 360 BC, recounted in his book *Timaeus* that Demiurge, the creator god, made the world out of the four elements: Earth, Air, Fire and Water. This world included the Earth and the celestial sphere of Moon, stars and Sun.

In formal magic the four elements are seen as providing natural energies for transforming wishes into actuality. Earth, Air, Fire and Water in this sense are not chemical elements, but symbols of the four forces that traditionally make up life on the physical, mental and spiritual plane, not only in mankind but throughout the universe. They combine to form the fifth element, ether or *akasha*, which represents pure spirit or perfection. Medieval alchemists worked at trying to create this elusive substance, often called the philosopher's stone, which was said to turn base metal into gold and, as an elixir according to the Eastern tradition, to cure all ills and offer immortality.

In Chapter 3 I described the elemental associations of various ritual tools and suggested ways in which the elemental symbols can be used within a magical space, frequently the magic circle, to build up energies into a focused source of power. But their application spreads far beyond formal magic, and they are most potent both for ritual and divination in the natural world from which these elemental powers derive.

The Four Elements

Earth

This is the element of order, both in nature and in spheres such as the law, politics, finance, health and education. It represents the female/yin/nurturing Goddess aspect, Mother Earth, the home and family, as well as money and security. Its elemental creatures are gnomes, with their stores of hidden treasure, wisdom and above all common sense. You may see them only fleetingly in your garden amid the autumn leaves. Its colours are green or brown and its quarter is north. The direction is night.

Air

This element represents life itself, logic, the mind, communication, health, new beginnings, travel, learning and healing, and the male/yang/God in the form of sky deities. Its elemental creatures are sylphs, gentle spirits of the air who can be seen fleetingly as butterflies and offer ideas, ideals and a reminder to enjoy happiness while you can. Its colour is yellow and its quarter is east. The direction is dawn.

Fire

This element represents light, the Sun, lightning, fertility, power, joy, ambition, inspiration and achievement, and also destruction of what is now no longer needed. Like Air, it represents the male/yang/God in the form of the Sun deities. The elemental creature is the salamander, the mythical lizard (though the name is now given to a species of amphibious newt) which lives within fire. Its colour is red and its quarter is south. The direction is the noonday Sun.

Water

This element represents love, relationships, sympathy, intuition, healing, and the cycle of birth, death and rebirth. Like Earth, it represents the female/yin/Goddess in the form of the Moon goddesses. Its elemental creatures are undines, spirits of the Water. The original Undine was created without a soul, but gained one by marrying a mortal and bearing him a child. However, she also lost her freedom from pain and her immortality. The colour is blue, the quarter is west. The direction is dusk or sunset.

A Source of Personal Power

Mankind was seen as made up of the four elements in different proportions, which explained predominant character types observed first by the Greeks. This tradition continued through Roman times to the Middle Ages and Tudor times. So Shakespeare could write of Henry V, knowing that his audience would understand him perfectly, '. . . he is pure Air and Fire; and the dull elements of Earth and Water never appear in him'.

In our own age, the psychologist Carl Gustav Jung identified the four elements with four basic ways of functioning: Earth with sensations, Air with thinking, Fire with intuition and Water with feeling. He paired these as two sets of polarities, thinking/feeling and intuition/sensation, and believed that all people have a predominant element, a secondary one and most importantly a shadow element, the opposite from our predominant element. This soul image, as he called the opposing element, was absent from the conscious life, but might emerge in dreams or in the choice of a future partner who reflected the missing function. So the thinking Air person, according to Jung's theory, has a Water or feeling soul-image; the intuitive Fire person has an Earth or sensation soul-image; the feeling or Water person has a thinking or Air soul-image; and the Earth or sensation person has a Fire or intuitive soul-image.

Tuning into Your Personal Elemental Strengths

It may be more productive not to think in magical terms that our predominant elemental type is set in stone for all time – although we may naturally veer towards, for example, a feeling or Water response rather than a thinking or Air response in our everyday interactions, as both Jung and the ancients suggest; what is more, we may find the opposite polarity harder to access.

Since the whole point of magic is to harness different strengths at the appropriate time, thereby increasing our overall potential for success and happiness, it can be useful to regard the elemental modes as potential ways of responding to a given situation. For example, the most logical or normally predominantly Air person may automatically switch into Water or feeling mode in a close relationship. More importantly, that person may benefit from deliberately bringing into the fore this Water element, using Water-strengthening rituals and artefacts at a time when tact and empathy are vital.

If we can discover in advance the strength that will be most helpful in a particular situation, we can maximise our opportunities and minimise potential conflict. The simplest way of finding your most useful element at a given time is to focus on a forthcoming event or issue and use as your guide an ordinary pack of playing cards, or if you prefer, tarot cards.

Your unconscious wisdom has an overall picture and is aware of factors that have not yet emerged into your conscious field of vision and awareness. Years of practising divination using tarot cards and runes with hundreds of people have led me to believe that somehow, in a way not yet explained or even acknowledged by science, our unconscious can affect our choice of cards or runes.

Playing card	*Tarot card*	*Element*
Diamonds	Pentacles or discs	Earth
Hearts	Cups or chalices	Water
Clubs	Wands or staves	Fire
Spades	Swords	Air

- Select the aces to tens in all four suits in a playing card pack or tarot pack, forty cards in all.
- Shuffle the cards.
- Deal these cards one at time face up on to a pile until you come to an ace.
- Put the ace down face up and use this as the base for a second pile. Continue dealing until you have another ace to start another pile, or a two of the same suit to lay on top of the aces.

- Continue dealing, turning over the unused cards and beginning again, laying threes on top of the twos, fours on top of the threes and so on, until you have completed a suit.
- The first suit to be completed gives you the elemental strength which is currently needed in your life.
- If you are concerned about the chance factor, record your first result and repeat the process as many times as you wish.
- If at the end of the ten or so deals any of the suits are equal in number, use only these, reshuffle and deal to get a single overall result. Remember to shuffle your cards in between each game.

Elemental Substances

For performing ritual magic certain substances can be used to symbolise the four elements.

Salt for Earth: Salt is the purest element and vital for human life. Kind and trustworthy people are often called the 'salt of the earth'. Use sea salt and keep it in a small unglazed pottery jar and a tiny pottery dish.

Incense for Air: Use different perfumes of incense for different rituals, for example: allspice for money rituals, bay for rituals concerning health, cinnamon for increasing psychic awareness, dragon's blood for sexual attraction and fertility, frankincense for success and new beginnings, myrrh for endings and banishing sorrow, rose for love, pine for courage, rosemary for memory and learning, sandalwood for protection.

Candles for Fire: Use different colours according to the need and astrological associations.

Oils for Water: Different fragrances evoke special powers, for example frankincense for courage, lavender for happiness and pine for positivity. Alternatively use either pure spring water from a sacred spring, such as Buxton water, or tap water left in the light in a crystal or clear glass container for a twenty-four-hour Sun-and-Moon cycle.

These forms of magic can be used separately, for rituals concerning the related areas, for example, Earth for the family, for legal and financial matters. Earth could also be used to help to take a practical ordered approach that may be necessary to deal with a forthcoming situation, especially if order is not naturally a strong point.

Salt Magic – the Magic of Earth

Often we think of Earth purely in terms of burying magic – that is, carrying out a ritual in which an object symbolising the habit we wish to kick or the sorrow we wish to banish is buried in Earth. It is certainly an effective way of dispelling pain, illnesses or regrets (see Chapter 1).

But Earth is also protective. In rural communities people used to cast a handful of earth in the wake of a departing child or loved one as a way of protecting them throughout the day.

Salt adds the dimension of life, growth, health and increase, albeit in the Earth's steady, calm way in which everything has a time and season. Salt is also associated with the increase of money, and many traditional folk spells on both sides of the Atlantic centre on a pot of money surrounded by salt. Salt is extracted from sea water and there are also inland sources (think of the salt mines). The old salt routes, used for centuries by traders in this vital substance, are among the oldest tracks known to mankind.

This is the history behind the following gentle ritual for preserving love or friendship, which can be especially valuable after a period of discord or separation. You cannot bind another person to you unwillingly, so you need to build into the ritual the other person's options. But if you and the other person have made a promise of fidelity, this is a powerful way of preventing others from interfering.

A salt and clay ritual for preserving fidelity

Take some clay, another symbol of the Earth and life (according to various mythologies, human beings were formed from clay by divine artisans). You can find clay naturally on some beaches, river banks and hillsides or buy it from an art or craft shop.

- Shape the clay into a shallow bowl to represent your relationship. As you work, visualise you and the other person being moulded together, whether spiritually, emotionally or physically, and recite: 'I mould [name] and myself closer together, smoothing out the differences, the dissent, so that we are one if he/she so chooses and so to remain.'

- Finally engrave your initials and his or hers in a twining, continuous pattern around the edge, while saying, 'May he/she and I be so entwined in mutual purpose if he/she so desires.'
- Allow the clay to dry, but do not fire or glaze it.
- Place on either side of the clay bowl two shallow glass dishes, one for you and one for the other person in the relationship, containing sea salt or unrefined rock salt.
- Take a tiny jug of slightly warmed pure spring water.
- From the salt representing yourself sprinkle a few grains into the dish, saying; 'I pour my essence into this union that it may be strong.'
- From the second dish sprinkle some more salt grains into the clay bowl on top of yours, saying; 'If what [name] has pledged is what he/she wills, I join his/her essence with mine that we may be strong.'
- Continue to add salt from each bowl, adding whatever you wish to the relationship – endurance, patience, loyalty in word and deed – as you mix the salt.
- Take some water on your finger and begin to work the salt into the clay, saying, 'Salt, clay, source and sustainer of life and our home, blend us in love, in joy and above all in free will that we may choose to be together.'
- Keep the pot safe, but I think it is better not to glaze it. If it does crack, create another and rededicate it – relationships change and you may want to add new strengths.

Incense Magic – the Magic of Air

Incense has been used for thousands of years in many cultures to carry petitions to the deities and as an offering of thanks. Now widely on sale commercially, in floral fragrances as well as the more traditional ones, it offers an instant focus for air magic if you need logic, or a new beginning or want to travel.

Herbs/incense	*Ruled by*	*Magic qualities*
Allspice	Mars	Money, strength, action
Bay	Sun	Healing, protection
Benzoin	Sun	Money, increasing mental acuity and concentration
Cedarwood	Mercury	Healing, cleansing redundant influences and negative thoughts
Cinnamon	Sun	Increases passion, money-bringer, psychic awareness
Cloves	Jupiter	Love, repelling hostility
Dragon's blood	Mars	Love, protection and passion
Fern	Mars	Bringer of change, travel and fertility
Frankincense	Sun	Courage, joy, strength and success
Juniper	Sun	Protection and healing
Lavender	Mercury	Love and reconciliation
Myrrh	Moon	Healing, peace and inner harmony
Rosemary	Sun	For love and happy memories
Sage	Jupiter	For wisdom and improved mental powers
Sandalwood	Moon	For spiritual and psychic awareness and healing

It is probably easiest to use a single fragrance to concentrate on a particular area in which you need your Air wisdom. Sometimes a fragrance may have a dual or even a triple quality – the property on which you are focusing is the one that will come to the fore, but you can widen your rituals to include the other qualities if you need them. A ritual is a magical way of setting specifics, a reason that home-devised spells work better than ones you follow even from the best books or teachers.

- You can buy incense sticks and cones which are combustible incenses, which are very hard to make at home. However what you can make is a non-combustible incense to burn on a charcoal block. Do so by grinding herbs, flowers, berries or leaves in a mortar and pestle (see table for their various properties). As you do this, repeat over and over again faster and faster your magical intention and the name of the herb, combined in a chant, for example: 'Clove, clove, bring me love.'
- When you burn the incense, if the smoke goes directly upwards your wish will come to fruition soon.
- If it goes to the left, others will help.
- If it goes to the right, you will succeed by your own efforts.
- If the incense goes out, relight it – you will succeed if you persevere.
- Place a fireproof plate or tray behind the incense smoke and see what symbol the smoke traces, which may give you an indication about the form your path will take.

An incense Air ritual for long-distance travel

- Be specific about the journey you wish to undertake, the destination, the purpose – to further your career, a holiday, love. Much magic is misdirected because we do not focus clearly on what we actually want.
- Use an actual map, or draw a sketch map of the direction and the location, and mark where you are right now with a stick or cone of incense on a fireproof dish.
- Use fern incense for travel, or one of the powerful Sun incenses such as frankincense for success and joy, especially if the place you wish to visit is a sunny one.
- Light a path of incense sticks across the map to your chosen destination, placing one stick or cone on each major place on the route. As you light each one in turn, beginning with the first, say, 'I am here, carry me far on your fragrant path, free as a bird, fleet as an arrow, to where I long to be.'

- When all the incense sticks are alight remove the map from beneath them, returning each stick to its place where it may safely burn as a fragrant trail marking the direction of your dreams.
- Carry out an action to further your plan, perhaps beginning to learn a new language, planning a budget to raise the money, so that the wish moves into the reality plane.
- Repeat the ritual regularly, and each time move your plan further in actuality.

Candle Magic – the Magic of Fire

Candles are also discussed in Chapter 4, which explains the astrological colours and tells you which to use for different needs. It is very easy to make your own beeswax candles for rituals. Pure undyed beeswax releases the gentle aroma of honey and has been used for thousands of years in rituals. The Mother Goddess was pictured on cave walls as a bee and, although formal beekeeping did not begin until around 2500 BC in Ancient Egypt, people have gathered beeswax from hollow trees since time immemorial.

You can buy sheets of beeswax, undyed or in naturally dyed colours, together with wicks, from many craft outlets. Making your own beeswax candles gives you the opportunity to enfold your wishes and needs in the candle by visualising your desires as you wrap the beeswax around the wick.

- The wick should be about ½ inch (1 cm) longer than the intended height of the candle.
- Place the wick at the edge of the sheet and roll the wax around it.
- Alternatively, mould tiny beeswax images for specific needs.
- As you create your candle or image, add such words as 'Golden honey bee, bring love/money/health/joy to me' over and over again, so that you imitate the sleepy humming of bees on a summer day. If you can work in the sunshine this will incorporate the power of the bees' natural element into the magic (see Chapter 13).

A candle ritual for speeding up a long-awaited change

Take a golden candle to represent the desired event.

- Draw up a desired timescale from the time of the ritual to the earliest possible time in earthly terms that the project can be completed or the aim fulfilled.
- If you are realistic in your aims, they are more likely to be fulfilled.
- Tie some small separate cords, each knotted in the centre – one for each day, week or month.
- Mark your candle with the same number of notches, beginning at the top.
- Light the candle and place it on a fireproof tray.
- Lay your cords in front of the candle. When the first segment of candle is burned down, consign your knotted cord to the flame, saying,

Time burn
Luck turn
Change to me,
Soon to see.

- Blow out the candle.
- At the same time the next night burn the next segment and burn the second knot.
- Continue this nightly ritual until the candle and knots are all burned.

Oil Magic – the Magic of Water

Oils are particularly good in rituals because they combine both the Water and Air elements when they are burned. But equally oils dropped on water, especially in a bath, can make energies flow, whether for calm or energy.

Oils for success, love, happiness and protection

For maximum effect, burn the oil or oils of your choice in a diffuser or oil burner. Baths in the appropriate fragrance are another way of empowering yourself or ensuring a night free from bad dreams.

Oil	*Magical quality*
Cedarwood	Health
Chamomile	Harmony, healing
Eucalyptus	Health
Geranium	Love
Lavender	Happiness, peace, mending of quarrels
Lemon	Driving away negativity
Orange	Divinatory abilities, heightened intuition, psychic development
Patchouli	Money
Peppermint	Protection
Pine	Purification of bad atmosphere, driving away negativity
Rose	Luck
Rosemary	Learning
Sandalwood	Spirituality, divinatory abilities, heightened intuition
Tea tree	Purification of bad atmosphere
Thyme	Learning

When using oils in baths, or indeed in any way in which they come into contact with the body, you need to be particularly careful.

Take care with oils

- Always follow the instructions on the bottle.
- Don't use cedarwood, rosemary or thyme in pregnancy.

- After contact with orange or lemon don't expose yourself to direct sunlight for at least six hours.
- Never add to a bathful of water more than three drops of peppermint, lemon or cedarwood.
- Never add to a bathful of water more than three drops of the more astringent or potent oils: orange, pine, rosemary, tea tree and thyme.
- The following oils are so mild that they are safe even for young children, and adults can use up to ten drops in a bath: chamomile, lavender, geranium, rose.

An oil bath ritual for attracting love

- Carve a heart on a tiny bar of soap. Inside the heart, entwine your initials and those of the person you wish to attract, or a question mark if the person is unknown.
- Run a bath, and when it is filled add lavender and rose, a drop at a time in turn, saying with each drop of lavender,

Flow love flow,
from my heart to his [or hers].

and with each drop of rose,

Return love, return
In my own heart to burn.

- Have a leisurely bath by candlelight, using a jasmine or neroli candle to inspire love. Let your soap dissolve, saying,

Melt, heart, melt,
And to me alone be true.

- When you have finished your bath, leave the soap until it has melted, then run cold water into the bath, swirl it round and let it flow down the plughole to the words

Love, love flow from me,
Wheresoever true love be.

15

Magical Times

When man first stood outside his cave and gazed at the heavens, he knew that the Moon, Sun and stars were of magical and spiritual significance and made them his deities. The Sun gave warmth and light and marked the seasons with growing or decreasing light. The Moon's phases mirrored the monthly cycle of women. The waxing, full and waning phases found echoes in the earthly passage from maiden to mother to wise woman, and also in the passage of maturity in men's lives. The stars guided the navigator across land and sea, heralding the seasons by their changing positions in the heavens.

The celestial sphere rotates around us like the dial of some gigantic timepiece, offering a highly accurate way of foretelling the seasons because some stars appear over the horizon only at certain times of the year. For example, the Ancient Egyptians relied on the rising of Sothis, as they called Sirius, to tell them when the Nile was going to flood.

As people began to divide time into finer units, from day and night to the months of the moon, to the hours of the day, they began to realise that certain times of the day were especially magical. They used the energies of time to strengthen their magic charms and to ensure the success of actions.

Although we now consult digital clocks rather than the Moon and Sun, the earlier measures of time, linked as they were to planetary and stellar energies, remain potent. If we can harness these special times, we can not only perform rituals more effectively but also tune into the specific aspects of protection or good fortune that we need at critical or change points in our lives.

Locked in office blocks or factories, we may lose track of the passage of the Sun through the day and through the year. Yet solstices that mark the times of maximum and minimum light, and the equinoxes, when there is equal day and night, offer the most powerful energies of all (see Chapter 13).

Living by the Sun and Moon

Before you begin working with the different energies of the Sun, Moon and stars, try to regain contact with the natural rhythms of the day by spending some time living in the old way before gas and electric lights turned night to perpetual jaundice-coloured day.

While on holiday in Spain in April 1998, each day I made a point of watching the dawn rise over the Mediterranean – I often went to bed quite early when my body told me I was tired, not long after dark fell. As day broke, the bats which fluttered all night around the palm trees – the night shift, as my children called them – were replaced by the dawn chorus of tiny coloured birds. On one magical dawn, the waning Moon shone brilliantly with two magnificent stars standing sentinel as the Sun rose over the sea. The early morning lights of the dark forms of fishing boats faded as they chugged across the scarlet sea, only to reappear as harbingers of morning as the rising Sun glinted on their nets and sails. By the end of a week of Sun and Moon time, I felt amazingly full of energy and much calmer. I shall always remember dawn over the palm trees and shingle shore.

- If possible, begin when it is summer and the days are long, preferably on the evening of the full Moon so that you can enjoy maximum light. If you are beginning this exercise in winter you can still experience the natural rhythms, although your outdoor activities will be more limited and you may rely more on candles for the longer evenings.
- Try to spend a long weekend or an unbroken two- or three-day period when you do not have to go to work or meet any

deadlines. If possible stay in unspoilt countryside in a cottage, hut or tent. If you do remain at home, switch off all phones and faxes; do not use electrical appliances unless necessary and do not answer the door except in an emergency.

- Stock up with provisions so that you do not need to go shopping.
- On the first morning, set your alarm to go off just before dawn so you can hear the birds beginning to sing as the light enters the sky. You are witnessing the first point of transition between night and day, darkness and light. Be aware of the special energies of dawn for new beginnings. This is a time for rituals to attract love, a time for optimism and original ideas.
- Eat your first meal as close as possible to first light and your midday meal when the Sun is at its height in the sky.
- Feel the power of the Sun at noon, the magical time for rituals for fertility, money, health and healing, a focus for confidence, heightened energy and clear vision.
- Spend the day out of doors or very quietly indoors if it is cold or wet, avoiding any form of artificial entertainment, seeing only your immediate family and special friends or remaining alone. Choose companions who will not make demands nor create anxieties nor awaken feelings of guilt or resentment.
- Be aware of time stretching out – not to be filled with frantic activity, but to be appreciated in quiet walks or conversations or just savoured for itself.
- As dusk falls let yourself relax, winding down with the passing of the light. This is another powerful time of transition – in Celtic times the beginning of the day, which ran from sunset to sunset. It is a time for banishing pain or worry, regrets, destructive habits and redundant relationships.
- Above all, it is a time for divination by candlelight and for looking into other dimensions. Use candles sparingly and savour the growing darkness. Before extinguishing them, look at the pictures in the flame and as you blow each candle out send its light to anyone who needs it.
- If it is practical, given your venue, do not draw the curtains at dusk to close out the night but welcome it as the shadow side of the day.
- If it is a clear night and the Moon is full, you will be able to see quite clearly even after dark.

- Explore the garden or the immediate vicinity by moonlight, and see what a very different world it is when dreams and intuitions rule and the cold logic of day is softened by magical moonlight, shedding its insights and instinctive wisdom.
- Go to bed when you feel tired.
- Set your alarm for dawn on the second day, although you may wake just before it and spend another day living by natural time.
- Monitor your own energies as they become more attuned to the natural cycles of day and night, and try to manage for an even shorter period with candlelight.
- In the evening, light a fire either outdoors or in a small grate and look at the fire fairies and pictures in the embers in the darkness.
- If you cannot light a fire, use a large beeswax candle and let the honey fragrance carry you back thousands of years to the time when the Paleolithic bee goddess was worshipped as the bringer of light in darkness.
- Listen to your inner voice, and you will find the answers to questions you had not even known you needed to ask.
- Go to bed even earlier but this time do not set your alarm. You may rise at dawn naturally. Even if not, you will wake refreshed, having had the sleep you need rather than the sleep that the world tells you that you must take.

Try to live by the light of the Sun and Moon at regular periods throughout the year. Children naturally adapt to this slower time and the rhythm works wonders for insomniac or hyperactive children, freeing them from artificial lighting and the flicker on computer and television screens that wreaks havoc enough with adult health and peace of mind.

The Aettir or Tides of the Day

As I have researched magical practices, I have discovered many powerful ways of focusing the energies of transition times of the day and night. One of the most potent spread through northern Europe and eventually across the Atlantic and even to parts of Australia and New Zealand where Viking or Anglo-Saxon descendants may be found.

In the Norse or Viking tradition each twenty-four-hour day was divided into eight tides, known as the aettir. A day tide or aett is three hours long, with a peak or chime hour in the middle of each. Each aett has special strengths, qualities and areas of focus. If you need a special energy or are worried about an aspect of your life, identify the most appropriate aett for your need and spend the chime hour looking either into a candle flame or into still water in sunlight. Let pictures filter into your mind that will offer wisdom and perhaps an answer. I have used the modern idea of beginning the new day at midnight, but if you wish you can use the traditional sunset-to-sunset time-frame for your magical work.

Below I have listed the strengths of the time periods, and certain issues or problems that concern you may fit into one or other of them. The times reflect the slower agricultural world where toil began early and any loving and learning were relegated to the evenings after work was finished. It follows on naturally from the Sun and Moon time. If you are a shift worker you can reverse the tides.

0430–0730: Morningtide

The time of awakening, fertility and new beginnings. The chime hour starts at 6 a.m. Use its energies for new beginnings and all matters concerning infertility, conception, pregnancy and birth of both babies and projects. Rather than lie awake worrying, if you do wake early set up and sort out unfinished paperwork. You can always rest later or go to bed earlier the following night.

0730–1030: Daytide

The time of work and money-making. The chime hour starts at 9 a.m. Use its energies for money problems, money-spinning ventures and success.

1030–1330: Midday

The time of endurance and perseverance. The chime hour starts at 12 p.m. Use its energies for matters that are proving wearisome or taking a long time to bear fruit, and for difficult people.

1330–1630: Undorne

The time for change, transformation and illumination. The chime hour starts at 3 p.m. Use its energies for exploring new horizons and making travel plans.

1630–1930: Eventide

The time of the family, of home and reconciliation. The chime hour starts at 6 p.m. Use its energies for questions concerning children of all ages, domestic matters, marriage and partnerships.

1930–2230: Night-tide

The time for love, passion and learning. The chime hour starts at 9 p.m. Use its energies for love relationships, close friendships and acquiring formal knowledge.

2230–0130: Midnight

For healing and restoration of mind, body and spirit. The chime hour starts at midnight. Use its energies for insight into illness, especially of the chronic kind, for the mending of quarrels and the world of the spirit.

0130–0430: Uht

The time of sleep and old age. The chime hour starts at 3 a.m. Use its energies for concerns over elderly relatives and ageing, and for calm sleep.

Solar Times of Power

Dawn, noon and sunset were also regarded as significant moments in the passage of time. When dawn or dusk fall on a chime hour the energies are especially strong: for this reason noon is always a peak time. Because the Celtic day began at sunset, Hallowe'en (the eve of All Hallows) and May Eve became more significant than the following days for magical rituals and energies.

Dawn

Good for magic involving new beginnings, change and gain, whether love, money, health or happiness. You do not need to perform specific rituals unless you wish, but let the colours of the dawn permeate your being, filling you with optimism and energy.

Noon

When the sun is overhead is the time for action, power and success. If it is a sunny day, leave whatever you are doing and stand for two or three minutes in the full sunlight, letting the warmth and light clear away any doubts and hesitation. This is pure yang in the Oriental tradition.

Dusk

For love, healing and banishing any guilt, resentment or regrets accumulated during the day. Send love to absent friends and family on the crimson sky, and if you can see the Moon welcome her gentler energies to guide you towards sleep.

Midnight

We often associate midnight with dark practices. But it is a good time for acceptance and balance; it is a time of what the Chinese would call pure yin energy. If you cannot sleep, light a purple candle fragranced with lavender and let the midnight energies whether moonlit or dark, wipe the slate clean so that you can sleep until dawn.

The Planetary Hours

This system in no way contradicts the aettir, but offers additional information so that you can add different energies at specific times according to your needs. If this seems complex, you do not need to use it or save it for times when you want to concentrate your energies or protective powers or carry out a specific ritual of great importance. Using it, you can tune into the old planetary energies attached to measured periods from sunrise to sunset and sunset to sunrise.

In this system the magical periods are not exact hours from 6 a.m. sunrise to 6 p.m. sunset, but are calculated from the actual varying daily sunrise to the actual sunset; these times can usually be found in a diary or daily newspaper.

The period is divided by twelve to give you the daytime hours, and so in summer each will be longer than an hour and in winter shorter. The only exception is at the equinoxes, when there is equal day and night. The sunset-to-sunrise divided by twelve will give you the night-time hours – these again will not be exactly sixty minutes but will vary according to the time of year.

Each of these periods, day and night, is ruled by a different planet according to the day of the week on which it falls. If, for example, you were carrying out a ritual for new love, you could begin at dawn, the first hour on Fridays, since both this period of time and the day are ruled by the goddess of love, Venus. Any rituals, visualisation or wishes at this time would attract the normal rising energies of dawn for new beginnings.

If you timed your ritual or desire at the right time of the year dawn would fall between 0430 and 0730 – morningtide – the time of awakening, fertility and new beginnings. This would be a perfect time to attract love, to turn new love into something more or if you wanted a baby to bless your union.

Alternatively if a developing or established love needed extra positive energies, or you wanted to increase passion in a relationship, you could wait until a day on which the Venus period fell during the night-tide, between 1930 and 2230, the natural time for love and passion.

If a love affair was causing you sorrow, or it had ended and you wanted to move on, you could use the Venus period that fell on a day when healing and reconciliation energies were at their height. This could be either 1630–1930, eventide, the time of the family, of home and reconciliation, or 2230–0130, the midnight period, for healing and restoration of mind, body and spirit.

This system only uses the original seven planets plus the Sun and Moon, because this way of dividing time is very ancient. I have, however, used methods where the more recently discovered planets Uranus, Neptune and Pluto are incorporated.

Daytime from Sunrise to Sunset

Add the hours and minutes from sunrise to sunset and divide the total by twelve to give you the periods for each day. If you wish, you can calculate a week or month ahead, using the table below as a basis – remember to allow for local and regional variations. The first hour period each day at sunrise is ruled by its day planet. As you will see, the planetary order has a regular pattern.

Sunrise

Hour	*Sunday*	*Monday*	*Tuesday*	*Wednesday*	*Thursday*	*Friday*	*Saturday*
1	Sun	Moon	Mars	Mercury	Jupiter	Venus	Saturn
2	Venus	Saturn	Sun	Moon	Mars	Mercury	Jupiter
3	Mercury	Jupiter	Venus	Saturn	Sun	Moon	Mars
4	Moon	Mars	Mercury	Jupiter	Venus	Saturn	Sun
5	Saturn	Sun	Moon	Mars	Mercury	Jupiter	Venus
6	Jupiter	Venus	Saturn	Sun	Moon	Mars	Mercury
7	Mars	Mercury	Jupiter	Venus	Saturn	Sun	Moon
8	Sun	Moon	Mars	Mercury	Jupiter	Venus	Saturn
9	Venus	Saturn	Sun	Moon	Mars	Mercury	Jupiter
10	Mercury	Jupiter	Venus	Saturn	Sun	Moon	Mars
11	Moon	Mars	Mercury	Jupiter	Venus	Saturn	Sun
12	Saturn	Sun	Moon	Mars	Mercury	Jupiter	Venus

Sunset

Hour	*Sunday*	*Monday*	*Tuesday*	*Wednesday*	*Thursday*	*Friday*	*Saturday*
1	Jupiter	Venus	Saturn	Sun	Moon	Mars	Mercury
2	Mars	Mercury	Jupiter	Venus	Saturn	Sun	Moon
3	Sun	Moon	Mars	Mercury	Jupiter	Venus	Saturn
4	Venus	Saturn	Sun	Moon	Mars	Mercury	Jupiter
5	Mercury	Jupiter	Venus	Saturn	Sun	Moon	Mars
6	Moon	Mars	Mercury	Jupiter	Venus	Saturn	Sun
7	Saturn	Sun	Moon	Mars	Mercury	Jupiter	Venus
8	Jupiter	Venus	Saturn	Sun	Moon	Mars	Mercury
9	Mars	Mercury	Jupiter	Venus	Saturn	Sun	Moon
10	Sun	Moon	Mars	Mercury	Jupiter	Venus	Saturn
11	Venus	Saturn	Sun	Moon	Mars	Mercury	Jupiter
12	Mercury	Jupiter	Venus	Saturn	Sun	Moon	Mars

Below, each day is listed with its ruling planet, metal and crystal. These can form a focal point for energies, both on their own day of the week and also during the specific planetary period you are using for rituals. So for your Friday love magic at dawn, or simply to attract love, you would incorporate a jade crystal and a copper coin.

You could carry these items throughout Friday to amplify love energies, whether or not you performed a specific ritual. If you have a metal and crystal to represent each day they can be a welcome addition to your magical store of energy. I have included the magical glyph for each planet, as traditionally these were engraved on the appropriate metal or crystal. You can use these in a talisman for concentrating your day energies and bringing yourself good luck.

Planetary Qualities

Sun

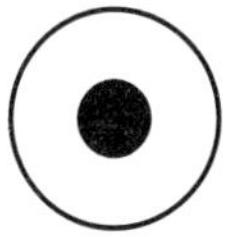

Sunday, the day of the Sun, is a good day if the main issues are personal ones, concerned with your identity and for prosperity, power and ambition. The Sun is linked with sparkling **clear crystal quartz** and other clear white crystals. Traditionally the Sun was associated with diamonds. Carry your Sun crystal when you need a new beginning but doubt yourself, or when you are tired and need a sudden boost of energy. **Gold**, the metal of the Sun, contains the pure masculine power and energy for success and achievement. **Brass** is frequently used as a less expensive substitute, especially in money rituals, as it too is ruled by the Sun.

Moon

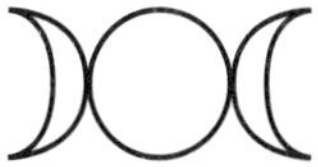

Monday, the day of the Moon, is a propitious day if you are concerned with partnership issues or need to make a choice, especially where there are no clear pointers ahead; also with emotions, the sea, home and gardening. The Moon is associated with the translucent **moonstone**, especially white ones, and other cloudy white or delicately coloured translucent stones. Carry your Moon stone if you need to get in touch with your inner self, or sleep with it to ensure creative dreams. **Silver**, the metal of the Moon, contains the pure feminine power of intuition and instinctive wisdom for spiritual and psychic understanding.

Mars

♂

Tuesday, the day of Mars, is a positive day if you are concerned with expansion in any field, face opposition or feel strongly about an issue. Mars is associated with red or **blood agate, rubies** and other vibrant red stones. Carry your Mars stone for courage when you feel under threat or when you need to make an unpopular change. **Iron** is the metal of Mars and offers the power to stand against injustice and protection from negative influences. **Steel** is often used in modern magic as a substitute for iron, and its gleaming surface can add a dimension of light to the protective qualities of traditional iron.

Mercury

☿

Wednesday, the day of Mercury, is a good day if you are concerned with travel, communication of any kind, money or business matters. Mercury is associated with sparkling yellow **citrine** and other vibrant yellow stones, both clear and opaque. Carry your Mercury stone when you need to communicate clearly, either verbally or in writing, or when you need to make an instant decision. **Mercury** is the metal of the planet: it contains the power to communicate and learn new things to interact with others and make a place in the world. But this metal is unstable and potentially lethal unless contained in a thermometer or barometer. **Aluminium** is used as a modern substitute in magic, as it too is ruled by the planet. You can also use **silver**.

Jupiter

♃

Thursday, the day of Jupiter, is a good day for divination on career matters, for examinations, learning and the law. Jupiter has as his stone **lapis lazuli**, eye of the gods, which is a dense purple/blue with flecks of iron pyrites (fool's gold), and all rich blue and purple crystals. Carry your Jupiter stone when you need wisdom to make the right decision, or when you need to apply yourself to learning a new skill or gaining deeper knowledge of a subject. **Tin**, the metal of Jupiter, provides the wisdom and idealism that make ventures worthwhile.

Venus

♀

Friday, the day of Venus, is a harmonious day for matters concerning peace, love, relationships, family and friendship. Venus has as her special crystal **jade** and all delicately shaded green and pink stones. Carry your Venus stone to find or nurture love or when you are seeking reconciliation. **Copper** is the metal of Venus: it contains the power to love and to attract love, and to encourage harmonious relationships with family and friends.

Saturn

♄

Saturday, the day of Saturn, is concerned with unfinished business, with endings that lead to beginnings and with the unexpected. Saturn is associated with **obsidian** (**apache tears**) and all black, grey and brown stones, especially those that reflect light. Carry your

Saturn stone when you feel at the mercy of blind fate, or when life seems an uphill struggle but you know you have to make a great effort. **Lead** is the metal of Saturn and offers mastery over fate, through recognising times of change and finding a way round difficulties. However, as lead is poisonous for many years **pewter** has been used as a substitute in magic. Pewter objects can be bought very cheaply in garage sales, boot fairs and secondhand goods shops.

The Magic of the Sun

The Sun has been worshipped as a symbol of life itself in many cultures since the dawn of humanity. The bonfires that our ancestors lit at midsummer, Beltane or Beltain (May Eve) and Samhain (Hallowe'en) were intended as rituals to encourage and strengthen the Sun on its journey throughout the year.

The Sun is invariably associated with good fortune. It is lucky to be born at sunrise, and also for a bride if she is bathed-in sunlight as she leaves the marriage place: 'Happy is the bride the sun shines on.'

At first the Sun was worshipped as a living being. Later, the Sun deities were thought to live in the house of the Sun. Wisdom and the arts of civilisation were believed to have been brought from the Sun by solar deities or early hero-gods who travelled from the east and returned to the west when their work was done. In Ancient Greece, the solar god, Helios, was praised each dawn as he emerged in the east and drove his chariot of winged horses around the sky before plunging into the ocean in the west at sunset.

The Sun, masculine, powerful, courageous and assertive, speaks of our conscious strength to succeed and direct our energies in a linear way. It corresponds to yang, to the left brain, to light, convergent thinking and to creativity.

It is often assumed that magic uses only the right side of the brain, the side associated with intuition and unconscious powers. But that is only half the story. The magic of the Aztecs, Greeks, Egyptians, Chinese and Celts, and of the alchemists who sought to combine the essence of King Sol with Queen Luna, acknowledged the need for powerful, direct solar energy and action as well as intuitive lunar powers.

By harnessing the power of the Sun as well as the Moon, left-brain, logical magic does not usurp, but supplements, the mystique of lunar powers. As well as recognising the cyclic nature of human lives and lunar magic, solar magic relies on a surge of direct, focused energy to project ideas into the real world. Women and men have within them energies that correspond to both the Sun and the Moon, and the power of the Sun can give to woman the focused energy to make dreams into reality, and put plans into action.

Solar or lunar magic?

Solar power is best for matters in the conscious, outer world and material matters, family matters, a better job, money or establishing a strong identity. Things of the spirit, inner issues and emotions, spells for love and kicking deep-seated habits or destructive relationships are better in moonlight, where the unconscious powers predominate.

Natural Sources of Solar Energy

You can use any or all of these natural sources of the Sun's power whenever you need energy, inspiration, health, optimism, self-confidence and pure, unbridled joy.

- Carry one or more of the crystals of the Sun.
- Eat the fruits and foods of the Sun.
- Wear gold jewellery and orange or yellow clothes.
- A dish of golden apples can form a focal point in a kitchen and exude health-giving energies. If you eat raw or unprocessed Sun foods you absorb *prana*, the life force.
- Place the flowers of the Sun in your home, or plant any yellow flowers in your garden or on waste ground.
- Use the Sun herbs to make tea, for cooking, and as essential oils to burn or in a bath; or plant up a Sun herb patch or window box.
- Find a Sun tree and feel its warmth and energy emanating from the trunk.
- Tie golden ribbons around the branches of your Sun tree and leave yellow flowers around the base.

Crystals and gems of the Sun include amber, carnelian, citrines, clear crystal quartz, diamonds and topaz.

Foods of the Sun include apricots, all citrus fruits (especially oranges), dates, figs, golden wheat, nuts (especially almonds and walnuts), olives and olive oil, peaches, saffron rice, spicy foods, sunflower seeds and sweet corn (maize).
Herbs, incenses and oils of the Sun include chamomile, cinnamon, cinquefoil, fennel, frankincense, garlic, St John's wort, saffron, sandalwood, turmeric, thyme and verbena.
Trees of the Sun include almond, ash, laurel, olive, palm and walnut.
Flowers of the Sun include buttercups, carnations, chrysanthemums, lavender, marigolds, roses (especially golden ones) and sunflowers.
Colours are red, gold, yellow and pure dazzling white.

Solar Days and Times

The days between the summer solstice and midsummer (around 21–24 June) are the most powerful of the solar days, so use them for asking for promotion or more money, applying for jobs, making important plans or making a new beginning (see Chapter 13). Sunday, the day of the Sun, is especially powerful for solar rituals.

Although Sun rituals frequently involve fire, you should not feel tied to specific associations. The following ritual harnesses the opposing element, Water, and is one that has proved very effective (see also Chapter 14).

A Sun ritual for gaining promotion or positive recognition

If you cannot find a suitable bridge you can use a large bowl of water and allow the flowers to float on the surface.

- You will need three golden flowers, each as large as possible, a small golden or brass bell and a tiny crystal quartz.
- At noon, the time symbolic of full solar power, or when the Sun is shining especially brilliantly during the afternoon, find a bridge and see your image reflected in the water, completely surrounded by the rippling sunlight.
- Let the golden energies fill you with confidence, and define either out loud or silently your current goal. Be specific. It can be very helpful to express exactly what you want, as sometimes this can take an unexpected twist as your inner voice speaks.

- As you cast the first flower off the bridge so that it floats down the stream, say,

Sun shine,
Give me power

- When it has floated out of sight, cast the second golden flower in the water and say,

Sun shine,
At this hour

- Ring your golden bell three times, holding it upwards so that the Sun glints on the gold, saying on the third ring,

Sun gold
Power hold

- Cast the third flower and say,

Sun light
Crystal sight.

- Finally cast your crystal into the water as a gift (see Chapter 2) and see the ripples break and re-form, showing you the picture of what you will achieve. This may be your new job or an entirely unexpected image of success and happiness.
- As the water is stilled, remain on the bridge until the Sun fades or you feel energised, letting the sunlight warm you and fill you with optimism and assurance of success.
- End your ritual by drawing the sign of the Sun, a circle enclosing a dot, with a stick in the earth at the opposite side of the bridge, or make it out of small stones in your garden if you are working there.

Moon

Just as the Sun became in many cultures associated with the Father, so the Moon became associated with the Great Mother. The cave, man's earliest home, was likened to the womb of the Mother and decorated with paintings of the creatures who provided food and clothing, the tallow torches around the walls representing the moonlight.

Because the cycles of the Moon mirror the human menstrual cycle, the Moon has continually been linked to motherhood through many ages and cultures. Women who wanted to become pregnant would sleep under the rays of the Moon from waxing to full to ensure conception.

A trinity of huge carved stone goddesses, representing the three main cycles of the Moon and dating from between 1300 BC and 1100 BC was found in a cave at the Abri du Roc aux Sorciers at Angles-sur-l'Anglin in France. Vestiges of Moon worship can be seen in the myths of less technologically developed cultures even today.

The Moon goddess ruled the night, as the Sun God did the day, and both were worshipped as the source of all life and goodness. When it was realised that the tides rose and fell with the Moon, the concept was applied to bodily fluids and even agriculture. In planting and reaping, the waxing Moon was said to increase all growth and ripening, while the waning Moon decreased the speed of growth and richness of fruit. Gardeners, particularly in country places, abide by these old maxims, which seem to work.

The Moon, feminine, mysterious, intuitive, nurturing, is the yin power, dark, unconscious wisdom, the right side of the brain, divergent thinking, equally powerful but operating in cycles of time, in alchemy Queen Luna or silver to King Sol or gold.

Natural Sources of Lunar Power

You can use any or all of these natural sources of the Moon's power whenever you need intuition, to share or keep secrets, to understand the hidden emotions of others, to develop your psychic abilities; also for fertility, quiet sleep, inner harmony, reconciliation and flowing naturally with the cycles of life.

- A tiny moonstone or silver charm in an egg on the bedroom windowledge from the new to full Moon can bring fertility and fresh growth of all kinds into the home.
- Plant herbs of the Moon (like all herbs on the waxing Moon)

three or four days before the appearance of the full Moon. The moment the Moon turns full is sometimes favoured for cutting, as the plant retains its full vitality. Essential oils are said to be richest in those herbs cut at the full Moon. These Moon oils and herbs will carry the power of the Moon if you bath in them and increase your own intuitive and psychic powers.

- Turn over a silver coin on the new Moon and bow three times, and you will attract money as the Moon waxes. A variant on this uses a silver locket or a silver ring.
- When you first see the crescent Moon in the sky, go into the garden and place the ring on your wedding finger or the locket around your neck and say:

New Moon
True Moon,
Moon in the stream,
Bring true love
In my dream.

- Place the heart or ring in a tiny silver-coloured purse or pouch under your pillow for three nights, and on the third night you will dream of the person who will make you happy. It is supposed to be doubly lucky if you can see the Moon reflected in a stream or any running water as you recite the rhyme

Crystals and gems of the Moon include moonstones and mother of pearl, sea-green aquamarine and pale golden beryl. Moonstones come in different hues – pink, yellow and blue as well as creamy white – so different coloured moonstones can represent the different phases; perhaps a pink moonstone for the waxing phase, white or yellow for the full Moon and blue for the waning Moon.
Foods of the Moon include aubergines, coconuts, cucumber, eggs, grapes, lettuce, melons, milk and watercress.
Herbs, incenses and oils of the Moon include calamus, camphor, jasmine, lemon and lemon balm, myrrh and sandalwood.
Trees of the Moon include any growing close to water but especially willow, mountain ash, mango, rowan, banana and cactus.
Flowers of the Moon include dog rose, gardenia, jasmine, lotus, night-scented stock, poppies and wallflowers.
Colours of the Moon are silver or misty white, cream and blue.

The Lunar Phases

The most effective way of beginning Moon magic is to choose a night when you can actually see the Moon. When it is waxing, the light is on the right and the illuminated Moon grows larger night by night from right to left until the disk is fully illuminated. When the Moon wanes, following the appearance of a full Moon the darkness increases from the right, covering the light on the left until it disappears, to return three days later as a crescent.

The Moon phases are usually to be found in daily newspapers, along with the times of sunrise and sunset. Many diaries also include the Moon dates. The cycle from one new Moon to the next lasts 29.5 days, but there is a retardation averaging about fifty minutes a day in the rising and setting of the Moon. It takes just over twenty-seven days for the Moon to complete its orbit round the Earth.

There are various ways of calculating the phases of the Moon. For example, the lunar month is counted as twenty-eight days, and on calendars the lunar phases are divided into four weeks: the week of the new Moon, the week of the first quarter, the week of the full Moon and the week of the last quarter. These quarter periods will vary between seven and eight days according to the month, which in turn varies each year. There are also eight recognised phases within the lunar cycle.

The easiest way is to use the two main phases, the waxing phase from the new Moon until the full Moon and the waning period from the full Moon to the dark of the Moon. This gives you two fourteen-day periods.

New Moon and Waxing Magic

This is the time to initiate new ventures. Rituals to increase money, especially on the day of the new Moon, are perhaps the most common waxing spells. These rituals are found in all cultures and date from the time when coinage was first used. They were handed down orally and were first recorded in about the eleventh century. Traditionally, the children of fishermen or sailors would bow to the new Moon three times and chant:

I see the Moon
The Moon sees me,
Guard the sailors
On the sea.

Full Moon Magic

The night of the full Moon was traditionally used by witches for their esbats or monthly covens. It is especially potent for love magic and matters of the heart, and for any rituals requiring a great deal of energy – perhaps for healing or for granting wishes.

Waning Moon Magic

If you have had a period of bad luck or poor health this can be very potent for removing pain or sickness, for banishing guilt or sorrow, or for ending peacefully a relationship that has run its course.

A waning Moon ritual to banish pain

This is especially good for chronic ailments, and can help children and adults who suffer from stress-related conditions. It is best carried out on the dark of the Moon – the last three days of the Moon cycle, as the Moon is on the cusp and the new Moon is not yet visible in the sky – but it is potent at any time during the last quarter.

You will need some herbs of healing cut on the waning Moon with a white-handled knife, for example rue and fennel. You will also need a sprig of yew, the tree of endings, also cut on the waning Moon, and some gardenia or wallflower seeds or seedlings.

- Take a small bone to represent the pain or sickness; if you do not like handling animal bones, use a similar-shaped stone.
- Scratch on it with a black-handled knife the symbol of the waning Moon, with the crescent shape on the left, and put a horizontal cross through the Moon.
- Wrap it in long fronds of rue and fennel tied in nine knots and enclose it in a dark square box or square purse made of some biodegradable material.
- Dig a hole in the earth or in a very deep flowerpot full of earth and place the box in it, saying

Old Moon,
Die soon.
Moon of sorrow,
Take my pain,
And bring again
Health on the morrow.

- Mark the spot with your sprig of yew.
- As the new Moon appears in the sky, you may feel some relief. But wait until three or four days before the full Moon to plant you gardenia or wallflower seeds or seedlings.
- You may need to repeat the ritual monthly.
- As a variation, people who had an illness or infection would catch the rays of the waning Moon in a silver dish and wash their hands in the water, chanting:

I wash my hands in thy waning light
Cleanse my sickness [or sorrow]
Oh Moon, this night.

Stars

In ancient lore, stars were thought to be the souls of either unborn children or those who had died and were awaiting rebirth. Shooting stars were therefore new souls falling to enter their new Earth forms.

In Native American myth the Milky Way was the road on which souls travelled on their journey after death, and the brightest stars were the campfires by which they rested on their travels. The Inuit in north-west Greenland say that the Aurora Borealis or Northern Lights dancing in the sky are deceased family members dancing round their fires at celestial festivals.

Wishing on a Star

We have all heard the expression 'wishing on a star'. However, it is making a wish on the first star of the evening that promises fulfilment. You should make the wish aloud three times, between each wish reciting this rhyme which is so old that we cannot date it:

Star light, star bright
First star I see tonight
Wish I may, wish I might
Have the wish I wish tonight.

Eclipses

Most magical of all are the eclipses, from earliest times symbols of cosmic power and catalysts for powerful rituals of both endings and regeneration.

A lunar eclipse occurs when the full Moon is covered by the Earth's shadow. The Moon does not disappear but becomes a dull coppery-red colour. Eclipses of the Moon occur only when the Sun, the full Moon and the Earth are completely aligned, so that the Earth blocks the Sun's light and casts its shadow on the Moon.

During total solar eclipses the Sun seems to vanish. Eclipses of the Sun occur when the Moon comes between the Earth and the Sun, briefly hiding it and casting a shadow on the Earth. The eclipse can only be seen in places covered by the shadow, which is less than 150 miles (240 km) wide.

An eclipse of the Sun was feared by early people, who believed that the source of light and warmth was lost forever. The effect of a total eclipse was so terrifying that those priests and magicians who could predict one and calm the population, promising to restore the light, held high office in ancient times.

Both solar and lunar eclipses were regarded in Chinese tradition as a great dragon eating up the Sun. Some Native American Indian tribes saw the Sun God as menaced by a giant demon toad who tried to swallow it. When it succeeded, there was an eclipse. As soon as the solar disc began to be obscured, the Indians would decorate their bodies with red and fire arrows at the Sun to drive off the toad. During the eclipse the Indians believed that their mother was dying. In contrast, some Inuit tribes believe that the Sun Goddess's face becomes so dirty that it is eventually blackened out, and the powerful magic of the shamans is needed to wash it clean.

On average there are 237 solar eclipses per century, so they are rare things. But they are well worth waiting for, as a major catalyst for change in almost any aspect of your life. You can use either a lunar or solar eclipse and carry out rituals even at times of partial eclipses, which are more frequent but are still effective magical forces.

The Magic of Transitions: Nine Steps to Happiness

You will need a gold-coloured candle for a solar eclipse or a silver-coloured candle for a lunar eclipse, together with nine black cords and nine white ones.

- Light your candle about ten minutes before the eclipse begins, and name each black cord in turn for a sorrow, a regret, an unresolved resentment or a broken dream.
- As you consign each named cord to the flames, say,

Sorrow, anger go from me,
Travel on the cosmic sea
Ride beyond the dark waves
Eclipsed in blackness may you be.

- Save the most painful or difficult burdens till last, and burn them as the sky becomes dark or the Moon turns coppery.
- When you have finished, extinguish the candle by snuffing rather than blowing it out – you can buy cheap candle snuffers in many stores. As you are plunged into darkness chant:

Eclipsed in blackness.
Forever be.

- In the darkness name each of your white cords as a step towards happiness and change.
- As the light slowly returns, relight your candle and one by one tie each white cord into a knot as you name its strength.
- Say as you pass each cord over the candle:

Be great, be bright,
Be glorious and light
Great power and joy
From black
To white.

- Circle the candle with each cord and then put it in a circle surrounding the candle, beginning in the east for rising energies.
- When all nine cords are in place, leave the candle to burn away naturally. Keep your circle of cords where it will not be disturbed, but where it is open to solar and lunar light.
- As you prepare to make each step, unknot a cord and wrap it in white silk until all nine are unravelled and you are on the way to achieving your aim.
- Use the nine cords to hold up plants as a reminder that you are travelling daily towards the light.

Further Reading

Wicca, Witchcraft and Spell-casting

BUCKLAND, Raymond, *Buckland's Complete Guide to Witchcraft*, Llewellyn, St Paul, Minnesota, 1997

CROWLEY, Vivianne, *Wicca, The Old Religion in the New Age*, Aquarian, 1989

CUNNINGHAM, Scott, *Wicca, a Guide for the Solitary Practitioner*, Llewellyn, St Paul, Minnesota, 1993

DUNWICH, Gerina, *Wicca Craft*, Citadel, Carol Publishing, New York, 1993

EASON, Cassandra, *Every Woman a Witch*, Quantum, 1996

FARRAR, Janet and Stewart, *Spells and How They Work*, Robert Hale, 1992

LYDDON MADDISON, Sarah, *The Modern Witch's Spellbook*, Citadel, Carol Publishing, New York, 1994

RAVENWOLF, Silver, *To Ride a Silver Broomstick, New Generation Witchcraft*, Llewellyn, St Paul, Minnesota, 1995

RAVENWOLF, Silver, *To Stir a Magic Cauldron, a Witch's Guide to Casting and Conjuring*, Llewellyn, St Paul, Minnesota, 1997

History of Witchcraft and Magic

BRIGGS, Robin, *Witches and Neighbours, The Social and Cultural Context of European Witchcraft*, HarperCollins, 1996

GUILEY, Rosemary Ellen, *The Encyclopedia of Witches and Witchcraft*, Facts on File, New York, 1989

Seasonal Magic and Old Festivals

BERRESFORD-ELLIS, Peter, *The Druids*, Constable, 1994
COOPER, J.C., *Aquarian Dictionary of Festivals*, Aquarian, 1990
GREEN, Marian, *A Calendar of Festivals*, Element, 1991
PEGG, Bob, *Rites and Riots, Folk Customs of Britain and Europe*, Blandford, 1981
STEWART, Bob, *Where Is St George? Pagan Imagery in English Folksong*, Blandford, 1988

Earth Energies, Spirits and Magical Beings

CUNNINGHAM, Scott, *Earth Power, Techniques of Natural Magic*, Llewellyn, St Paul, Minnesota, 1997
DEVEREUX, Paul, *Shamanism and the Mystery Lines*, Quantum, 1992
GREEN, Marian, *The Elements of Natural Magic*, Element, 1989
HESELTON, Philip, *The Elements of Earth Mysteries*, Element, 1991
MOLYNEAUX, Brian Leigh, *The Sacred Earth*, Macmillan, 1995

Herbs, Oils, Trees and Flowers

CUNNINGHAM, Scott, *Complete Book of Oils, Incenses and Brews*, Llewellyn, St Paul, Minnesota, 1991
DUNWICH, Gerina, *Wicca Garden, A Modern Witch's Book of Magical and Enchanted Herbs and Plants*, Citadel, Carol Publishing, New York, 1996
GORDON, Lesley, *The Mystery and Magic of Trees and Flowers*, Grange, 1995
LIPP, Frank J., *Herbalism*, Macmillan, 1996

Colour Magic

BUCKLAND, Ray, *Practical Color Magic*, Llewellyn, St Paul, Minnesota, 1996

Useful Addresses

Crystals and New Age Suppliers

Australia

Future Pastimes, 24a Collins St, Kiama, New South Wales. Tel: 0242–32–2594. (General supplies. Mail order.)
The Mystic Trader, 125 Flinders Lane, Melbourne 3000. Tel: 03–650–4477. (Mail order as well as personal service.)
Mysterys, Level 1, 314–322 Darling Street, Balmain, New South Wales. Tel: 02 98–18–2274. (Wiccan supplies. Mail order.)

South Africa

The Wellstead, 1 Wellington Avenue, Wynberg, Cape 7300. Tel: 797 8982. (Mail order.)

UK

Futhark, 18 Halifax Rd, Todmorden, OL14 5AD. Tel: 01706 813205. (Occult, magical and alchemical supplies of all kinds. Mail order.)
Mandragora, Essex House, Thame, OX9 3LS. Tel: 01844 260990. (Mail order.)
Merlin's Mantelpiece, 376 Richmond Rd, Twickenham, TW1 2DX. Tel: 0181 891 6140. (Mail order.)
Mysteries, 7 Monmouth St, London WC2H 9DA. Tel: 0171 240 3688. (Shop/mail order: absolutely everything for the New Age, plus good advice.)

Pentagram, 11 Cheapside, Wakefield, WF1 2SD. E-mail:pentagram@psinet.demon.co.uk. Tel/fax: 01924 298930. International: + 44 192 429 8930. (Mail order and personal service: everything for the New Age, Wiccan and occult.)

USA

Eye of the Cat, 3314 E. Broadway, Long Beach, CA 90803. Tel: (213) 438–3569. (Mail order crystals and other New Age commodities.)
The Crystal Cave, 415 West Foothill Blvd, Claremont, CA 91711. (Mail order. Stocks a huge variety of crystal and stones, including unusual ones.)
Open Door Metaphysical Shoppe, 428 North Buchanan Circle, Suite 16, Pacheco, CA 94553. Tel: 925 676 3858. Fax: 925 676 3813. (Mail order.)
Spirit Search Emporium, Sun Angel Innovations, 3939 W. Windmills Blvd, # 2060 Chandler, Arizona 85226. Tel: 1 800 256 3551. (Mail order.)

Earth Energies

UK

British Society of Dowsers, Sycamore Barn, Hastingleigh, Ashford, TN25 5HW
Findhorn, Findhorn Foundation, The Park, Forres, IV36 OTS. (Workshops and courses on meditation, consciousness and nature spirits.)

USA

American Society of Dowsers, PO Box 23, Damville, VT 05828. Tel: 1 800 711 9530 (toll free).

Essential Oils by Mail Order

Australia

Toona Essential Oils PTY, 6 Tagigan Road, Goomboonian, Queensland 4570. Tel: 61 7 5486 5216.

UK

Fleur Essential Oils, Pembroke Studios, Pembroke Road, London N10 2JE. Tel: 0181 444 7424, Fax: 0171 444 0704. (International mail order.)

USA

Moonrise Herbs, Mail Order EG, 826 G Street, Arcata, CA 95521. Tel: 1 800 603 8364 (toll free.)
Les Herbes, 9 Gerry Lane, Huntington, NY 11743. Tel/Fax: 001 516 271 4246

Herbal Suppliers

UK

G. Baldwin and Co., 171–173 Walworth Rd, London SE17 1RW. Tel: 0171 703 5550. (Largest range of herbs and herbal products in the UK; extensive mail order.)
Island Herbs (Vicki and Ian Foss), Sunacre, The Terrace, Chale, Ventnor, Isle of Wight, PO38 2HL. Tel: 01983 730228. (Wide variety of culinary and medicinal herbs for garden and window box All plants grown on site. Send SAE for list.)
Gerard House, 736 Christchurch Rd, Bournemouth, BH7 6BZ. Tel: 01202 434116. (Good for dried herbs by mail order.)

USA

Joan Teresa Power Products, PO Box 442, Mars Hill, NC 28754. Tel: (704) 689–5739. (Mail order, especially for unusual herbs, plants, oils, incenses etc.)
The Sage Garden, PO Box 144, Payette, ID 83661. Tel: (208) 454 2026. (Herbs, oils, amulets, incenses; mail order.)

Paganism

There is a great overlap between this and the Wiccan section, and the divisions have been made purely on name.

Australia

Novocastrian Pagan Information Centre, Laren, PO Box 129, Stockton, New South Wales 2295
The Pagan Alliance PO Box 823, Bathurst, New South Wales 2795. (An umbrella movement for pagan organisations.)

UK

The Pagan Federation, BM Box 7097, London WCIN 3XX

Pagan Federation International: National and Regional Coordinators

Belgium: Joanne Agate and Stefan van der Ende, Postbus 241, 2100 Deurne 1, Antwerpen
Canada: David Springer, PO Box 32, Station B, Ottawa K1P 6C3
France: Julie Renshaw, 1 Allée des Eméraudes 85220 Landvieille
Germany: Joint Secretaries and Regional Co-ordinators for Hanover area: Claudia and Tom Wehmeyer, Wittekindstr. 5333615 Bielefeld
Regional Co-ordinator for Southern Germany (Bavaria): Natascha Heinhaus, Werner-Haas-Str. 3a, 86153 Augsburg
Regional Co-ordinator for Rhein/Main/Taunus area: Birgit Kapraun, Ruesselsheimer Allee 86, 55130 Mainz
Regional Co-ordinator for Ruhrgebiet (east) and Niederrhein: Barbara Stiller, Wuppertalerstr. 48–50, 42653 Solingen
Regional Co-ordinator for the Pfalz and South-West: Ian MacWatt, PO Box 610251, 684242 Mannheim
Regional Co-ordinator for Northern Germany: Oliver Greeff, Lilienthaler Heerstr. 6, 28359 Bremen
Regional Co-ordinator for Berlin: Jutta Hofmann, Wollankstr. 25, 13359 Berlin
Joint Regional Co-ordinator for Munsterland and Ruhrgebiet (west): Frauke Diemel and Ish-Thar Bockholt, Marke 13, 48361 Beelen

Iberia and Brazil

Isobel Andrade, Federacio Paga – Portugal e Brasil, Apartado 24170, 1250 Lisbon

Netherlands

The Lady Bara and Morgana, PO Box 473, 3700 AL Zeist

Norway

Paul Greenslade, c/o Nordisk Paganistforbund, Postboks 1814, 5024 Bergen

Sweden

Laila Wiberg, Holmvagen 20, 19435 Upplands Vasby

Switzerland

Daniel Paris, Kaktusbluete, Steinberggasse 8, 8400 Winterthurland

Wicca/Goddess Organisations

UK

Fellowship of Isis, Huntington Castle, Bunclody, Enniscorthy, Eire. (A worldwide network of Goddess worshippers.)

USA

Circle Sanctuary, PO Box 219, Mount Horeb, WI 53572. Tel: 608-924-2216. Contacts with 700 pagan groups, networks etc.
Covenant of the Goddess, PO Box 1226, Berkeley, CA 94704.
Living Wicca Foundation, PO Box 4186, Dunellen, New Jersey 08812. (Continues the work of the late Scott Cunningham.)
The Witches' Voice Inc., PO Box 4924, Clearwater, Florida 33758–4924. (A resource organisation with worldwide links.)

Index

action 34
aettir/tides of the day 226–8, 229
Air viii, 23, 25–6, 29, 31, 58, 60–2, 81, 187, 210, 211, 212, 213, 214, 216–19
akasha (fifth ether) 23, 210
altar xii, 21, 22, 33, 193
amulet vii
Ancient Babylon/Babylonians 5, 6, 37, 39
Ancient Chinese 8
Ancient Egypt/Egyptians 8, 39, 40, 41, 223
Ancient Etruscans vi
Ancient Greece vi
Apollo, Ancient Greek god 42, 103
Archangels xi, 192
astrological associations 166–8
athame (air dagger) 25–6, 31, 34, 35, 90
attracting magic 5
autumn equinox 120, 174, 189, 192–4, 207

bagua, Chinese 97, 98
banishing and protective magic 5, 108–10
bells 24–5, 32, 104, 177, 238
Beltain/Beltane 168, 198, 201–4, 236
black magic 131–2
Book of Shadows or Grimoire x, xi
bottles 50–1, 109–10
Bride's Eve 199–200
broom/broomstick 57, 126

cakes and ale xiii, 35–6
candles viii, ix, xii, xiii, 12, 15, 20, 22–3, 28, 29, 33, 44, 55, 88–90, 91, 93, 95, 96–7, 113, 126, 153, 190, 195, 199, 200, 206, 207, 208, 214, 219–20, 225, 246–7
cauldron 27–8, 57, 90, 91
ceremony 32–6
Cerne Abbas Giant, Dorset 4, 122
chakras 49
chalice 27, 30, 33, 35, 57, 90, 91–2
chants and words ix, 20, 34, 36, 135, 149
Christian/ity vi, 127, 128, 188, 192, 199, 204, 205, 209
Christmas tree vii, 3
clouds xi, 171–3
colour magic ix, 12, 23, 39–56, 238
computers ix, 63–8
coins 16, 96–7
contagious magic 4, 5, 93

coven x, 21, 130–1
crystals ix, xii, xiii, 12, 16, 24, 31, 43, 50, 53, 55, 85, 93, 95, 96, 101–3, 110–12, 112, 114, 116, 181, 188, 190, 193, 195, 200, 206, 233, 234, 235, 237, 238, 241

dawn 198, 229, 230
days of the week 47–8
daytide 227
daytime 230–3
defensive magic 107–16
deities xii, 14, 154, 211
Devil 41, 128
dew 169–71
Diana, Ancient Greek goddess 42
divination x
dreams xi
Druids vi, 18, 119, 124, 154, 168, 169, 171, 190, 192, 208
drum 12
dusk 229

Earth viii, 4, 23, 24–5, 26, 28, 29, 31, 35, 36, 38, 40, 41, 42, 58, 59–60, 81, 110, 119, 126, 153, 188, 189, 192, 194, 195–6, 209, 210, 211, 213, 214, 215–16
Easter 15, 127, 187–8
eclipses 245–7
eightfold year 196–209
elemental substances 29–30, 211–12, 214–22
elemental magic, modern 58–65
Eostre, Anglo-Saxon goddess of spring 15, 187
esbats 30, 33, 129, 135
eventide 228, 230

fairies vii, 41
Feng Shui 71
Feyja, goddess of love and fertility 5
Fire viii, 23, 26–7, 29, 31, 58, 62–3, 81, 189, 210, 211, 212, 214, 219–20
flowers viii, xi, 16, 24, 60, 71, 85–8, 125, 135, 161–6, 166–7, 188, 190, 238, 241
focus, the 33–4
food 51–2
formal magic viii, ix, 20–38
four leaf clover vii

garden, magical 79–82
Gerald Gardner xi, 129
gifts 14–19
  of love 18–19
Great Rite 3
Goddess, the xi, 37, 128–9, 199, 200, 201, 205, 219
guardians xi, xii, 80–3, 112, 119–26

Hallowe'en/Samhain 14, 18, 26, 28, 129, 197, 198, 199, 207–9, 236
hearth, magical 72–3
hedge witch 131
herbs viii, xii, xiii, 3, 60, 62–3, 75, 76–8, 85–8, 100, 112–13, 135, 136–53, 166–7, 188, 190, 192, 200, 202, 206, 208, 217, 238, 241
high priestess x
home, magical 71–82
Horned God 23, 128–9, 197
housework, magical 74–6

I Ching x
Imbolc/Oilmec/Brigantia 198, 199–201
incense xii, 14, 29, 55, 92, 153, 177, 192, 200, 202, 206, 208, 214, 216–19, 238, 241

journal x–xi
Judas Iscariot vi, 41

Jupiter 41, 235

karmic wheel 114–15
knot magic viii, 5–7, 33, 34, 61, 89, 93, 109–10, 153, 161, 220, 246–7

Lammas/Lughnasadh 15, 198–9, 200, 205–6
Long Man of Wilmington, East Sussex 122
love magic 18–19, 83–93
luck vi, vii, 78
lucky charm vii
lunar phases 242–4

magic circle xiii, xiv, 30–2, 34
  salt and water circle 32
  incense circle 32
magical area 21
magical number squares 7–13
mantra 47, 66, 111
Mars 39, 40, 79, 234
materials of ritual magic 28–30
May Eve 4, 28, 170, 197
Mercury vii, 41, 100, 234
metal 78–9, 103–6, 191, 233, 234, 235
midday 227
midnight 228, 229, 230
Midsummer Eve 3
midwinter/winter solstice 120, 127, 174, 175, 192, 194, 198, 209
mirror vii, 88–90, 97–8
modern magic 57–68
money vii, x, 17, 94–106
money bottle, 72, 73–4
Moon viii, 6, 18, 20, 22, 23, 28, 33, 38, 42, 50, 82, 88, 91, 97–8, 100, 115, 120, 129, 131, 135, 153, 170, 188, 203, 211, 223, 224–6, 233, 239–44, 245
morningtide 227, 230
music 47

Native Americans 10, 41, 112, 123, 172, 244, 245
natural magic 135–68
Newgrange, Eire 120
night-tide 228
noon 229
Northern tradition 13
numerology 9
  and colours 44–7

oils ix, xii, 28, 74, 75, 76, 97, 149, 214, 220–2, 238, 241
Osiris, Ancient Egyptian god 41
ouija board 107

pentacle 25, 33
pentagram 31, 33, 64–5, 153
personal preparation 30
planetary hours 229–35
planetary qualities 233
poppet 33, 136, 150–3
power 34–5, 212
prana (life-force) 49
psychic attack 107
psychic protection xi–xii, 80–3, 83–4, 108, 110–16
Pythagoras/Pythagorean 8, 9, 40, 45

rain 180–1
rainbows viii, 181–3
Ra, Ancient Egyptian god 42
Ran, Viking sea goddess 15
Ridgeway, the 124
rituals viii, ix–x, xi, xii–xiv, 3, 6–7, 16–18, 52–6, 67–8, 84–5, 88–90, 90–2, 92–3, 95–6, 96–7, 97–8, 99–103, 104–5, 136–53, 160–1, 165–6, 169–71, 177–80, 181, 182–3, 188–9, 190–2, 193–4, 195–6, 200–1, 202–4, 206, 208–9, 215–16, 218–19, 219–20, 222, 238–9, 243–4

Romans vii, 14

sabats 129, 197, 201
salt vi, 28, 29, 84, 95–6, 214, 215–16
Satanism 131–2
Saturn 40, 42, 235–6
scrying 28
seasonal magic 186–209
sex magic 36–8
shadow time 198
shaman 12, 13
Shony, sea god 14
smudge sticks 112–13
solar tides 186–7
solar times 228–9, 238
spider vi–vii
spring/vernal equinox 15, 120, 127, 175, 184, 187–9, 194, 198, 201, 207
St John's Eve 3–4
stars viii, 223, 224, 244–5
statues ix, 23–4
stones, magic 100–3
storms viii, 183–5
summer/midsummer solstice 120, 176, 187, 189–92, 197, 204, 238
Sun vii, viii, 22, 28, 40, 42, 55, 100, 120, 153, 159, 160, 166–7, 168, 169, 188, 191–2, 194, 196, 203, 209, 211, 223, 224–6, 233, 236–9, 245
superstitions vii
sympathetic magic 4, 5

talismans 7, 11,12, 13, 42, 55, 188
tarot 74, 213
tea leaves x
technological magic 65–9
time of light 198–9
time, magical 223–47
tools 24–8
  elemental 24–8
trees vi, viii, 71, 80, 99, 135, 153–61, 166–7, 238, 241
traditional magic 3–13

uht 228
undorne 227

vampires vii
Venus 41, 42, 87, 100, 230, 235

Winston Churchill vi
wand 26–7, 31
Water viii, 23, 27, 29, 31, 58–9, 63, 81, 192, 210, 211–12, 213, 214, 220–2, 238
weather magic 169–85
Wicca xi, xiii, 21, 33, 37, 128–32
wells 14, 123–5
wind, and magic 173–80
winter 194–6
witches vii, 10, 57, 126–32, 197
wizards 57
Woden, Anglo-Saxon Father God 78
wood 26–7

yang 23, 35
yin 23, 35

Zeus vi, 40